Kunst und Politik
Band 10/2008

KUNST UND POLITIK
JAHRBUCH DER GUERNICA-GESELLSCHAFT

Begründet von Jutta Held

Herausgegeben von Martin Papenbrock und Norbert Schneider

KUNST UND POLITIK
JAHRBUCH DER GUERNICA-GESELLSCHAFT

Kunst und Politik
Band 10/2008

Schwerpunkt:
Bildwissenschaft und Visual Culture Studies in der Diskussion

Herausgeber dieses Bandes:
Andrew Hemingway
Norbert Schneider

in Verbindung mit
Markus Buschhaus
Asko Lehmuskallio

V&R unipress

– Veröffentlichung des Universitätsverlags Osnabrück bei V&R unipress –

Redaktion:	Martin Papenbrock (Leitung), Bettina Franke, Julia Frohnhoff, Anna Greve, Dirk Janßen, Barbara Martin, Isabel Steppeler
Redaktionsadresse:	Guernica-Gesellschaft, Klauprechtstraße 19, 76137 Karlsruhe, Tel. 07 21/3 52 93 79
Erscheinungsweise:	Jährlich im Herbst
Abonnement:	Der Preis für ein einzelnes Jahrbuch beträgt EUR 22,50 im Abonnement EUR 19,50

Gedruckt mit Unterstützung der Stiftung Kritische Kunst- und Kulturwissenschaften und des Ulmer Vereins

Bibliographische Information Der Deutschen Bibliothek

Die Deutsche Bibliothek verzeichnet diese Publikation in der Deutschen Nationalbibliografie; detaillierte bibliografische Daten sind im Internet über <http://dnb.ddb.de> abrufbar

1. Aufl. 2008

Einbandgestaltung: Tevfik Göktepe

Gedruckt auf säurefreiem, total chlorfrei gebleichtem Werkdruckpapier. Alterungsbeständig.
Printed in Germany

ISBN 978-3-89971-530-9

Inhalt

WEITERE THEMEN

INTERNATIONALE BERICHTE

BESPRECHUNGEN

MATERIALIEN

ANHANG

BILDWISSENSCHAFT UND VISUAL CULTURE STUDIES IN DER DISKUSSION

Vorwort

Die Konzeption dieses Jahrbuchbandes geht auf Jutta Held zurück. Als Herausgeberin von *Kunst und Politik* und als Lehrkörpermitglied des Karlsruher Graduiertenkollegs *Bild – Körper – Medium* hatte sie im Sommer 2006 gemeinsam mit Markus Buschhaus und Asko Lehmuskallio über die Planung dieses 10. Bandes diskutiert. Von Anfang an war daran gedacht, ihn mit einer Tagung vorzubereiten, die – wie auch die früheren Konferenzen zur *Kunstgeschichte im Nationalsozialismus* und *Kunstgeschichte in der Nachkriegszeit* oder zur *Politischen Kunst heute* – am Institut für Kunstgeschichte der Universität Karlsruhe stattfinden solle (durchgeführt wurde sie dort am 23./24. Februar 2008).

Das Ergebnis des Meinungsaustauschs und ihre eigenen Überlegungen fasste sie in einem Exposé zusammen: Darin heißt es:

> »Die neue Disziplin oder der Projektverbund ›Bildwissenschaft‹ wird einerseits – auf Seiten der KunsthistorikerInnen – noch weitgehend ignoriert, obwohl die kunsthistorischen Gegenstände längst den massenmedialen Wirkungsmechanismen und medialen Bildpraktiken eingepasst werden und Grund besteht, diesen Vorgang zu reflektieren. Andererseits – auf Seiten der BildwissenschaftlerInnen – wird der neue wissenschaftliche Zugang bereits prospektiv an die Stelle der als veraltet geltenden Kunstgeschichte gesetzt. Die wissenschaftliche Analyse von Bildern, die einmal die Domäne der Kunstgeschichte war, ist in der Tat zunehmend von anderen Disziplinen ›usurpiert‹ worden.
>
> Eine kritische Bestandsaufnahme der bisherigen Diskussionen und Ergebnisse bildwissenschaftlicher Forschungen scheint uns an der Zeit zu sein.
>
> In dem geplanten Band sollen theoretische Reflexion und empirische Fallanalysen verbunden werden mit dem Ziel, das Verhältnis der Bildwissenschaften, der von unterschiedlichen Disziplinen praktizierten Zugänge zu Bildern, zu der ›alten‹ bildrelevanten und bisher die Bildkompetenzen monopolisierenden Kunstgeschichte klären zu helfen.
>
> Die Frage, welche politischen und sozialen Semantiken durch die Bildwissenschaft erschlossen werden, welcher politische Gebrauch der Bilder und welche Bilderpolitiken durch die Bildwissenschaft erschlossen (oder auch gestärkt) werden, ist bei jedem einzelnen Thema zu stellen.
>
> Darüber hinaus fragen wir nach dem wissenschaftspolitischen Projekt einer Bildwissenschaft. Der Verdacht liegt nahe, dass sie einen Faktor innerhalb des kulturpolitischen Kalküls bildet, die ›alten‹ geisteswissenschaftlichen Disziplinen auszutrocknen und in neue, transdisziplinäre Projekte mit unmittelbarem Aktualitätsbezug aufgehen zu lassen.

> Folgende Themenkomplexe bzw. Fragestellungen und Perspektiven sind vorgesehen:
>
> Globale Bilder – lokalisierte Bilder
>
> Was leistet die Bildwissenschaft über die Kunstgeschichte hinaus?
>
> Konturen einer bildwissenschaftlich dimensionierten Kunstgeschichte
>
> (Subversive) Bildpraktiken im Alltag
>
> Brennpunkte der Bildpolitik. Welche Semantiken, Funktionen und Geltungsbereiche des politischen Bildes sind festzustellen?
>
> Visual Studies in den USA und in Großbritannien
>
> Der wissenschaftliche Weg eines ›Bildwissenschaftlers‹: W.J.T. Mitchell (Skizze einer intellektuellen Biographie).«

Die Trauer über ihren Tod am 27. Januar 2007 hat uns lange gelähmt und gehemmt, das von ihr initiierte Projekt wieder aufzunehmen, das sie in ihrer singulären, bewundерungswürdigen Tatkraft gewiss bald zügig auf den Weg gebracht hätte, immer darauf dringend, dass die gesteckten Ziele und Kriterien auch beachtet würden, damit eine zwar fazettenreiche, aber in sich geschlossene Sammlung von Texten entstehe, die sich als kritische und politisch reflektierende Position von den inzwischen zahllosen Sammelbänden erkennbar abhebt.

Im April 2007 begann ich, auf der Grundlage ihrer Notizen, die auch eine Liste anzuschreibender Autorinnen und Autoren enthielt, Kontakt mit den ins Auge gefassten Subherausgebern, so besonders mit Asko Lehmuskallio (da Markus Buschhaus inzwischen beruflich stark absorbiert war) und einzelnen Mitgliedern des Jahrbuch-Beirates aufzunehmen. Sehr engagiert wurde ich über die Monate von Andrew Hemingway unterstützt, der innerhalb dieses Gremiums den besten Überblick über die Diskussion der *Visual Culture Studies* im angloamerikanischen Bereich hat. Ihm ist es zu danken, dass nun – mit ihm – fünf profilierte Autorinnen und Autoren aus den USA und Großbritannien sich an unserem Band beteiligen und diese kritische Sicht einbringen. Hatte Jutta noch den Hauptakzent auf das funktionsanalytisch und methodenkritisch zu bestimmende Verhältnis von Bildwissenschaft zur Kunstgeschichte gelegt, so hat sich bei der Suche nach Autoren bei Wahrung dieser Fragestellung eine leichte Verschiebung ergeben, und zwar hin zu einem kontrastierenden Vergleich von Bildwissenschaft und *Visual Culture Studies*, der, wie wir sahen, bei ihr durchaus auch vorgesehen war.

Die *Visual Culture Studies* oder kürzer: *Visual Studies*, um mit ihnen zu beginnen, waren in den 1970er und 1980er Jahren noch vom theoretischen und politischen Impuls des von Raymond Williams initiierten *Cultural Materialism* oder des Birminghamer *Centre for Contemporary Cultural Studies* unter der Leitung von Stuart Hall getragen, haben heute jedoch, nach etlichen Wandlungen und Häutungen, vor allem durch kontinuierliche Integrierung postmoderner Theorieversatzstücke, vielfach ihr gesellschaftskritisches Potential verloren. Dennoch erscheinen sie, denkt man etwa an Nicholas Mirzoeffs *Introduction to Visual Culture* (London 1999, 4. Auflage 2004) oder John A. Walkers und Sarah Chaplins gleichnamigen Band, immer noch stärker an politischer Aufklärung über die bewußtseinsdeformierende Kraft von in den Medien strategisch eingesetzten Bildern interessiert als hierzulande einzelne – durchaus dominante – Richtungen innerhalb des Disziplinpostulats »Bildwissenschaft«, die mehr essentialistisch eine Ontologie des Bildes betreiben.

Zwar gibt es bei den bildwissenschaftlichen Modellen im deutschsprachigen Bereich vereinzelt auch Berührungspunkte, ja Überschneidungen mit medienwissenschaftlichen Ansätzen, doch ist in diesen Fällen die empirische Analyse des funktionalen Gebrauchs und Einsatzes von Bildern, wenn sie denn überhaupt betrieben wird, oft überdeckt von spekulativen idealistischen Theorien im Umfeld von später Phänomenologie und Dekonstruktivismus. Man kann sich fragen, ob und wie viel die Apostrophierung postmoderner Theorielabels Erkenntniszuwachs bringt. Manchmal kann man sich des Verdachts nicht erwehren, dass sie im Sinne sozialer Distinktion mehr der Demonstration einer Zugehörigkeit zu einem privilegierenden akademischen Diskurs dienen soll.

Nicht immer ganz frei von solch modischen Referenzen erscheinen auch Arbeiten innerhalb der Bildanthropologie. Dennoch sind an ihr die durch trans- oder interkulturelle Vergleiche gewonnenen Einsichten hervorzuheben, die im Zeichen der Globalisierung zu Beobachtungen gelangen, wie sie auch für die *Visual Culture Studies* charakteristisch sind. Wissenschaftshistorisch ist daran zu erinnern, dass die Bildanthropologie aus kunstgeschichtlichen Forschungen zu den divergierenden Funktionen von Bildern im Mittelalter und in der Neuzeit hervorgegangen ist. Man denke etwa an Hans Beltings epochemachendes Buch *Bild und Kult*. Eine seiner impliziten Thesen läuft darauf hinaus, dass im Übergang vom Kult- zum Ausstellungswert der Bilder (um mit Walter Benjamin zu sprechen), von der religiösen zur ästhetischen Funktion das Bewusstsein des Nachwirkens bildmagischer Praktiken und ihrer atavistischen Potenz bei technisch produzierten oder massenmedial verbreiteten Bildern zwar verblasste, diese mentalen Strukturen aber dennoch unterschwellig virulent sind. Die herkömmliche Kunstwissenschaft hat dieses sonst mehr von Ethnologie und vergleichender Religionswissenschaft reflektierte Moment überwiegend ignoriert oder verdrängt. Es wieder ins Bewusstsein gehoben zu haben, stellt zweifellos einen bedeutsamen Erkenntnisgewinn dar.

Zu beobachten ist freilich, dass die Konzentrierung auf die magisch-subrationalen Momente letztlich dazu geführt hat, sie repetitiv nur an einem sehr eng gesteckten Gegenstandsbereich herauszuarbeiten, in dem sie offensichtlich sind. Das Gros dieser bildwissenschaftlichen Arbeiten befasst sich in auffälliger Wiederholung mit Themen wie Schleier, Maske, Spiegel, Abdruck, *vera icon* usw. So ist gleichsam unter der Hand ein bildanthropologischer Kanon entstanden, der, wenn man seine Genese rekonstruiert, im Wesentlichen von Georges Didi-Huberman initiiert wurde. Er war es auch, der die zur Bildwissenschaft erweiterte Kunstgeschichte zu einer metaphysischen, ja theologischen bzw. mystischen Reflexion hin geöffnet hat (»Das Bild als Riss und der Tod des Fleisch gewordenen Gottes«), die zwar im Hinblick auf das den Bildern innewohnende Thanatosmoment bedenkenswerte Züge hat, bei der man sich freilich aber auch fragen kann, wieweit sie sich nicht in projektive Spekulationen versteigt.

Bei einem derart ausgerichteten Erkenntnisinteresse ist unübersehbar, dass die meisten bildwissenschaftlichen Interpretationen – ob geflissentlich oder nicht, sei dahingestellt – einen ganz entscheidenden Aspekt ausblenden, nämlich ihren politischen und sozialen Kontext sowie die ihre Produktion generierenden Interessen. Sie bewusst zu machen, heißt aber zugleich, die Funktion von Bildern im Spannungsfeld von Hegemonie und Subversion in antagonistisch strukturierten Gesellschaften zu bestimmen. Hier scheinen mir die angloamerikanischen *Visual Culture Studies*, welcher postmodernen Korrosion auch immer sie in den letzten Jahren ausgesetzt waren (worauf der Beitrag von Andrew Hemingway hinweist), entschiedener auf den ideologischen Charakter der Bilder als letztlich politisch determinierende (und determinierte) Signifikanten im sozioökonomischen Prozess abzuheben.

Dabei geht es diesem Forschungsparadigma immer auch um das Problem der Repräsentation der realen Verhältnisse in den Bildern, also um ihre mimetische Funktion, zugleich aber nicht zuletzt darum, in welchem Maße und in welcher Weise sie dazu beitragen, Machtverhältnisse und Machtdiskurse zu stützen oder sie zu unterminieren.

Von Anfang an war daran gedacht, dass dieser Band mit seinen – erkennbar unterschiedlichen Kontexten entstammenden – Beiträgen sowohl selbst eine Diskussion abbilden als auch zu weiterführenden Debatten einladen soll. Theoretische Homogenität war nicht angestrebt. So finden sich bei den auf die Bildwissenschaft bezogenen Texten zum einen solche, die deren Grundannahmen teilen, dagegen wiederum andere, die ihren Thesen, etwa der einer *a priori* gegebenen Prävalenz von Bildern vor allen anderen Zeichensystemen, nachdrücklich widersprechen. Die sich auf die *Visual Culture Studies* beziehenden Aufsätze akzentuieren von einer materialistischen Sicht aus, bei der partiell die Kritik der Kulturindustrie durch die Frankfurter Schule wieder eine erkenntnisleitende Rolle spielt, die politische Dimension von Bildern und der sie reflektierenden Theorien, deren Entwicklung ihrerseits mit den realen sozioökonomischen Veränderungen der letzten Jahrzehnte in Verbindung gebracht wird.

Norbert Schneider

Andrew Hemingway

From Cultural Studies to Visual Culture Studies: An Historical and Political Critique

It is virtually self-evident that the disciplinary – or more accurately ›anti-disciplinary‹ – model that set the agenda for Visual Culture Studies in Britain and the United States was the cognate development known as Cultural Studies. Not only are there important precedents in the analysis of the visual forms of mass culture in specific investigations issuing from the University of Birmingham's Centre for Contemporary Cultural Studies – particularly those concerned with advertising and imagery of women in magazines[1] – but the refusal of established disciplinary boundaries was a key aspect of the Cultural Studies project and this, along with many of the theoretical tools it assembled, was taken up by the advocates of Visual Culture Studies. In fact, almost from the outset, Cultural Studies was understood as a major ally in the assault on conventional art history that the New Left launched in Britain. The main organ of that tendency, *Block*, not only published quite numerous instances of Cultural Studies-type analyses, but when the editors of the defunct journal assembled an anthology of selected highlights, they published it under the title *The Block Reader in Visual Culture*.[2] Cultural Studies thus turned out to be one element in the *nouveau mélange* that went by the name of the New Art History and from which Visual Culture Studies issues. Correspondingly, it may be noted that Stuart Hall, who was acting director and then director of CCCS from 1968-79, is co-editor of an Open University volume that calls itself *Visual Culture: The Reader*.[3]

My argument here is that the political factors that increasingly debilitated Cultural Studies as a critical practice also compromise Visual Culture Studies, and to an even greater degree. I should acknowledge that while I take the work of the Birmingham Centre as paradigmatic of the Cultural Studies project, it was not the only place in which Cultural Studies was made. However, it was, in the initial stages, the acknowledged nexus for all that was most vital and critical about it.

CCCS, as it was generally known,[4] was initiated in 1964 by Richard Hoggart, professor of modern English literature at the University of Birmingham, as a research institute to continue the line of inquiry he had pursued in his 1957 book, *The Uses of Literacy: Aspects of Working-Class Life, with Special References to Publications and Entertainments*. Although he was socialist in his sympathies, Hoggart was not of the New Left. Stuart Hall, on the other hand, who was with the Centre from its opening, and who succeeded him as director, was among its leading figures.[5] In his retrospective accounts of the formation of Cultural Studies, Hall has been careful to put a certain distance between it and Marxism. The New Left, in his account, »always regarded Marxism as a problem, as trouble, as danger, not as a solution«.[6] For him, classical

Marxism was deformed by a »class reductionism« that prevented it from »dealing with cultural questions seriously«.[7] At times Hall's references to ›traditional‹ and ›classical‹ Marxism seem like a straw man, and there is little sense in his writing of Marxism as a complex tradition of thought, which, particularly in its German-language variants, had long been concerned with problems of culture and consciousness. Moreover, nearer the time he described the Centre's »break into a complex Marxism« in more positive terms.[8]

For ease of summary in defining the Cultural Studies problematic, I refer here mainly to Hall's various essays and to Richard Johnson's *What is Cultural Studies Anyway?* of 1983. (Johnson was the Centre's third director.) To understand the particular methodology of Cultural Studies it is important to register how it conceptualized its object. According to Johnson »culture« remained useful »not as a rigorous category, but as a kind of summation of a history. It references in particular the effort to heave the study of culture from its old inegalitarian anchorages in high-artistic connoisseurship and in discourses, of enormous condescension, on the not-culture of the masses«[9]. The term »Culture« had value as a »reminder« rather than a »precise category«, and as such it encompassed »consciousness« and »subjectivity« in the realm of everyday life.[10] In sum: »*Our* project is to abstract, describe and reconstitute in concrete studies the social forms through which human beings ›live‹, become conscious, sustain themselves subjectively.«[11]

The reason that Cultural Studies was marked by »openness and theoretical versatility« was that »cultural processes do not correspond to the contours of academic knowledges, as they are«. No single academic discipline fully registered their complexity, and thus Cultural Studies had to be inter-disciplinary in tendency.[12] The different approaches to the study of culture such as the literary, historical, and sociological all revealed aspects of it, but none was adequate to »the subjects of culture as a whole«[13]. The reason that what Hall called »the dialogic approach to theory«[14] was necessary was also because Marxism in its received forms could not deal adequately with questions of gender and race. The fact that those at the Centre were forced to address these questions was a result of the rise of the woman's movement and second-wave feminism in the 1970s and the increasing tensions around race in British political life in that and the following decade.[15]

The context for CCCS's work in the 1970s and 1980s was given by the paradox that Britain had simultaneously a working class with a strong culture of class solidarity and an immensely powerful trade union movement, but at the same time a feeble social-democratic party with no effective commitment to socialism.[16] Moreover, its founding texts had assumed that the relative working-class affluence of the 1950s and 1960s and the rise of consumerism and mediatic forms of mass entertainment were having corrosive effects on the communal and class conscious aspects of working-class culture. The work of the Centre also registered that despite extraordinary levels of union militancy in the 1970s, the politics of the Labour Party were shifting markedly to the right after mid decade.[17]

Some of the main causes of Labour's weakness were tellingly summarized by Paul Willis in a paper on shop-floor culture published in 1975, a year after the Labour Party had won a General Election with less than 40% of the vote – a figure that took it back to a level of support it had not experienced since the 1920s and foretold the swing of working-class votes to the Conservatives in 1979.[18] Although shop-floor culture was »full of political *significance*« wrote Willis, it was »deeply *unpolitical*«:

> »Its riveting concern the workplace … prevents the connecting up of work experiences, issues and social structure; it prevents a true political practice. The inherent and deeply charged contradiction of a culturally threadbare working class politics having such a richly threaded, but essentially unpolitical base, is right at the heart of the problems facing strategists of class liberation.«[19]

Of course there was more to »the problems facing strategists of class liberation« than this, and I am not claiming that the perception of a crisis in labour and socialist politics prior to the 1979 election debacle that brought the first Thatcher government to power was uniquely concentrated in CCCS. However, I am suggesting that the work of the Centre had long acknowledged the crisis and that as a collective it was particularly well-placed to identify at least some of its causes precisely because it had registered that they were in important respects cultural. Indeed, in the late 1970s and early 1980s the Centre had published a series of volumes that addressed key problems in the areas of education, race relations and law and order – all of which were hot points in the breakdown of the social-democratic consensus from which Thatcherism drew its energies.[20]

The key political context for the application of the CCCS critique seems superficially a surprising one for a New Left formation in that it was provided mainly by the Communist Party's monthly magazine *Marxism Today* and a number of related book-length publications issued by its publishing house Lawrence and Wishart. The basis for this conjuncture lies in the effects of Thatcherism's political success on the Communist Party, in that it hardened divisions between the grouping centred on its daily paper *The Morning Star* and that centred on *Marxism Today*, which had enjoyed significant circulation growth since 1977. Conventionally this is seen as a division between Stalinist and Euro-Communist wings of the party, but such schematic characterization does not do justice to what was at stake. In relation to my concerns, the most important features of *Marxism Today's* position are that its rejection of what it perceived as economism went so far that it conceived struggles over women's issues, racial issues, gay rights and youth interests as being effectively outside or independent of class struggle. After Thatcher's second electoral victory in 1983, the corresponding notion of a Popular Front type alliance against her government was embraced to the extent that the magazine aligned itself with the right of the Labour Party rather than with those MPs who still continued to call for a socialist alternative.[21] By the end of the decade the magazine could be described not inaptly as »more or less the theoretical organ of Labour revisionism«[22].

Key statements that lay behind this strategy included Eric Hobsawm's 1978 Marx Memorial Lecture, published in *Marxism Today* later that year as »The Forward March of Labour Halted?«, and then as the centre-piece of a volume recording the ensuing debate, and Stuart Hall's essay »The Great Moving Right Show«, published in *Marxism Today* in January 1979, which served as the opening essay of the anthology Hall edited with the magazine's editor Martin Jacques under the title *The Politics of Thatcherism* of 1983.[23]

Hall's analysis in »The Great Moving Right Show« focused on the causes of the increasing political dominance of the Thatcherite Right both within the Conservative Party and over the Labour Party, causes that he identified primarily – but not exclusively – in terms of the categories of ideology and hegemony. The theoretical repertoire that underpinned these categories was drawn from Althusser, Gramsci, and Ernesto Laclau's recent book *Politics and Ideology in Marxist Theory*.[24] The key question for Hall was that of why social democracy had lost the assent of such a large swathe of the electorate, including many working-class voters. The answer lay partly in the contradictory form of social democracy itself, within which the so-called party of Labour claimed to be the representative of the working class, but not only worked with capital it also used state power to seek to »*discipline* the class and the organizations it represents«, namely the trade unions.[25] It was a form in which the party had no interest in popular mobilization, but used the state's resources to make piecemeal reforms to the conditions of working-class life so long as they did not interfere too much with the requirements of capitalist accumulation.[26] It was thus relatively easy for Thatcherism to mobilize popular support against Labour's »statism«, since Labour in power always treated its constituency simply as a passive object. The genius of Thatcherism was its ability to forge a »historic bloc«, in Gramsci's term, between »sections of the dominant and dominated classes«, and to devise a language of »the people« that was »unified behind a reforming drive to turn the tide of ›creeping collectivism‹« on the one hand, and, on the other, to »›make Britain *Great* once more‹« by reestablishing social discipline and combating various enemies within associated with trade union radicals, alien black elements and aspects of youth culture.[27] The term that Hall devised to characterize this ideological ensemble was »authoritarian populism«.[28]

That this hypothesis had explanatory power was widely acknowledged on the left, but it was also criticized for its »ideologism«, for generating »an excessive concern with the mass media and ideological production at the expense of political and economic organization«, and diverting attention from the state's problems of »economic and political *crisis-management*« and the shifting relations within the real power bloc.[29] In sum, it tended to reify Thatcherism into a more coherent whole than it actually was and overlooked some of the contradictions both within its ideological ensemble and within its social support base.[30] Hall was drifting into a discourse theory approach – a charge he denied, but which his opponents reiterated.[31]

In the late 1980s analysis of Thatcherism in *Marxism Today* mutated into a broader debate on the Left's future that went by the name of »New Times« and issued in a volume under that title edited by Hall and Jacques that appeared in 1989.[32] In the »New Times« analysis, the crisis of British capitalism and social democracy was now located as essentially a response to a global phenomenon that – in a nod to Gramsci – was dubbed »Post-Fordism«, and this in turn was linked with the new cultural trend known as postmodernism. An epochal shift was taking part, equivalent to the transition from entrepeneurial to monopoly capitalism in the late nineteenth century, and one with major cultural concomitants.[33] The Left showed itself particularly inept in this conjuncture because it had »lost touch with change and the world outside itself«, and become in many ways »a culturally conservative force«. Thatcherism claimed to represent the »New Times«; the task for the Left was to show that it could respond to the new conditions more effectively within the bourgeois democratic order.[34]

One feature of the new condition was the emergence of »new identities and political subjects«, »new social movements, new collective identities«, a »proliferation of the sites of antagonism and resistance«.[35] This proposition was filled out in the article »After the Masses« by Dick Hebdige, author of a well-known study of youth subcultures that grew out of a CCCS MA thesis.[36] Hebdige argued for the need to articulate a »new kind of socialism … without the masses«, one that acknowledged that the »two great collective identities through which the masses came together to ›make history‹ in the last two hundred years« – those of nation and class – were breaking down in the developed world, but new collectives were emerging and partly taking shape through the new media. Faced with a bewildering range of »communities, interests, and histories«, a new flexible politics was needed to counterpose to the capacity of Thatcherism to use language in ways that interpellated a compelling sense of national identity and unity. Significantly, Hebdige contrasted the failings of the Left to reenvisage the subject of late twentieth-century society with the success of market research in categorizing and mapping popular desires. The sociological flimsiness of these formulations and their lack of theoretical precision is notable. But so are the assumptions that socialism could be discussed not as an alternative to capitalism but merely as a »commitment to social justice, equality of opportunity, and social welfare«, to achieve which »a relaxation of the old critical and judgmental postures« was needed.[37] We are already at a premonition of the New Labour agenda, *avant la lettre*.

The implications of this are made dismally clear in the essay by another CCCS graduate Frank Mort, »The Politics of Consumption«, which asserted that »*our* conception of politics must again be prised open« [my emphasis] to accommodate »consumer individualism«. The market, Mort claimed, had broken up »postwar class certainties« and contributed to a lifestyle segmentation that was closely linked with the politics of identity. The notion of »fixed subjects« was stale, »early 20th century«. »*We*« [my emphasis] all carried »a bewildering range of different, and at times conflicting, identities around with us in our heads at the same time«.[38] The Left was over-preoccupied with production and needed to adapt to the dominance of consumption in an age of affluence – it needed to discard its masculinist assumptions about the priority of the former, and engage with the feminized realm of the latter. Labour was historically obsessed with austerity and should embrace »consumer democracy«.[39] Against the Left's socialist moralism, Mort affirmed that the »new consumerism« was »all about floating visual images, pleasures and impossible dreams«. And what these amounted to was not merely ideology. Indeed, advertisers it turned out were offering a social service:

> »A more serious look at advertising's dialogue with the market puts paid to the cliché that consumption is foisted on gullible populations by hype and the lust for profits. Advertisers and marketers are not simply the slaves of capital. They are the intermediaries who construct a dialogue between the market on the one hand and consumer culture on the other. Marketers will tell you that this is a two-way process; it doesn't simply come from above […] to fail to recognize that marketing taps something of our pleasures and aspirations as consumers is ignore the how and why of its success.«[40]

What is astonishing here is the complete inversion of the critique of consumer culture on which Cultural Studies was partly founded, indeed the abandonment of any notion of critique and the complete capitulation to the capitalist order.[41]

To conclude with I want to sketch briefly some of the continuities between Cultural Studies and Visual Studies. For the purposes of my exposition here, the differences between its various exponents such as Mieke Bal, Nicholas Mirzoeff, and the Bryson/Holly/Moxey triplet are of little consequence.[42] I noted earlier Cultural Studies' embrace of the postmodern as an aspect of its political accommodation to the present. Visual Studies, at least as formulated by Mirzoeff, is an even more unequivocally postmodern phenomenon – in his words, »Postmodernism is visual culture«, while »visual culture is a tactic with which to study the genealogy, definitions and functions of postmodern everyday life«[43]. Indeed, reading expositions of the Visual Studies problematic is like going through a check list of trite postmodern propositions. In particular, there is an embrace of epistemological relativism and of interpretative contingency, and a rejection of historical modes of explanation– although there are some differences among the names listed above on this latter score.[44] Ontology and epistemology are simply *passé* concerns, doubtless to be consigned to what another exponent calls »a tedious and traditional corpus of knowledge«[45]. Underlying all is a rejection of Marxism and a refusal of causal hierarchies of determination.[46] Which is also to say that if Visual Studies has an intellectual guiding star its name is Foucault. The Foucaultian claim that the academy itself is an institution of power and domination and that claims for »objectivity« are just a form of »caste privilege« are linked with an insistence on the necessary positionality and political character of all knowledge production and a corresponding imperative to make it respond to the particular demands of contemporary politics.[47] But the politics involved is only one of difference and not one of systemic or anti-capitalist critique. Not only is the model of scientific knowledge in the anglophone sense of the term ruled out, but so is the model of *Wissenschaft*. Disciplinary boundaries are just so many impediments to the investigator's playful alignment of methods and theories according to the needs of the moment.[48] (Whatever else, Visual Studies embraces the flow of the New, and exemplifies the valorization of relentless change so often seen as a signature of postmodernity).[49] The term »discipline« has become non-U because it suggests the academy, while visual culture should be a »tactic«, a style of interpretation that »hopes to reach beyond the traditional confines of the university to interact with people's everyday lives«[50] Visual Studies, like Cultural Studies, is thus unabashedly populist in its claims,[51] and one of the notable things about some of its defenders is their tendency to confuse the demands of making higher education syllabi relevant or popular with students (and there is often a slippage between the two) and the demands of knowledge production. The instrumentalism of the Foucaultian conception of knowledge is embraced in a double sense.

There is not space here to lay out yet again a Marxist critique of Foucault.[52] At this point, I only wish to echo the artist Silvia Kolbowski's point that it should not be assumed »the loss or blurring of boundaries is always *socially* progressive«.[53] The refusal of academic disciplines has always been intrinsic to the Marxist project, which has its own critique of the knowledge/power relationship that goes by the name of ideology. But unlike Foucaultian theory, Marxism does not of course see truth as inherently a ruse of power but rather as the evolving knowledge of nature and the historical process through social struggles and the dialectic. Disciplines are objectionable to the extent that they fragment the totality of the social whole and obscure the complex causal mechanisms that bind it together. To begin with, at least, Cultural Studies in Britain had a clearer idea both of the nature of its object and of that object's role in the social order than Visual Culture Studies does of its, and the creation of another reified object of inquiry under the name »visuality« (as currently conceived) is unlikely to advance understanding of either society or history.

---

1 E.g., Trevor Millum: *Images of Women: Advertising in Women's Magazines*. London 1975; Janice Winship: *Advertising in Women's Magazines: 1956-74*. CCCS Stencilled Occasional Paper No. 59, University of Birmingham 1980.

2 George Robertson et. al.: *The Block Reader in Visual Culture*. London/New York 1996.

3 Jessica Evans, Stuart Hall (ed.): *Visual Culture: The Reader*. London 1999.

4 The University of Birmingham closed the centre in 1991, and replaced it with a Department of Cultural Studies and Sociology. This was in turn closed in 2002.

5 Lin Chun: *The British New Left*. Edinburgh 1993, pp. 13–16; »The formation of a diasporic intellectual: An interview with Stuart Hall by Kuan-Hsing Chen« In: David Morley, Kuan-Hsing Chen (ed.): *Stuart Hall: Critical Dialogues in Cultural Studies*. London/New York 1996, pp. 491–98.

6 Stuart Hall, »Cultural Studies and its theoretical legacies« In Morley, Chen 1996 (as n. 5), pp. 270, 264, 265.

7 »The formation of a diasporic intellectual« (as n. 5), p. 499. For Hall's conception of updated Marxism, see especially his »The problem of ideology: Marxism without guarantees« In: Morley, Chen 1996 (as n. 5), pp. 25–46. For critiques of this position, see Jorge Larrain: »Stuart Hall and the Marxist concept of Ideology«, and Colin Sparks: »Stuart Hall, Cultural Studies, and Marxism« In: Morley, Chen 1996 (as n. 5), pp. 47–70, and 71–101.

8 Stuart Hall: »Cultural Studies and the Centre: Some Problematics and Problems« In: Hall et. al. (ed.): *Culture, Media, Language: Working Papers in Cultural Studies*. London 1980, pp. 25–26.

9 Richard Johnson: *What is Cultural Studies Anyway?* CCCS Stencilled Occasional Paper No. 74, University of Birmingham, 1983, p. 8. (Also published in: *Social Text*, no. 16, Winter 1986–87, pp. 38–80). Cf. Raymond Williams's formative essay »Culture is Ordinary« (1958) In: Williams: *Resources of Hope: Culture, Democracy, Socialism*. London/New York 1989, pp. 3–18.

10 Johnson 1983, pp. 11, 2.

11 Johnson 1983, pp. 13.

12 Johnson 1983, pp. 2, 9. Cf. Hall 1980 (as n. 8), pp. 37, 38.

13 Johnson 1983, p. 7. Cf. Hall 1980 (as n. 8), pp. 42–47.

14 Hall 1996 (as n. 6), p. 264.

15 Hall described »the emergence of feminism« as »the most profound challenge to any attempt to establish a Cultural Studies ›orthodoxy‹« – Hall 1980 (as n. 8), pp. 38-9.

16 See especially Ralph Miliband: *Parliamentary Socialism: A Study in the Politics of Labour*. London 1961.

17 See Leo Panitch, Colin Leys: *The End of Parliamentary Socialism: From New Left to New Labour*. London/New York 2001, chapters 5–6.

18 I am referring to the election of February 1974.

19 Paul E. Willis: *Human Experience and Material Production: The Culture of the Shop Floor*. Stencilled Occasional Paper No. 33, Centre for Contemporary Cultural Studies, University of Birmingham, 1975, pp. 13–14.

20 Stuart Hall et. al.: *Policing the Crisis: Mugging, the State, and Law and Order*. London 1978; CCCS Education Group: *Unpopular Education: Schooling and Social Demoracy in*

England since 1944. London 1981; CCCS: *The Empire Strikes Back: Race and Racism in 70s Britain*. London 1982.

21 My analysis here is based on Lee Pitcairn: »Crisis in British Communism: An Insider's View« In: *New Left Review*, series 1, September/October 1985, no. 153, pp. 102–20.

22 Michael Rustin: »The Politics of Post-Fordism: or the The Trouble with ›New Times‹« In: *New Left Review*, series 1, May/June 1989, no. 175, p. 56.

23 Eric Hobsbawm: »The Forward March of Labour Halted?« In: *Marxism Today*, September 1978, pp. 279–86; Martin Jacques, Francis Muhlern (ed.): *The Forward March of Labour Halted?* London 1981; Stuart Hall, Martin Jacques (ed.): *The Politics of Thatcherism*. London 1983.

24 Ernesto Laclau: *Politics and Ideology in Marxist Theory*. London 1977.

25 Stuart Hall: »The Great Moving Right Show« In: Hall, Jacques 1983 (as n. 23), p. 27.

26 Hall, Jacques 1983 (as n. 23), p. 32–24.

27 Hall, Jacques 1983 (as n. 23), p. 30–31.

28 Stuart Hall: »Popular Democratic vs. authoritarian-populism: two ways of ›taking democracy seriously‹« In: Alan Hunt (ed.): *Marxism and Democracy*. London 1980, pp. 157–85.

29 Bob Jessop, Kevin Bonnett, Simon Bromley, Tom Ling: »Authoritarian Populism, Two Nations, and Thatcherism« In: *New Left Review*, series 1, September/October 1984, No. 147, pp. 37, 52, 53.

30 Jessop, Bonnett, Bromley, Ling 1984 (as n. 29), p. 42. For the ensuing debate, see Stuart Hall: »Authoritarian Populism: A Reply to Jessop et al« In: *New Left Review*, series 1, May/June 1985, No. 151, pp. 116–18; Bob Jessop et. al.: »Thatcherism and the Politics of Hegemony: a Reply to Stuart Hall« In: *New Left Review*, series 1, September/October 1985, No. 153, pp. 87–101.

31 Jessop, Bonnett, Bromley, Ling 1984 (as n. 29), p. 37; Hall 1985 (as n. 30), pp. 121–122; Jessop et. al. 1985 (as n. 30), p. 95. The discourse theory politics of Ernesto Laclau and Chantal Mouffe, on which Hall drew, was subjected to sustained critique at the time. See, for instance: Peter Osborne: »Radicalism Without Limit? Discourse, Democracy and the Politics of Identity« In: Peter Osborne (ed.): *Socialism and the Limits of Liberalism*. London 1991, chapter 8. Osborne provides a bibliography of other critical responses (n. 3, 222) and also notes Hall's »lack of clarity« on the »philosophical issues underlying the application of discourse theory to politics« (n. 38, 224).

32 Stuart Hall, Martin Jacques (ed.): *New Times: The Changing Face of Politics in the 1990s*. London 1989.

33 Stuart Hall and Martin Jacques: »Introduction« In Hall, Jacques 1989 (as n. 32), p. 12.

34 The »New Times« line was again criticized by Bob Jessop, Kevin Bonnet, and Simon Bromley, in »Farewell to Thatcherism? Neo-Liberalism and ›New Times‹« In: *New Left Review*, series 1, January/February 1990, No. 179, pp. 81–102.

35 Hall, Jacques 1989 (as n. 32), pp. 15, 17. Cf. pp. 36–37.

36 Dick Hebdige: *Subculture: The Meaning of Style*. London 1979.

37 Dick Hebdige: »After the Masses« In: Hall, Jacques 1989 (as n. 32), pp. 93, 90–91, 89–90.

38 Frank Mort: »The Politics of Consumption« In: Hall, Jacques 1989 (as n. 32), pp. 171, 169.

39 Ibid., 164–165.

40 Ibid., pp. 169, 167. Hall's position on civil society and consumerism was at least more nuanced – see Stuart Hall: »The Meaning of New Times« In: Hall, Jacques 1989 (as n. 32), pp. 130–131.

41 See for instance, Raymond Williams: »Advertising: the Magic System« In: Raymond Williams: *Problems in Materialism and Culture: Selected Essays.* London/New York 1997, pp. 170-95. This was originally written for one of the founding texts of Cultural Studies, namely Raymond Williams: *The Long Revolution.* London 1961, but omitted. It was first published in abbreviated form in *New Left Review*, series 1, July/August 1960, No. 4, pp. 27–32. The contrast between Mort's position and that of CCCS critique in the 1970s could hardly be greater – cf., for instance: Janice Winship: *Woman Becomes an »Individual« – Femininity and Consumption in Women's Magazines 1954–69.* Stencilled Occasional Paper No.65, Centre for Contemporary Cultural Studies, University of Birmingham 1981.

42 For a parading of these differences, see Mieke Bal: »Visual essentialism and the object of visual culture«, and »Responses to Mieke Bal's ›Visual Essentialism and the object of visual culture‹« In: *Journal of Visual Culture*, Vol. 2, 2003, No. 2, pp. 229–68.

43 Nicholas Mirzoeff: »What is Visual Culture?« In: Nicholas Mirzoeff (ed.): *The Visual Culture Reader.* London/New York 1998, pp. 4, 5. This proposition is linked to large claims about the dominance of »the visual« in the contemporary order and the leveling of established hierarchies of cultural value. Bal attacks these claims in Ball 2003 (as n. 42), p. 6.

44 E.g. Michael Ann Holly takes exception to Bal's »presentism« in »Responses to Mieke Bal's ›Visual Essentialism and the object of visual culture‹« (as n. 42), pp. 240–241. Yet for Holly »As long as the historical reading is appropriate, rich, full of thought, tied to sources and bound to ›images‹ of many colors, it doesn't matter if the meaning is the ›correct‹ one«. (241). The aestheticism of this formulation and its indifference to the responsibility of knowledge production is obvious.

45 Irit Rogoff: »Studying Visual Culture« In: Mirzoeff 1998 (as n. 43), p. 21.

46 E.g. Norman Bryson, Michael Ann Holly, Keith Moxey (ed.): *Visual Culture: Images and Interpretations.* Hanover, NH/London 1994, p. xix. Of course the Marxism described is like some Stalinist caricature and unrecognizable as such to anyone with a real knowledge of the Marxist tradition.

47 E.g. Bryson, Holly, Moxey 1994 (as n. 46), p. xxvii; Rogoff 1998 (as n. 45), p. 23.

48 For the »playfulness« of Visual Studies, see Holly in »Responses to Mieke Bal's…« (as n. 44), p. 238.

49 For a characteristic valorization of the new, see Michael Ann Holly: »Saints and Sinners« In: *October*, No. 77, Summer 1996, p. 41.

50 Mirzoeff 1998 (as n. 43), p. 11. Cf. Bryson, Holly, Moxey 1994 (as n. 47), p. xxix.

51 Mirzoeff even claims that left-wing defenders of art history often come out of Ivy League universities – Mirzoeff 1998 (as n. 43), p. 10.

52 E.g., Peter Dews: »The Nouvelle Philosophie and Foucault« In: *Economy and Society*, No. 8, May 1979, pp. 127–171; Peter Dews: *Logics of Disintegration: Post-Structuralist Thought and the Claims of Critical Theory.* London/New York 1987, chapters 5–7.

53 »Visual Culture Questionnaire« In: *October*, No. 77, Summer 1996, p. 48.

Stewart Martin

Visual Culture or Art?

Over the last decade or so there have been a number of articles, books and special issues of journals registering and reflecting on the emergence of ›visual culture‹ as a new field of research, and ›Visual Culture Studies‹ as a new academic discipline oriented to it. As one of its foremost proponents recently remarked: »Visual culture now stands [...] at the threshold of definition«.[1] One might add that it is also at, or perhaps past, the threshold of its institutional consolidation. Visual culture and its study is the scene of various hopes, anxieties and controversies, principally about what is to be gained and lost by its emergence. Minimally, it is just a new shuffling of academics and curricula. Maximally, it is a symptom of profound cultural transformation.

One of these controversies concerns the consequences for the study of art, both theoretically and practically. Visual Culture Studies looks set to become the preferred, if not default, disciplinary self-understanding for the practice and theory of art, thereby displacing Art History – at least in the Anglo-American academy. The rubric of ›Art History‹ is likely to be very resilient, but this is little substitute for methodological legitimacy. (As for the other historical and theoretical disciplines around art, these are quite unstable and complex. Art Criticism does not tend to have a strong disciplinary character, and what is often referred to as Critical Theory and Art Theory are frequently makeshift assemblages. The Philosophy of Art remains marginal.) The routine justification for this displacement of Art History by Visual Culture Studies is that visual culture presents an expansion of the field of art, opening it to the arena of low art and non-art. In its destruction of the exclusivity of high art, Visual Culture Studies is presented as corresponding to, if not blazing a trail for, the anti-conventional and transgressive character of much contemporary art practice. So while Visual Culture Studies makes no claim to be an exclusive theory of art, it is routinely content to incorporate art as one of its objects of study.

And yet, contemporary art practice cannot be described as essentially visual or encompassed by the field of visual culture or ›visuality‹, except perhaps in a deeply contested sense. Such a description would exclude many seminal works and widely recognized revolutions in the formation of what contemporary art has become. This multiplicity and non-identity of contemporary art practice may present difficulties for any theoretical discipline, but Visual Culture Studies is clearly not even geared to this end.

We are therefore confronted with an ironic situation, in which the *expansion* of the field of visual culture effectively leads to a *contraction* of the field of art. This situation could be appropriately described as repressive: Visual Culture Studies represses the expansion of contemporary art practice through condensing it, and thereby displacing it, with the expansion of visual culture. This repression is not the result of a simple opposition between cultural spheres, since it is reproduced within the contemporary artworld. This can be discerned in the way that expanded art practices tend to be situated or enfranchised (or perhaps just publicized) within arenas that retain a link to formally ›visual‹ arts, such as Documenta or many Biennials, which present a peculiarly suspended, yet persistent, link to painting and sculpture. This is equally evident in certain pervasive forms or dimensions of the contemporary artwork – the Readymade is exemplary of this suspended, yet persistent, link between painting and art in general. But, however much one can retrospectively construe as ›visual‹ those arts where the breakdown of the arts took place most insistently, this does not exhaust the consequences of this breakdown. Neither does it grasp this breakdown's emergence from avant-garde and romantic projects to overcome the reification of life within the delimitations of the arts. These dimensions of the expanded field of art also tend to be repressed within the expanded field of Visual Culture Studies.

This situation reveals deep tensions, if not a crisis, within the disciplinary self-understanding of art and visual culture. Visual Culture Studies should be able to resolve this if it gives up the claim to be a theory of art. Certainly, in some respects it does not make this claim and is not compelled to. Still, there remain important respects in which Visual Culture Studies is inextricably tied up with, and invested in, an expanded discourse about art. To this extent the problem remains.

The self-understanding of art faces a more insistent crisis, since, however limited Visual Culture Studies may be, it is not clear that there is a better alternative available. What would be the theoretical self-understanding of the expanded field of contemporary art practice? The lack of a good answer, especially from Art History, is a highly notable feature of the debates surrounding visual culture. In some ways, the difficulty of this question justifies the very limits of Visual Culture Studies – »let's at least specify this unwieldy field according to the visual«. And there are many ways in which Art History has historically shared this specification. But this answer misses the significance of the question, not just for the study of art, but for the study of contemporary culture more broadly.

The first and foremost thesis of this essay has already been outlined, namely, that *the expanded field of art is repressed by Visual Culture Studies*. But this essay is not ultimately concerned with shifting the ground of academic departments. Its purpose is not to lament the colonization of Art History by Visual Culture Studies, or even to defend the academic sovereignty of art. Rather, its fundamental orientation is towards the critique of capitalist culture and how this is at stake within the disputes over visual culture and art. It probably goes without saying that the critique of capitalist culture is an all too neglected criterion of the current division of academic labour. Capitalist culture is scarcely grasped by any particular academic discipline, so its critique requires a trans-disciplinary approach. This must draw on both Art History and Visual Culture Studies, but they do not exhaust the significance of the expanded field of art. Therefore, the second, but overdetermining, thesis proposed here is that *the expanded field of art presents a dramatic scene of contemporary capitalist culture, and that if we are to grasp the latter we need to grasp the former.*

To reiterate, the contention here is that there is a deep affinity between the nominalism of contemporary art practice and the nominalism of contemporary or late capitalist culture; that the flexible and transferable arts that go into contemporary artworks mimic the flexible and transferable skills that characterize certain evolved forms of wage labour; that the dissolution of art's autonomy from non-art and everyday life mimics some of the ways in which the boundaries between wage labour and everyday life have become eroded. More broadly then, the claim here is that late capitalist culture has many affinities with the ambitions of the early avant-gardes and romantics, but that it produces a perversion of their utopian ambitions: Art is dissolved into everyday life, not as communism, but as consumerism and the integration of wage labour and the self-valorization of capital into the reproduction of all aspects of social life. This perversion does not exhaust these avant-garde ambitions. Indeed, it is recognition of their force. Contemporary critical art practice continues to draw on these ambitions with good reason, but it is faced with an altogether more implicated relation to capitalist culture than it had in the 1910s and 1920s. This tension has made contemporary art practice the scene of both the affirmation of capitalist culture and its critique or negation. One only needs to look at the combination of radical politics and radical commercialism at some of the recent Biennials to recognize how the contemporary artworld is a persisting realm of bourgeois radicalism, with all the contradictions of freedom and capitalism that entails.

This characterization of the relation of art and capitalism may remain unconvincing for some, but at one level the proposition here is simply that contemporary art is part of capitalist culture and so is inevitably made out of, and against, its forms. More specifically, the contention is that in order to grasp this relation of art to capitalism one needs to grasp the very nominalism, multiplicity or non-identity that links them. It is this that Visual Culture Studies represses or occludes; hence the issue it poses for a critique of contemporary capitalist culture.

Staking out visual culture

There is no manifesto of Visual Culture Studies. Perhaps it has yet to be written, or perhaps a consensus has yet to be reached that one or other of the programmatic texts that have been written should have this status. In any case, controversies surround Visual Culture Studies, both at its borders and within it. But it is possible to discern a number of propositions that stake out its field, if only as points of contention. These reveal that art is an important but rather tangential concern.

One proposition would be that *Visual Culture Studies is a new discipline, with a new field, object and/or subject.* This is, perhaps inevitably, a point of considerable discussion among the proponents of Visual Culture Studies, as well as among its opponents. The former seem generally rather sceptical about the very attempt to forge disciplines, principally because of what they exclude, although W.J.T. Mitchell has notably claimed that Visual Culture Studies is not merely an »indiscipline«, but rather an »interdiscipline«[2]. Jessica Evans and Stuart Hall describe it as a partition of the broader and encompassing field of the semiotic analysis of culture.[3] Thus, without quite saying the words, they define it as a sub-discipline of Cultural Studies. Indeed, it is very compelling to view Visual Culture Studies as primarily a ›post-Cultural Studies effect‹; one consequence of re-ordering the Humanities within the transformed field of Cultural Studies. (›Spatial Culture Studies‹ would be another less renowned product.) With respect to the object and/or subject of Visual Culture Studies, Mitchell claims that it concerns »a new and distinct object«, which he sometimes calls »visuality« and sometimes »the visual field«. This produces his definition: »Visual culture is the study of the social constitution of the visual field, and the visual construction of the social field«.[4] Mieke Bal has nonetheless maintained that lack of clarity on what … [Visual Culture Studies'] object domain is remains its primary point of pain«[5]. And she proposes to resolve this by attention, not to the object, but to the subject of visual culture, or the »possibility of performing acts of seeing«[6] – so a quasi-transcendental account.

Visual Culture Studies is the product of a pictorial turn. Mitchell, who coined this phrase, has come to regret it as too crude a claim both historically and conceptually. He maintains, as does Bal, that vision is essentially synaesthetic. However, this merely begs the question of dedicating a discipline to it exclusively. Why not Synaesthesia Studies? Evans and Hall justify Visual Culture Studies as a corrective response to the obscuring of the study of visual culture by Cultural Studies as a result of the latter's predisposition to the semiotic analysis of the visual in terms of the textual. As they also point out, this was despite the importance of issues of vision and images for the foundational influences on Cultural Studies, such as Benjamin, Barthes, Foucault and Lacan.

Visual Culture Studies is a response to the emergence of new visual technologies and their cultural influence, if not dominance. According to some versions, it is a response to the emergence of a visual epoch of surveillance, spectacle, scopic regimes, and so on. It is perhaps here that Visual Culture Studies comes closest to understanding itself directly as a critique of capitalist culture. Although this critical task needs to be won from an altogether more uncritical relation, a suspicion articulated by the OCTOBER »Questionnaire« on Visual Culture Studies: »the suggestion is that visual studies is helping, in its own modest, academic way, to produce subjects for the next stage of globalized capital«[7]. However, whether affirmatively or critically, there appears to be little interest in articulating this relation in terms of an expanded conception of art.

Visual Culture Studies is a critique of iconophobia. In other words, it is a revaluation, if not affirmation, of images and our relation to them.[8] In the more inflected versions of this proposition, it is not proposed as an uncritical iconophilia, but rather as a critical discourse on images that does not regard them as mere lies or reduce them to some non-imagistic truth.

Visual Culture Studies presents an anthropological turn. This is a comparatively minor, but nonetheless interesting claim. Broadly, the contention is that Visual Culture Studies introduces considerations of the optical faculty of human beings and its transformation, which is frequently presupposed by other historical disciplines.[9]

Finally, then, we turn to Visual Culture Studies' explicit relation to art. Perhaps the first thing to note is how surprisingly under-articulated this relation is. Insofar as it is articulated at all, the proposition at stake might be formulated as: *Visual Cultural Studies is the result of the end of art, or its expansion beyond its traditional limits (and, relatedly, the end of Art History).* Susan Buck-Morss – a proponent of sorts for Visual Culture Studies – has expressed this view. But she is not concerned with an expanded notion of art. Rather, she speculates about whether the image is now outmoded by information, leaving specifically »aesthetic experience« as what is not accounted for. [10] Griselda Pollock is one of the few in the published debates about Visual Culture Studies to indicate how it has inflected her engagement with art.[11] But she is not concerned with the problem of art's multiplicity, or that the visual may be a constraint on considering it. Thomas Crow has made the case for the prosecution, pointing out how ironic it is that Visual Culture Studies restores the privilege of opticality that was subject to such criticism by Conceptual Art. In fact, he extends this critical capacity to the tradition of Western painting.[12] He thereby maintains the value of painting, not a multiple notion of art beyond the arts. In reply, Mitchell has rejected Crow's objection and others like it, as a »myth« about Visual Cultural Studies. Instead, he claims that it »encourages reflection on the differences between art and non-art« as well as on visual and non-visual, and that this is enabled precisely through the transgression of boundaries and a more encompassing field of research that allows this critical demarcation.[13] However, it is clear that vision and the visual remain the centre of gravity, and the problem of how this represses the expanded idea of art and its critical traditions remains.

Art's expanded field

So let us return to what Visual Culture Studies has repressed. In one sense, of course, it might be said that this is simply the non-visual arts, such as music or perhaps poetry. But music and poetry indicate alternative divisions of the arts, not a non-division. To this extent they do not ultimately challenge the fact that Visual Culture Studies indicates an alternative division of the arts; they merely draw attention to what is outside or overshadowed by it. Thus, it is possible to propose an alternative division of the arts according to visual culture, sonic culture, spatial culture, etc. However, there is a fundamental difference between competing conceptions of division and conceptions of non-division. It is this latter conception of art, discernable within various artistic programmes since the nineteenth century, which is more profoundly incompatible with Visual Culture Studies. The non-division of visual culture is also a re-division of the visual and non-visual. The condensation of the non-division of art with the non-division of visual culture thereby displaces this idea of art with a re-division according to visual culture. This is the repressive function of Visual Culture Studies. Undoubtedly, art is also liable to this re-division – say, between what is art and non-art. And yet, various radical programmes self-consciously opposed this, seeking in art's non-division a transformation of totality. Such programmes are also effectively repressed by the routine self-understanding of Visual Culture Studies.

This idea of art's non-division may be elaborated through a rough sketch of its history. The origin of this history is not the past, but the present, namely, the conjunction of Visual Culture Studies, art and capitalist culture that has already been outlined. If we consider the pre-history of this present the obvious next step is the 1960s, and the conspicuous crisis of the system of fine arts, that had in some sense been in place since its consolidation in the mid-eighteenth century. Clement Greenberg is probably the seminal figure here, since he has came to stand for the very idea of a differentiation of the arts, and then its crisis, and provided the common point of rejection for a series of alternative notions of art not based on the differentiation of the arts. Greenberg's ideas are highly familiar, but there are some common misperceptions that should be addressed in this context. Principally, it is important to recognize that he did not argue for the supremacy of painting over the other arts; he defended painting as one of the arts, internal to an inherently multiple and non-hierarchical system of arts. (In this Greenberg departs from the many systems of the arts developed from Kant to Heidegger; indeed, he is far more original in the history of systems of the arts than he is generally credited for.)[14] Thus, opposition to Greenberg is not simply a matter of re-asserting the rights of other arts besides painting, as is often assumed. He already maintained this himself, at least formally. Rather, fundamental opposition would require challenging the very idea of a system of different arts.

There certainly were a number of such challenges in the 1960s. A relatively tentative one was formulated in Donald Judd's notion of ›specific objects‹, which is no longer preoccupied with what is painting or sculpture, or, indeed, distinctions between art and non-art. These considerations are replaced by the considerations of something's ›specificity‹. Joseph Kosuth's notion of art is also no longer an issue of the arts, but of art as such or in general; furthermore, of new definitions of what art is. Another particularly resonant instance here would be Allan Kaprow's notion of ›Happenings‹, as events that would overcome the division of the arts and thereby the division of art from life. Similarly, Joseph Beuys's expansion of the task of art into that of an emancipated society is emblematic. Many other examples might be cited. Without overlooking the differences of such proposals, what is shared is a broad commitment to a conception of art beyond the arts.

It is worth considering whether such proposals of the 1960s shared common causes and motivations beyond the artworld, perhaps as a basis for their commonality. One such impulse was the pervasive aversion to bureaucratic ›specialisms‹ and divisions of labour, which was transposed into the realm of art as an aversion to its reification as yet another specialism, making it part and parcel of a broad critique of Fordist/Taylorist forms of industrialized work. (Clearly, Judd and Kosuth have an ambivalent relation to this context.) The persistence of this anti-specialism of art into the present – moreover, its persistence within a deeply commodified artworld, against which art's anti-specialism was frequently proposed – contributes to the sense in which late capitalism has managed to accommodate anti-Fordist forms of work, at least in certain spheres, and that contemporary art's multiplicity has become as much a symptom of this development as an objection to it.

The 1960s crisis of the arts is in many respects foundational for the formation of Visual Culture Studies. The undermining of the delimitation of the arts exposes art to non-art, and legitimates the introduction of ›culture‹ as a new common field of this indifference. This is therefore a condition of the possibility of then re-dividing this field according to the visual and non-visual, whether as a response to disenfranchised art historians, or the general desire to divide up this expanded field. And yet, this division also breaks up the emancipatory horizons of the dissolution of the arts.

This is only enforced if we look to earlier episodes than the 1960s, and particularly to those of the 1910s and 1920s, which are vital in this context. As in many other respects, the crisis of the arts in the 1960s repeats the crisis of the arts in those decades. However, it appears that the problem of the delimitation of the arts is articulated more fully and urgently in the 1960s than it had been earlier. The programmes from the 1910s and 1920s are frequently preoccupied, not so much with the problem of the arts, precisely understood, but with art as such. And they focus less on overcoming the delimitation of the arts, than on overcoming the delimitation of art as a whole – that is, its alienation from life. One of Alexander Rodchenko's ›Slogans‹ is exemplary in this regard: »Constructivist life is the art of the future«[15]. There are indications that the problem of the arts becomes more urgent within the comparatively narrowed political horizon of 1960s, as a revolution *within* art, rather than *beyond* art. This distinction between overcoming the specialism of the arts and overcoming the specialism of art altogether, is articulated well by that 1960s avant-garde that, tellingly, maintained more of the political ambition of the early avant-gardes, namely, the Situationist International – in particular Mustapha Khayati's claim that: »Dada realized all the possibilities of language and forever closed the door on art as a speciality … The realization of art – poetry in the Situationist sense – means that one cannot realize oneself in a ›work‹, but rather realizes oneself period«.[16]

One might point to a third episode of this prehistory of the present in the revolutionary programmes of the nineteenth century. While these do not turn against the idea of art as such in the way, or to the extent, that the programmes of the 1910s and 1920s did, they nonetheless propose a critique of the division of the arts, and their overcoming as a means to social revolution. Richard Wagner's notion of the »Gesamtkunstwerk«, as outlined in his essay *The Artwork of the Future* (1849), is exemplary in this respect. The limitations of the different arts would be overcome, while also being sustained, in a unified artwork, through which humanity could recover a unity that it has lost in modernity. Wagner expresses a sentiment here that is shared by a number of critics, namely, that the modern system of the arts canonized in the eighteenth century was not merely the classificatory achievement of human reason that the Encyclopaedists claimed, but symptomatic of humanity's alienation. There are certain ways in which this critique of the arts persists into the present, but in a form rendered profoundly ambivalent by the development of capitalist modernity.

And what of Visual Culture Studies? It seems very remote from this history. And, in large part, this is precisely the point: that this radical tradition of criticism of the division of the arts is effectively repressed by Visual Culture Studies; and that despite its claim to produce an expanded field – which seems to continue this tradition in certain respects – the stakes and politics of this tradition are largely neutralized and rendered an academic concern. Certainly, this radical tradition has become deeply ambivalent within contemporary capitalist culture. However, its ambivalence – the conflicts between the utopia of an art of life or a dissolution of art into life, on one hand, and, on the other, late capitalism's dystopia of a dissolution of art into a life of capital – does not structure the field of Visual Culture Studies, at least not as a self-conscious commitment. An exception would be in the commitment to Guy Debord's programme of a critique of the society of the spectacle – a critique of the visuality of capitalist culture. However, Debord proposed a revolutionary programme. To date, Visual Culture Studies has not. But in any case, it seems likely that we need to question whether the intensified subsumption of social life by contemporary capitalism is still grasped adequately by the notion of spectacle.

The contention of this essay is not that art offers a simple solution to the issues of visual culture and its Studies. It is rather that Visual Culture Studies does *not* offer a solution to the problem of art, but instead tends to repress it. Moreover, that this problem of art remains a prism through which both the negation and affirmation of the expanded art of capitalist culture is refracted. This is what gives the study of art such significance for the inevitably transdisciplinary study of capitalist culture, or what might be called Capitalist Culture Studies.

1 W.J.T. Mitchell in »Responses to Mieke Bal's ›Visual Essentialism and the Object of Visual Culture‹« In: *Journal of Visual Culture*, vol. 2 (2), 2003, p. 250.

2 W.J.T. Mitchell: »Showing Seeing: A Critique of Visual Culture« (2002) in his: *What do Pictures Really Want? The Lives and Loves of Images*. Chicago/London 2005, p. 356.

3 Jessica Evans, Stuart Hall: »What is Visual Culture?« In Jessica Evans, Stuart Hall (eds.): *Visual Culture: The Reader*. London/New Delhi 1999, p. 3.

4 Mitchell 2003 (as note 1), p. 152. This reformulates his definition in »Showing Seeing«.

5 Mieke Bal: »Visual Essentialism and the Object of Visual Culture« In: *Journal of Visual Culture*, vol. 2(1), 2003, p. 6.

6 »Instead of visuality as a defining property of the traditional object, it is the practices of looking invested in any object that constitute the object domain: its historicity, its social anchoring and its openness to the analysis of its synaesthetics. It is the possibility of performing acts of seeing, not of the materiality of the object seen, that decides whether an artefact can be considered from the perspective of visual culture studies«. Ibid., p. 11.

7 »Visual Culture Questionnaire« In: OCTOBER 77, Summer 1996, p. 25.

8 An emblematic book here would be Martin Jay: *Downcast Eyes: The Denigration of Vision in Twentieth-Century French Thought*. Berkeley/Los Angeles/London 1993.

9 Mitchell has referred to the primal scene of visual culture as the face-to-face origin of society. See Mitchell 2005 (as note 2), p. 351.

10 »Visual Culture Questionnaire« 1996 (as note 7), p. 30.

11 See her contribution to »Responses to Mieke Bal's ›Visual Essentialism and the object of visual culture‹« 2003 (as note 1), pp. 253–60.

12 »Preoccupation with the optical entails a failure to recognize that painting in particular achieved its high degree of self-consciousness in Western culture by virtue of its antagonism towards its own visuality.« »Visual Culture Questionnaire« 1996 (as note 7), p. 36.

13 Mitchell 2005 (as note 2), pp. 342–343.

14 Greenberg's key essays on the arts are probably »Towards a Newer Laocoon« (1940), and »Modernist Painting« (1961).

15 Alexander Rodchenko: »Slogans« (1920–21) trans. S.-O. Khan Magomedov. In: *Rodchenko: The Complete Works*. London 1986.

16 Mustapha Khayati: »Captive Words: Preface to a Situationist Dictionary« In: *Internationale Situationniste*, no. 10, March 1966, translated by Ken Knabb in: *Situationist International: Anthology*. Berkeley 1981, pp. 171–72.

Norbert Schneider

W.J.T. Mitchell und der ›Iconic Turn‹

Anlässlich der im Jahre 2005 veranstalteten Wiener Tagung *Iconic Turn – Pictorial Turn?* erschien im Internet ein Foto, das den in Chicago lehrenden Anglisten und Kulturwissenschaftler W.J.T. Mitchell und den in Basel tätigen deutschen Kunsthistoriker Gottfried Boehm in einträchtiger Verbundenheit zeigte. Der beigegebene Kommentar apostrophierte beide als die »zwei Grand Seigneurs der Bildforschung«[1]. Dem unbefangenen Leser musste sich der Eindruck aufdrängen, es handele sich um eine seit langem bestehende Harmonie von gleichgesinnt an einem gemeinsamen Projekt arbeitenden Gelehrten. Wer sich aber in den wissenschaftlichen Sozialisationen von Mitchell und Boehm bloß ein wenig auskennt, konnte gegenüber der suggestiven Botschaft dieser massenmedialen Präsentation nur skeptisch sein. Mir jedenfalls erschien sie der Konstruktion eines Mythos verdächtig, und so möchte ich hier die Doktrinen bzw. Positionen beider Autoren einer vergleichenden Analyse unterziehen.

Ein gewichtiges *Tertium comparationis* für beide Protagonisten ist offensichtlich, dass sie Schlachtrufe ausgegeben haben, die einen Paradigmenwechsel in den Humanwissenschaften auslösen sollten. Im Märzheft des Jahrgangs 1992 der Zeitschrift *Artforum* publizierte Mitchell einen Artikel mit der programmatischen Überschrift »Pictorial Turn«; zwei Jahre später ließ Boehm in dem von ihm herausgegebenen Band *Was ist ein Bild?* die Proklamation eines *Iconic Turn* folgen. Auf den ersten Blick schien das eine Koinzidenz der Interessen anzudeuten, allenfalls nur eine minimale graduelle Verschiebung. Indem Boehm ein amerikanisierendes Logo wählte,[2] durfte er auf eine über die zentraleuropäischen Landesgrenzen hinausreichende internationale Wirkung hoffen, nicht zuletzt, da sich dergestalt eine Verklammerung mit Mitchells inzwischen erfolgreicher Devise ergab. Der ins Amerikanische transgredierte Terminus wendete unmerklich, aber werbewirksam das Konzept der Ikonik seines Bochumer Habilitationsbetreuers Max Imdahl, das in der bundesdeutschen Kunstgeschichte lange Zeit ein eher insulares Dasein fristete (mit Zentren in Bochum und Gießen und einem Epizentrum in Konstanz) und mehr von Künstlern, Kunstlaien und Kunstpädagogen als von den meisten Fachgenossen favorisiert wurde, in ein Modell mit hegemonialem Universalanspruch. In dem Maße, wie sich viele der vormals kritischen Kunstwissenschaftler in den achtziger und neunziger Jahren zurückzogen oder entpolitisierten, konnte, so ge›turnt‹, die marginale Ikonik in ein Vakuum und damit in die vorderen Reihen vorstoßen.[3]

Boehm, von Hause aus Philosoph, der bei Gadamer promoviert hat, gelang dies, indem er die immanentistische Analytik Imdahls mit intellektuellen Diskursen verknüpfte, die für ihre Begründung zuvor nie eine Rolle gespielt hatten. Allenfalls hatte Imdahls Methode der Untersuchung von syntaktischen Strukturen und Formrelationen, bei der die Analyse der Komposition von religiösen Konnotationen nicht frei ist (die Bild-ordnung galt Imdahl gelegentlich als ein Zeichen für die Präsenz der »Ewigkeit« Gottes)[4], eine zeitweilige Affinität zu einzelnen Aspekten des Strukturalismus und der informationstheoretischen Ästhetik Max Benses. Darüber hinaus bestanden, mehr aus freundschaftlichen Bindungen als faktisch hinsichtlich der methodischen Orientierung, Berührungen zum *Poetik und Hermeneutik*-Kreis.

Boehm machte diesen Ansatz anschlussfähig für Theorien etwa des späten Merleau-Ponty oder Lacans und rief als weitere Kronzeugen für die »neue Legitimität des Bildes« Philosophen wie Kant (sic!), Kierkegaard, Nietzsche, Freud, Wittgenstein, Husserl und Heidegger auf. Sekundiert von dieser eindrucksvollen Reihe großer Denker, verfocht er eine These, die auf einer seit den frühen achtziger Jahren propagierten aufklärungskritischen, mindestens -skeptischen, Tendenz aufsatteln konnte, nämlich dem Logozentrismus-Verdikt. Dessen Anfänge gehen bekanntlich auf Michel Foucault zurück und entfalteten in der jüngeren französischen Kunstwissenschaft eine große Breitenwirkung. Namentlich Georges Didi-Huberman zog gegen die Ikonologie der zweiten Warburg-Schule zu Felde, der er eine im vermeintlichen Gefolge des Neukantianismus sich bewegende logoszentrierte Interpretation von Kunstwerken vorwarf.[5] Stattdessen hätte man sich, so seine Argumentation, auf die magischen subrationalen Kräfte des Bildes ungeschützt einzulassen und in Anmutungserlebnissen ihre mystischen Dimensionen zu erfassen.[6] (Ein Blick in den stets umfangreichen und gelehrten Anmerkungsapparat von Didi-Huberman lehrt indessen, dass er das, was er als eigene unmittelbare Erfahrung »devant l'image« ausgibt, sich der vorgängig gründlich angeeigneten Kenntnis ikonologischer Forschung verdankt, die er dann denunziert.)

Diese Mystagogik Didi-Hubermans ist Boehm, der eher ein kühler, begrifflich scharf denkender Theoretiker ist, zweifellos fremd. Denn er geht weniger von Emotionen und diffusen Empfindungen als von eidetischen Gegebenheiten aus, wobei sein frühes Vorbild Konrad Fiedler ist, dessen Werk er Anfang der siebziger Jahre herausgab.[7] Fiedlers zentrale Kategorie ist bekanntlich die Anschaulichkeit von Gemälden mit der methodischen Maßgabe, dass die Werkbetrachtung auf die reine Visualität unter Ausklammerung aller referentiellen Konnotationen eingegrenzt wird. Mit Didi-Huberman, dessen Buch *Vor einem Bild* bereits 1990 erschien, teilt Boehm jedoch die Auffassung, dass Bilder sowohl eine historische als auch eine kognitive Priorität vor der Sprache haben. Boehms ›historische‹ Begründung stützt sich auf überkommene Reste vorgeschichtlicher Höhlenmalerei, die für uns letztlich auch ein – m. E. jedoch, da es hierzu sehr konträre Hypothesen gibt, nicht zwingendes – Zeugnis für ein Wissen biete, »dass Bilder eine eigene Kraft und einen eigenen Sinn haben«[8]. Dass Visualität der Sprachfähigkeit immer schon vorausliege, wird zum triumphalen Beweisgrund dafür, dass der Bildwissenschaft im Gefüge der Humanwissenschaften letztlich der Rang einer Leitdisziplin zukomme.

Wenn Boehm von »Bildwissenschaft« oder gar von der »Rückkehr der Bilder« spricht, so legt dieser allgemeine Begriff des Bildes nahe, dass sich unter ihn wertfrei bzw. normindifferent alle nur erdenklichen visuellen Phänomene subsumieren lassen. In der Tat hat Boehm auch den Katalog potentiell thematisierbarer Bilder zehn Jahre nach seinem programmatischen Aufsatz von 1995 ein wenig erweitert und damit Konzessionen an die bei anderen Autoren inzwischen erfolgte Expansion von Bildtypen gemacht, die von den sog. bildgebenden Verfahren über epistemische Bilder im Dienste der Illustration wissenschaftlicher Erkenntnisse bis hin zu imaginären Bildern oder Metaphern reichen können. Dieses Spektrum ist bekanntlich ja schier unendlich.

Dennoch fällt auf, dass sein Interesse – neben dem anthropologisierenden Verweis auf prähistorische ›Urformen‹ – nach wie vor auf die Malerei der klassischen Moderne konzentriert ist, beginnend bei Paul Cézanne, über Henri Matisse, Josef Albers und Yves Klein, bis hin zu den amerikanischen Farbfeldmalern.

Dieses »Laboratorium der Moderne«, wie er es nennt, wird zum Demonstrationsfeld für die Methode der Ikonik,[9] deren gegen die Ikonologie gerichtetes Credo es ist, dass Bilder nicht als Platzhalter einer ganz anderen Logik betrachtet werden dürfen, es vielmehr nur auf ihre eigene Logik ankomme. Der Sinn von Bildern emergiert diesem Modell zufolge nicht aus bestimmten Motivanlässen, aus ästhetischen Überlieferungszusammenhängen und soziokulturellen Kontexten, sondern ist ein völlig selbstreferentieller Prozess einer oszillierenden Wahrnehmung von Kontrasten oder des Austauschs von Bildgründen (wie bei Matisses *La danse*). Vorzugsweise wird das an zur Abstraktion tendierenden Bildern demonstriert. Diesen wird dabei in hypostasierender Weise, in der Verwechslung von Urheber und Werk, die Potenz einer Selbstreflexivität zugesprochen, als wären sie selbst Subjekte. Kaum jemand wird die von Imdahl und Boehm so genannte »ikonische Differenz«, die letztlich auf das gestalttheoretische Modell der Figur-Grund-Relation bzw. auf Ingardens phänomenologische Unterscheidung von Sinnschichten zurückgeht,[10] bestreiten. Zweifellos schärft ihre Beachtung die Sensibilität für immanente Strukturen. Sie ist indessen nur *ein* methodischer Aspekt im Vorstadium der Analyse. Verselbständigt sie sich, wie das bei Imdahl geschieht, so erwächst daraus eine spiralige, in Sackgassen mündende Zirkularität des Denkens, das einem Glasperlenspiel gleichkommt.[11] Das geschieht umso mehr, als, wie von Boehm gefordert, alle anderen Bestimmungsgründe künstlerischer Produktion unter dem Stigma der Abbildtheorie kategorisch als unbedeutende, letztlich vernachlässigenswerte Externa abgetan werden, die das Eigentliche der Bilder nicht berühren. Hier entfernt sich Boehm sogar entschieden von der Favorisierung des Mimesis-Konzepts seines Lehrers Gadamer, der in der Kategorie der »Darstellung« ein entscheidendes Constituens von Bildern sah.[12]

Betrachten wir nun die bildwissenschaftliche Theorie des anderen *Grand Seigneur*, W.J.T. Mitchell, so fällt erst einmal auf, dass dessen intellektuelle Entwicklung nicht über eine immanentistische Hermeneutik lief, deren latente Politik nach wie vor die Verbannung alles Politischen ist, sondern immer eine sozialkritische Dimension hatte. Mitchell ist maßgeblich von marxistischen Theoriediskussionen geprägt, namentlich Althussers Theorie der ideologischen Apparate,[13] die bekanntlich das ältere Basis-Überbau-Modell zu überwinden suchte. Neben Althusser spielte für ihn immer auch die Theorie eines *Cultural Materialism* von Raymond Williams eine entscheidende Rolle,[14] wie er denn stets auch auf die Schriften von Marx selbst rekurrierte, so besonders auf dessen Theorie des Fetischcharakters der Ware (»commodity fetishism«).[15] Noch unlängst wandte er den Marxschen Begriff des Mehrwerts (»surplus value«) auf Bilder an.[16] Wenn Mitchell, der den Begriff der »Ikonologie« (*Iconology*) nicht verwarf, sondern lediglich uminterpretierte, Panofskys Ansatz kritisiert, dann geschieht dies nicht dezisionistisch von einer immanentistischen Warte aus, sondern auf der Grundlage einer hochdifferenzierten marxistischen Theorie. Entsprechend bestimmt er die Funktion der abstrakten bzw. zur Abstraktion tendierenden Kunst, die für Boehm das »Laboratorium« für die Bildwissenschaft abgibt, entschieden politisch, indem er sie konsequent historisch evaluiert. Das zeigt sich besonders in seiner Kritik an einigen Protagonisten der (ehemals trotzkistisch eingefärbten) Zeitschrift *October*, die wie Rosalind Krauss im Gefolge von Clement Greenberg oder Alfred H. Barr eine Gleichsetzung von abstrakter Kunst und Moderne vornehmen. Wo Imdahl bei Jasper Johns' Flaggenbildern die Frage stellte: »Is it a flag or is it a painting?«[17] und sie phänomenologisch-relationistisch zu beantworten suchte (was unweigerlich in eine Aporie führen musste)[18], geht Mitchell der Bedeutung dieses Motivs für den Künstler, der als »discharged soldier« aus dem Korea-Krieg zurückkehrte, nach und kontextualisiert es mit parafaschistischen Tendenzen in der McCarthy-Ära bzw. im Kalten Krieg.

Während Boehm den Gegenstand der Bildwissenschaft im Grunde genommen auf das Feld der klassischen Avantgarde und ihrer neueren Derivate eingrenzt und jüngst als kleinen Appendix im Repertoire gerade noch kognitive Bilder in der Art von Diagrammen gelten lässt, ist Mitchells Interesse prinzipiell auf die visuelle Kultur (*visual culture*) insgesamt gerichtet. Dabei sind ihm zufolge »cultural« und »social« zwar nicht theoretisch, jedoch meistens *in praxi* auswechselbare (»interchangeable«) Begriffe. Kunst spielt für Mitchell innerhalb von Kultur als Teilbereich zwar durchaus eine Rolle, in gleicher Weise müssten aber auch alle Phänomene der »vernacular visuality« wie Massenmedien, Massenkultur, Kitsch oder kommerzielle Kunst in den Blick genommen werden.[19]

Sosehr Boehm für die Ikonik einen Universalanspruch über eine angebliche Anthropologie der Bilder reklamiert, verbleibt er unübersehbar im Horizont einer institutionell selegierten Hochkunst, deren führende Rolle nachträglich durch das Kriterium der »ikonischen Differenz« begründet wird, obwohl dieses sich als Projektionsstrategie, konsequent beachtet, ohne Schwierigkeiten auch auf jede Form von Werbung anwenden ließe, die heute oft viel mehr »sophisticated« ist als etwa in ihrer immanenten Strukturiertheit meist schnell durchschaubare *Colour field paintings*. Gegenüber dieser enthistorisierenden Phänomenologie des Bildes besteht Mitchell nachdrücklich auf einer historischen Orientierung und soziologischen Analyse, wobei für ihn Pierre Bourdieus Distinktionstheorie[20] einen wichtigen Parameter abgibt.

In der neueren Bildwissenschaft wird gern von der Kreuzung der Blicke gesprochen. Auch Boehm rekurriert auf diese Topik, die sich aus den späten, teilweise kryptischen, Schriften Merleau-Pontys herleitet, so etwa in *Der Zweifel Cézannes* oder *Auge und Geist*. Auch bei Lacan und Sartre gab es schon das, so Boehm, »chiastische Modell der Bildverschränkung«[21]. Gegenüber Husserls Theorem der Intentionalität, der Gerichtetheit des Blicks (die Boehm zufolge sozusagen auf eine Einbahnstraße hinausläuft) entwickelte Merleau-Ponty den Gedanken, dass das, was wir anblicken, uns gleichfalls anblickt. Dieses Sehen auf Bilder, also hier die Fügungen von Farbe, Form und Linien bei Cézanne, sei letztlich ein selbstreflexiver Akt, der auf den eigenen Körper (*chair*) gerichtet sei.[22]

Solcher solipsistischen Einzäunung steht bei Mitchell, der auch auf die Bedeutung des Blicks eingeht, eine dezidiert soziologische bzw. politische Auffassung entgegen. Lacans Theorie, die, wie bereits dargelegt, auch Boehm adaptiert hatte, verbindet Mitchell bezeichnenderweise mit Emmanuel Levinas' »encountering the other«[23], ja er weitet sie im Sinne des antikolonialistischen Befreiungskampfes auf Frantz Fanons Kritik des diskriminierenden Blicks der Unterdrücker aus.[24] Mit Ralph Ellison[25] betont er, dass rassistische Vorurteile es verwehren, einen Menschen als Individuum wahrzunehmen: »a racist regime renders whole classes of people both *hyper*visible as a class (Look! A Negro! is Fanon's symptomatic utterance) and *in*visible as an individual.«[26]

Wie Boehm beharrt auch Mitchell auf der fundamentalen Andersartigkeit von Bild und Sprache. Schließlich war er es, der Richard Rortys Diagnose eines *Linguistic Turn*[27] in die des *Pictorial Turn* transformierte. Mitchell hatte auch vor Boehm bereits auf Wittgenstein hingewiesen, der anfänglich einem *Pictorialism* gehuldigt habe (woran Boehm sich festklammerte), später aber wieder zur Prävalenz der Sprache vor dem Bild zurückgekehrt sei. Insofern war und ist Wittgenstein für Mitchell letztlich kein Kronzeuge seiner Theorie.

Im Umfeld der Linguistik und des transzendentalen Lingualismus ist, so schon bei Saussure, die Semiotik zu sehen, deren Theorie und Systematik der Zeichen vorwiegend am Modell der Sprache orientiert ist. Da die Semiotik lange Zeit beanspruchte, als universelles Explikationsmodell auch visuelle Phänomene erklären, mindestens kategorisieren zu können, mussten sich die meisten Bildwissenschafter zwangsläufig mit ihr auseinandersetzen. Während sie hierzulande meist ohne nähere Begründung über sie ein Anathema verhängen, hat Mitchell zu ihr seit *Iconology* (1986) eine differenzierte Auffassung entwickelt, nicht zuletzt vielleicht auch, weil er in seinen Anfängen vom Paradigma des Strukturalismus (ähnlich wie Jonathan Culler oder Frederick Jameson) stark berührt war. Ihre Validität weiß er durchaus zu schätzen; er lehnt sich nur gegen ihre ausschließliche und schematische Anwendung auf.[28] Vor allem weist er auf die höchst verschachtelten Strukturen der *mixed media* hin, die es nicht gestatten, von einem einfachen Verweischarakter zu sprechen.[29] Seit seinen frühen Blake-Studien[30] interessierte ihn in besonderem Maße die Text-Bild-Relation, womit sich ihm notwendig eine semiotische Problemstellung aufdrängen musste. Von dieser zeichentheoretischen Orientierung älterer Observanz hat er sich zunehmend insofern entfernt, als für ihn von Interesse ist, was sprachliche und visuelle Äußerungen auf je spezifische Weise (oder in ihrer Kombination) politisch leisten. Eine essentialistische Bestimmung von Bildern, wie sie in Boehms ontologisch gemeinter Fragestellung »Was ist ein Bild?« anklingt, liegt ihm fern. Wo Boehm den Abbildcharakter von Bildern perhorresziert, betont Mitchell geradezu das Moment der »representation«[31], das für ihn konstitutiv ist für Kultur (*culture*): »Culture-as-representation helps to remind us that culture itself is a fractured concept, suturing of convention and nature and not a homogeneous terrain. [...] It leads us to ask not merely what these forms mean, but what they *do* in a network of social relations«[32].

Es dürfte deutlich geworden sein, dass zwischen den beiden *Grand Seigneurs* himmelweite Unterschiede bestehen. Boehm grenzt seinen Bildbegriff weitgehend auf sein schon früher bevorzugtes Terrain der klassischen Moderne ein und bevorzugt eher eine quietistische Betrachtungsweise. Diese versteht sich im Erfassen der »ikonischen Differenz« in der Selbstreflexivität als »prozeßhaft« (was aber bloß ein zerebraler Prozess der Verschachtelung der Thematisationsebenen ist), verharrt aber schließlich vor dem »dichten Schweigen« und der »innewohnenden Fremdheit« der Bilder wie vor einem Numinosen, einem *Ineffabile*.[33] So prädiziert er den Bildern nach Art der negativen Theologie und auch der Mystik Qualitäten des Absoluten.

Mitchell dagegen hat, bei allen modischen Annäherungen an postmoderne Diskurse, das politische Ferment seiner *Picture Theory* nie aufgegeben. Sein Erkenntnisinteresse richtet sich nicht auf eine diffuse Macht von Bildern als ästhetischen Reiz, der uns irgendwie ergreift, sondern im Sinne der Ideologietheorie auf ihre bewusstseinsbildende (bzw. -deformierende) Funktion in den sozialen Antagonismen. Sein Horizont bleibt nicht auf die Kunst beschränkt, sondern bezieht die technischen Bildmedien in gleicher Weise ein, von denen viele in seiner Sicht heute mehr denn je einem »global corporate fascism« Vorschub leisten. Dagegen setzt er »the hope for new and critical pictures of the public sphere«, die Hoffnung auf neue und kritische Bilder der öffentlichen Sphäre.[34]

---

1 Das grobgerasterte Foto der »beiden Koryphäen«, die man in Wien »erstmals« »im Doppelpack erleben« konnte – so der Bericht von Annegret Gerleit (26.04.2005) – kann man jetzt finden in dem Band von Hans Belting (Hg.): *Bilderfragen. Die Bildwissenschaften im Aufbruch.* München 2007, S. 26. In dem Buch folgt dann ein Briefwechsel zwischen Boehm und Mitchell, in dem ersterer letzteren umwirbt, sich seinem Programm des Iconic Turn anzuschließen.

2 Die deutsche Formel »Ikonische Wende« wäre wegen ihrer anderen semantischen Konnotationen vermutlich schnell verhallt. Besonders delikat ist, dass Boehm bei »iconic« auf einen Terminus der Peirce'schen Semiotik (»icon«) zurückgreift, die er ja gerade, wie unten zu zeigen sein wird, radikal ablehnt. Vgl. Charles Sanders Peirce: *What is a Sign?* 1894, § 3. Siehe auch Umberto Eco: *Einführung in die Semiotik.* München 1972, S. 197–201. Es kann gar keine Frage sein, dass Imdahl seinen Begriff der Ikonik der semiotischen Diskussion der 1960er Jahre entnommen hat. Es genügt hier, auf Max Bense zu verweisen, der den zeichentheoretischen Ikon-Begriff immer wieder, z. B. bei der Analyse von Konkreter Poesie, verwendet. Vgl. Max Bense: »Konkrete Poesie« In: *manuskripte. Zeitschrift für Literatur, Kunst, Kritik*, 11, Juni-September 1964, S. 1–3.

3 In seinem Briefwechsel mit Mitchell versucht Boehm die tatsächliche Abhängigkeit von ihm zu vernebeln, in dem er sich und Mitchell als »Waldläufer« stilisiert, die unabhängig voneinander »den gleichen, kaum bekannten Kontinent der bildlichen Phänomene und der Visualität durchstreift hatten« (G. Boehm: »Iconic Turn. Ein Brief« In: Belting 2007 [wie Anm. 1], S. 27) Abgesehen davon, dass er sich hier ein besonderes Arkanwissen im Bereich der Erkenntnis von Bildern zuerkennt, waren alle seine Hinweise auf Rorty, Wittgenstein usw. bereits in Mitchells »What is an Image« zu finden (in: ders.: *Iconology. Image, Text, Ideology.* Chicago 1986, S. 7 ff.). Diese zur Sicherung der vermeintlich eigenen Originalität vorgeschützte Ignoranz erscheint kaum glaubwürdig.

4 Max Imdahl: *Giotto. Zur Frage der ikonischen Sinnstruktur.* Miesbach 1979, S. 38. Dazu: Jutta Held, Norbert Schneider: *Grundzüge der Kunstwissenschaft. Gegenstandsbereiche – Institutionen – Problemfelder.* Köln 2007, S. 333 und Anm. 832.

5 Georges Didi-Huberman: *Vor einem Bild.* Aus dem Französischen von Reinold Werner. München 1990.

6 So demonstriert an Fra Angelicos Verkündigung (ca. 1440/41) im Kloster San Marco in Florenz. Vgl. Georges Didi-Huberman: »Die Kunstgeschichte in den Grenzen ihrer einfachen Praxis« In: Didi-Huberman 1990 (wie Anm. 5), S. 10–60, bes. 24 ff., wo die weiße Fläche auf dem Fresko uns die Annuntiatio angeblich unmittelbar bewusst werden lässt.

7 Konrad Fiedler: *Schriften zur Kunst.* Text nach der Ausgabe München 1913/14. Hg. v. Gottfried Boehm. 2 Bde. München 1971.

8 Gottfried Boehm: »Jenseits der Sprache. Anmerkungen zur Logik der Bilder« In: Christa Maar, Hubert Burda (Hg.): *Iconic Turn. Die neue Macht der Bilder.* Köln 2004, S. 28–43, hier S. 29.

9 Diese Ansicht vertrat auch sein damaliger Gießener Hochschulassistent Bernd Growe, der – gewiss mit Billigung seines Institutsleiters, der gerade eine eigene, auf die Ikonik eingeschworene Werkmonographie-Reihe im Insel-Verlag gestartet hatte – die von Klaus Herding begründete »Kunststück«-Reihe im Fischer-Verlag als »Stück-Werk« abtat, da sie ikonologisch und sozialgeschichtlich orientiert sei sowie ideologische Implikate rekonstruiere, statt sich von der Moderne als Norm der Interpretation leiten zu lassen: »...gleichwohl, ob man es wahrhaben will oder nicht, bleibt die Moderne die Bedingung unserer Erfahrung der Geschichte! Tradition ist so gesehen immer ›nur‹ der Sonderfall der Moderne. Erst an der Kunst der Moderne hätte sich die Tragfähigkeit der vorgeschlagenen Zugangsweise zu bewähren. Kunststück!« (Bernd Growe: »Stück-Werk. Zur Physiognomie einer kunstgeschichtlichen Reihe« In: *Merkur. Deutsche Zeitschrift für europäisches Denken*, Nr. 447, 40/1986, H. 5 (Mai), S. 432–437, hier 437. Es gab aber nicht nur Angriffe von Imdahlianern auf linke Kunsthistoriker, sondern sogar auch verwegene Aneignungsversuche: Growe und andere versuchten, einen marxistischen Autor, nämlich Max Raphael, im Imdahlschen Sinne umzudeuten (was schon einer Umfälschung nahekam), so in der bei Suhrkamp erschienenen Werkausgabe Raphaels. – Boehm, der so sehr auf Seherfahrung und dem Vorrang des Bildes vor der Sprache abhebt, unterlässt es zumeist, spezifische Qualitäten von Bildern zu benennen. Stattdessen deckt er sie mit dem Logos seiner unentwegt repetierten, festgezimmerten Theorie zu, die nur insistierend beschwört, was Bilder angeblich vermögen. Selbst an seinem Lieblingsgegenstand, der modernen Kunst, gerinnt das Meiste nur zur Formel: »Alles, was er malte, handelt von der Seherfahrung«, heißt es z. B. über Giorgio Morandi. Vgl. Gottfried Boehm: »Giorgio Morandi. Zum künstlerischen Konzept« In: *Giorgio Morandi. Gemälde, Aquarelle, Zeichnungen, Radierungen.* Hg. v. Ernst-Eberhard Güse u. Franz Armin Morat. München 1993, S. 11–22, hier S. 13. Wie diese Seherfahrung konkret aussieht und sich den Werken mitteilt, erfährt man nahezu gar nicht.

10 Vgl. Roman Ingarden: *Das literarische Kunstwerk.* 4. Aufl. Tübingen 1972 (1. Aufl. Halle/S. 1931). Hierin enrwickelt Ingarden die Theorie vom »polyphonen Kunstwerk« mit einer Mehrschichtigkeit der Bedeutungseinheiten, die vom Rezipienten im Akt des Lesens entdeckt und eigentlich erst realisiert werden. Ingarden kann in dieser Hinsicht als Ahnherr der neueren Rezeptionsästhetik (Wolfgang Iser, Hans Robert Jauss) gelten.

11 So lautet das Ergebnis von Imdahls Interpretation von Picassos Guernica-Bild: Das »Kohärieren von Inkohärenz und Kohärenz ist die eigentliche Botschaft« (Max Imdahl: »Zu Picassos *Guernica*. Inkohärenz und Kohärenz in moderner Bildlichkeit« In: Rainer Warning, Winfried Wehle (Hg.): *Lyrik und Malerei der Avantgarde*. München 1982, S. 521–565, hier 560).

12 Vgl. Hans-Georg Gadamer: *Wahrheit und Methode. Grundzüge einer philosophischen Hermeneutik.* Tübingen 1960 u.ö., S. 142 f.

13 Vgl. Louis Althusser: *Ideologie und ideologische Staatsappartate. Aufsätze zur marxistischen Theorie.* Hamburg u.a. 1977.

14 Vgl. Raymond Williams: *Marxism and Literature.* New York 1977.

15 Vgl. Mitchell 1986 (wie Anm. 3), S. 191. Zu Marxens Camera obscura-Metapher vgl. ebd., S. 168–172.

16 W.J.T. Mitchell: »The Surplus Value of Images« In: Ders.: *What Do Pictures Want?* Chicago/London 2005, S. 76–110.

17 Max Imdahl: »›Is it a Flag, or Is It a Painting?‹ Über mögliche Konsequenzen der konkreten Kunst« (1969) In: ders.: *Zur Kunst der Moderne* (Gesammelte Schriften, Bd. 1). Hrsg. v. Angeli Janhsen-Vukičevič. Frankfurt/M. 1996, S. 131–180.

18 Imdahls Untersuchung blendete jeglichen Kontext aus. Nicht einmal das Nächstliegende, die Definitionsmacht der Institution Museum, die dieses Gemälde kategorial von einer Flagge unterschied, kam ihm in den Sinn. Zu dieser Zeit hatte bereits Arthur C. Danto die Differenzqualität von Andy Warhols *Brillo Boxes* gegenüber realen Verpackungskartonagen mit einer Institutional Theory zu erklären versucht. Vgl. Arthur C. Danto: *The Transfiguration of the Commonplace*. 7. ed. Cambridge, Mass. u.a. 1996. – Zuvor schon George Dickie: »Defining Art« In: *American Philosophical Quarterly*, 6/1969, S. 253–266.

19 Die von Kunsthistorikern ausgebildeten Kriterien der »art appreciation« könnten, wendet er ein, durchaus leicht ins Wanken geraten, wenn man sie nicht in deren institutionell ausgebildeter Normativität blindlings akzeptiert, sondern dem Bildmaterial unvoreingenommen (»with an open mind«) gegenübertritt. Vgl. Margaret Dikovitskaya: »An Interview with W.J.T. Mitchell, Gaylord Donnelley Distinguished Service Professor of English and Art History, University of Chicago, 11 January 2001« (humanities.uchicago.edu/faculty/mitchell/Dikovitskaya_interviews_Mitchell.pdf), S 17.

20 Dikovitskaya 2001 (wie Anm. 19), S. 15. Vgl. Pierre Bourdieu: *Die feinen Unterschiede. Kritik der gesellschaftlichen Urteilskraft*. Frankfurt/M. 1987 u. ö.

21 Gottfried Boehm: »Die Wiederkehr der Bilder« In: Ders. (Hg.): *Was ist ein Bild?* München 1994, S. 11–38, hier 24.

22 Vgl. Maurice Merleau-Ponty: *Das Auge und der Geist*. Hg. u. übs. v. Hans Werner Arndt. Hamburg 1984 (Philosophische Bibliothek, Bd. 357). Dazu Norbert Schneider: »Leib und Bild bei Maurice Merleau-Ponty« In: *Kunst und Politik. Jahrbuch der Guernica-Gesellschaft* 6/2004, S. 87–102.

23 Vgl. W.J.T. Mitchell: »Showing Seeing. A Critique of Visual Culture« In: Mitchell 2005 (wie Anm. 16), S. 337–356, hier 351.

24 Vgl. Frantz Fanon: *Aspekte der algerischen Revolution*. Frankfurt/M. 1969. – Frantz Fanon: *Das kolonisierte Ding wird Mensch. Ausgewählte Schriften*. Leipzig 1986 (Reclams Universal-Bibliothek 1147). – Frantz Fanon: *Schwarze Haut, weiße Masken*. Übers. von Eva Moldenhauer. Frankfurt/M. 1980. – Frantz Fanon: *Die Verdammten dieser Erde*. Frankfurt/M. 1966.

25 Vgl. Ralph Ellison: *Invisible Man*. London u.a. 1965 (dt.: Der unsichtbare Mann. Aus dem Amerikanischen von Georg Goyert. Zürich 1995).

26 Dikovitskaya 2001 (wie Anm. 19), S. 8.

27 Richard Rorty: *The Linguistic Turn. Recent Essays in Philosophical Method*. Chicago 1967.

28 »Semiotics may be understood [...] as a promotional strategy for elevating the dignity of all sorts of signs and communicative activities. It is hardly an accident that semiotics breaks down the preserves of ›literariness‹ and aesthetic elitism, that it fans out into the fields of popular culture, ordinary language, and into the realms of biological and mechanical communication. Signs are everywhere; there is nothing that is not potentially or actually a sign.« (Mitchell 1986 [wie Anm. 3], S. 62).

29 Vgl. W.J.T. Mitchell: »Addressing Media« In: Mitchell 2005 (wie Anm. 16), S. 201–221.

30 W.J.T. Mitchell: *Blake's Composite Art*. Princeton 1977.

31 W.J.T Mitchell: »Representation« In: Frank Lentricchia, Thomas McLaughlin (Hg.): *Critical Terms for Literary Study*. Chicago 1995, S. 11–22.

32 W.J.T. Mitchell: »Conclusion: Some Pictures of Representation« In: *Picture Theory*, S. 423.

33 Boehm 2004 (wie Anm. 8), S. 43. So hat bereits Pseudo-Dionysius Areopagita Gott als in Schweigen gehüllt beschrieben (»De divinis nominibus« I, 1 In: Jacques-Paul Migne [Hg.]: *Patrologia Graeca*. Bd. 3. Paris 1889, Sp. 589 B). Komplementär zum Schweigen Gottes

fordern die Mystiker eine Sigetik von den Gläubigen, so z.B. Meister Eckhart und Johannes Tauler. Interessant ist aber, dass hier das Schweigen als der Grund des Sprechens und der Sprache und nicht etwa von Bildern aufgefasst wird.

34 W.J.T. Mitchell: »Pictures and the Public Sphere« In: *Picture Theory*, S. 369.

Angela Miller

Beyond the National Self: Cross-Cultural Exchange and Postcolonial Studies

In the past two decades, postcolonial and postmodern critiques of canonical art histories have reorganized how we define the subject of art.[1] Unlike German *Bildwissenschaft*, visual studies – in the context of the American academy – largely lacks a consistent theoretical position, serving instead as a clearinghouse for a range of new interpretive and analytic tools. In the process, it has vastly enlarged the object set constituted by traditional art history by reaching out to vernacular, mass cultural, and non-singular forms, as well as by tilting the field of inquiry away from the producer of art to issues of circulation, visual consumption, and the active and fluid creation of meaning by audiences. Visual studies focuses – according to one definition – on the *event* that occurs at the juncture of the object (or visual sign), the act of perception (mediated in many cases by technologies of vision), and the perceiving agent.[2] Among its first contributions was to challenge some of the central premises of art history as a discipline by broadening our focus from the high art productions of cultural elites to a range of artifacts produced by groups marginal to the centers of power.[3] Despite such changes, art historians too often bring these new instruments in the production of knowledge about visual worlds to bear on the usual suspects: works of fine art by representatives of European avant-gardes. Key hierarchies remain in place: named over anonymous producers; European over non-western; fine arts over vernacular or applied arts; aesthetic over functional. While issues of reception – and of variability of meaning as it takes shape in different historical moments and among distinct audiences – have come to play a much more important role in art historical studies, the role of the object in transactions and exchanges between cultures – the object, that is, as a medium of communication between groups with radically different positions in the world – has been slighted. What happens when we shift our thinking from the object as embodying specific national, regional, or ethnic cultures, to the object as a »transformer«, a node in a circuit of cultural energies, a point at which those energies shift from one modality to another? What happens when we move our focus from aesthetic product to cultural process?[4]

The epistemological framework of the human sciences has been centrally involved with defining identities in terms of essential characteristics, a process that occurs through *differentiation*. Identity formation – in psychoanalysis, philosophy, cultural history, and theories of national self-definition – is framed in terms of a conflictual model wherein fully achieved selfhood (or nationhood) emerges through a process of negation, rejection, or abjection of an other: children in relation to parents, individuals in relation to family, and communal selves in relation to ethnic ›strangers.‹ The powerful hold of identity and difference on post-Enlightenment philosophical patterns of thought has withstood assault from many directions over the past century. As binaries, »self« and »other« have also structured how we have understood the processes of cultural exchange that have played an increasingly central role in the history of the arts.

Exchange implies reciprocity; in place of older art-historical models of influence – grounded in a one-way movement of forms, ideas, and materials from one agent to another – it suggests a mutual transfer of ideas, materials, forms, or experiences in which both parties to the exchange are transformed in some manner. Exchange furthermore shifts attention from the object as the carrier of change to the cultural subjects who both make and use the object in their everyday transactions. By contrast, the concept of influence embeds certain assumptions about the nature of the cultural producer, tied to fixity and stability. Influence involves a process of adding on, a kind of value supplement wherein an object acquires other characteristics that do not essentially alter its identity. It is not surprising that the concept of influence dominated the early history of art history, a period coinciding with the formation of nation-states and the coalescence of nationalist art histories directed at identifying the key characteristics of national schools.[5] The model of a one-way borrowing or transfer of cultural material from object to subject also recalls the history and process of extractive capitalism; colonized cultures as the source of raw material available for extraction and appropriation by a more powerful culture unprepared to acknowledge the debt.

To fully engage the concept of exchange requires that we redefine our working concept of cultural identity as something reshaped and expanded by intersubjective and intercultural exchange, rather than as something requiring constant defense in order to preserve its core integrity.[6] Art history has paid close attention to the conversation between the object and its audiences, but in this model the artist speaks ventriloquistically through the object, communicating through his work from a position of centered subjectivity and artistic selfhood. Haunting this figure of a self-contained creative producer is a model of identity as clearly bounded, formed in opposition to various cultural others, and in which creative expression serves to buttress both personal and collective aims. Gendered as defiantly masculine, the artistic producer forges his identity through a process of differentiation in which his embattled individuality is tested and fortified. The voyaging self does change, does evolve, but only in a manner that refines and purifies that which is already there, the untested, not fully matured subjectivity of the artist.

Nation-centered narratives of artistic development – taking shape in the twilight of the romantic nationalism of the 19th century – in many ways recapitulate this underlying model of the individual journeying, in a heroic self-realizing fashion, toward a fully developed and autonomous selfhood.[7] Identity formation – on both the individual and the cultural/national level – is shaped by an agonistic conception of self, pitted against the world and struggling to defend its boundaries against the corroding or complicating effects of encounters with others. In a kind of national *Bildungsroman*, or coming-of-age narrative, mid-twentieth century histories of American art traced the emergence of cultural self-consciousness through a series of trials and encounters that set into high relief the moral outlines of the nation-state. National selfhood was centered on the cultures of northern Europe for the most part, clustered on the East Coast. This national »self« in turn was formed out of exclusions; sealed off from disruptions – hybridizing encounters with other groups – that threatened its integrity or violated its boundaries. These cultural »others«, as they would be termed in postcolonial discourse, were there in the form of the Spanish, the French, peoples of indigenous and African descent, but their main function was to act as catalysts that sparked a unitary national tradition into life, and helped define the proverbial »new man, the American«, in J. Hector St. John de Crèvecoeur's endlessly repeated phrase of these years.[8] Human nature on the American continent emerged out of the singularly privileged conversation this new man, the American, had with himself. These histories did acknowledge the influence of Europe as a source of the formative conversation that took place – in the *Bildungsroman* model – between parent and child.[9] Greater symbolic emphasis, however, was put on the pre-social communion between the artist and the »wilderness« of the New World. Such a perspective echoes in the American Studies »myth and symbol« texts that emerged in the two decades following World War II: the ideal of the American Adam as supreme individualist forging a transparent relationship to the universe beyond the self. Nationalist mythologies of the Cold War era carried the imprint of this heroic agonistic version of subjectivity.

Raymond Williams pointed out decades ago that the term culture is a palimpsest of historically distinct meanings, several of which continue to shape how we currently conceive of artistic and material production. »Culture« carries an older association with husbandry, that is, with »the tending of natural growth«. Romanticism further encouraged the idea that cultures and their productions were intimately linked to unique and localized histories, environments, and traditions. »Community« would come to be synonymous with a specific and binding ethnic heritage of »custom, ritual, and way of life« referring back to »a shared history and shared provenance or homeland«.[10] Onto these organicist meanings, two others were layered: one referring to »a general process of intellectual, spiritual and aesthetic development«, and the other to »the works and practices of intellectual and especially artistic activity«.[11] All these definitions are haunted by a lingering personalism, the idea, that is, that cultures are like individuals, and that – like individuals – they are organized around a core subjectivity – a selfhood – toward which their central operations of material and aesthetic expression, social systems, and historical self-narration are oriented. Cultures, like selves, are born, flourish, and die. Such similarities issued from a common root: a body of ideas concerning the interior and holistic character of fully realized cultures and selves, as opposed to the exterior and mechanical character of the market and of abstract economic processes.[12] Organicist philosophies of social thought defined the individual within the social, as distinguished from the »aggressive individualism« of theorists of democracy. Yet – while communal in nature – such definitions of culture pivot upon the pursuit of a defining whole to which the individuals who comprise it submit, and which by extension excludes those elements that do not fall within its purview. Cultures and individuals – as they grow to a perfected maturity – do so by realizing an internal principle of development. Modern western nation-states, as David Theo Goldberg has argued, »are predicated on the (usually unspoken) assumption of cultural homogeneity organized around ›universal‹ liberal-individualist secular values.«[13]

The predisposition to think of cultures according to trajectories of individual development and growth regulated around principles of organic unity stems in part from a broader historical reaction to the Industrial Revolution and its assaults upon the perceived autonomy and spiritual integrity of the individual. In this context, culture – in both the English and the German traditions – came to be associated with the power of critical self-reflection itself: »a court of human appeal, to be set over the processes of practical social judgement ... as a mitigating and rallying alternative.«[14] The »moral and intellectual activities« associated with art, literature, and philosophy found their grounding throughout this period in an oppositional stance which pitted the critical intellectual against the motive forces of the material, the economic, and the industrial realms.

As we now know, nationalist narratives grounded in the pursuit of self-definition according to largely ahistorical and essentialist premises ignored or pushed to the margins many phases of cultural production in the New World that didn't reinforce the central story of the rise to national self-consciousness. This is one of several reasons why the arts of encounter – those objects that expose the processes of cultural hybridization on the boundaries between Native and European – were so consistently quarantined off by academic sub-disciplines, into their own distinct fields, which only now are beginning to take their place within a more integrated history of New World arts.[15]

The lingering ideal of the national self encouraged an approach to the arts as expressions of identity in the face of other cultures who threatened the autonomy of the youthful nation-state. But the history of colonization itself has also contributed to a set of governing conceptions about identity as forged out of radical difference; as oppositional; and as contingent on the power to abject cultural others.[16] This – as will become clear shortly – was true not only for the imperial colonizers, but also for those colonized cultures whose movement into self-awareness was so hard fought and hard won.

The reinstatement of so-called »minority« traditions – those associated with colonized cultures and their diaspora, as well as with internal colonizations of indigenous populations – began in the 1990s. It coincided with the rise of what would come to be known as identity politics, a movement with its roots in the 1970s. Identity politics generated a range of philosophical, political, social, and theoretical debates over the past twenty years, most notoriously as a significant aspect of the so-called »culture wars« of the early 1990s. Identity politics represented an important way station in the emergence of postcolonial ontologies of self. But while the insistence on ethnic identities served as a powerful instrument of political and social rights by asserting a sense of cultural belonging and collective agency, and by substituting ethnic affiliation for national affiliation, it also generated a powerful new form of post-colonial exclusivity which may have proven politically expedient but which appears in retrospect to have been increasingly out of step with a world in which the rate of cultural exchange and ›border crossings‹ has burgeoned exponentially. Such politics – entrenched in notions of ethnic and gender essentialism, and fostered by powerful historical grievances – ironically mirror the very tyrannies of the imperial center, a point made passionately by Edward Said in 1991.[17] One of the less fortunate legacies of colonization was what Said has termed the »epistemology of imperialism«, a way of organizing knowledge about the world according to narrowly exclusionary categories of identity, categories that served the caste-based social systems that underwrote imperial rule in Asia and Africa, and which thereafter served the frequently savage identitiarian energies of postcolonial movements and of the internecine conflicts which wracked eastern and central Europe following the collaps of Communism, driven by racial, ethnic, religious, or cultural claims. A range of postcolonial theorists from Said to Paul Gilroy have argued forcefully against the entrenched identities fostered by »ethnic absolutisms«, in his phrase, identities that foster »patterns of inclusion and exclusion«. In their place are calls for greater »worldliness«, or, in Gilroy's phrase, new forms of »planetary humanism«.[18]

Thus a primary challenge of any postcolonial visual studies is to imagine new forms of communication which allow »different cultural communities [to] live together and attempt to build a common life while retaining something of their ›original‹ identity«, in the words of Stuart Hall, among the most prominent and consistent theorist of a politically engaged postcolonial cultural studies.[19] The invocation of a »common life« exists at this point as a utopian promise only, but one increasingly part of the everyday experience of permeability fostered by globalization of media and consumer goods, travel, and a hyperincrease in the mobility of images. Such newly mobile forms of everyday life in no way guarantee that the boundaries of self and nation will become more pliable, however; indeed in some cases of fundamentalist backlash, the opposite has occurred. What is needed in order for more fluid and multitudinous pathways to emerge between and among identities is a reassessment of our longstanding propensity to understand identity as the product of agonistic models of struggle, opposition, and difference.[20]

Along with new more intersubjective models of identity that move beyond the »abjection« of otherness toward an »identification across and through difference«, in Kelly Oliver's words, a second issue involves the uneven nature of cultural exchange between colonizers and colonized. Postcolonial approaches to art history and visual culture studies are premised on such asymmetries of power, and much postcolonial visual culture is directed at deconstructing the resulting value hierarchies that reduce the subaltern or colonized culture to a condition of voicelessness.[21] What happens, however, if we return to a historical moment when power shifted back and forth between the parties to the encounter, a time and space of more or less equal exchange theorized by Richard White as the cultural »middle ground«?[22] It is worth noting here that the concept of the middle ground has no precise counterpart in postcolonial theory, heavily based as it is on European colonization of India and Africa. Resting as it does on this very different historical ground, the American example – from the early colonial period – allows us to imagine a different kind of space at the meeting point of cultures. Terence Malick's film of 2005, *The New World*, offers an example of how one filmmaker has struggled to imagine a time when the cultural field is – if certainly not a *tabula rasa* – then at least a space where there is room for many more possible encounters and many more possible outcomes than those usually allowed by our history-haunted imaginations. Power relations between the British and the Native Algonquian Indians –seen at a point of first encounter in the 1607 founding of Jamestown (the film takes as its point of departure the story of Pocahantas and John Smith) – fluctuate back and forth over the course of the film, in a manner that exposes a range of different possible scenarios. But what is significant here is how Malick nonetheless opens the film with a moment of aesthetic revelation that resonates with the utopian promise of the first encounter between Old and New worlds, a moment – and a place – to quote F. Scott Fitzgerald, »commensurate to man's capacity for wonder«.[23]

What would an object situated at this juncture between precariously balanced cultures look like? That is, an object that abjures its identity as object in favor of its *function* as a form of communication between cultures? A pipe-tomahawk from 1770 brings these issues vividly to life – and with them a different understanding of aesthetic objects as active agents in new forms of identity. The pipe-tomahawk represents a still early phase of encounter between Europe and the New World.[24] Its type finds no ready counterpart outside the eastern region of what would become the United States. It is a hybrid, combining an implement dedicated to war – the tomahawk – with one used for ceremonial purposes of diplomacy and peacemaking – the pipe. Its hollow wooden shaft is beaded with Native quillwork, while its hatchet is of European pewter, engraved with the names of maker and owner, and with familiar cultural emblems such as the heraldic sun. If we read objects as in some sense declarations – pronouncements – this one offers two opposed propositions: war, or peace; violence, or diplomacy; and two forms of agency: to cleave or to unite. These possibilities can only be activated by two people rather than by one acting alone, making the pipe-tomahawk a very suggestive example of the role of objects in mediating cultural encounters. For it takes two parties to make war, or to forge treaties. The pipe-tomahawk gives us a glimpse of a very different Euro-American frontier than the one that has been enshrined in cultural myth over the past two centuries as a space of presocial, solitary danger. This older mythic frontier tests – and helps form – what D. H. Lawrence famously described as the hard, stoic, isolate American soul. The pipe-tomahawk opens into a very different history: of intimate social exchange and of identities that oscillate between cultures, making borders hard to define. The pipe-tomahawk serves the two parties to the encounter simultaneously; its semantic force only comes into focus as it is *used* by each of the two parties to the encounter. Such an object has no inherent meaning; it does not exist, semantically, apart from its circulation and use, and any effort to discuss it must necessarily abstract it from this dense web of social relations. Its identity, as a signifier of culture, is entirely bound to its position at the boundary *between* cultures.

This position at the juncture of cultures is signaled not only by its usage but in the very constitution of the object itself. Its manufacture combines the metalsmith skills of an English gunsmith – Richard Butler – and an unnamed Native woman who created the plaited quillwork covering the shaft, crossing not only cultural but gender boundaries and hierarchies. The pipe-tomahawk is culturally double-coded; its materials and decorative motifs drawn from Native and European sources, it suggests simultaneous participation in two distinct cultural orders – European and Native – seamlessly connected. One cannot choose one without the other, and the implicit proposition – war? Or peace? – is extended equally. The hierarchy of European over Native, colonizer over colonized, cultural self and other, gives way to equivalence, deliberation, choice. To handle the pipe-tomahawk is implicitly to participate in both systems at once; the object is activated through a cross-cultural gesture, yet the instrument of the gesture *itself* embodies the intertwined identities of colonizer and colonized, self and other, in a manner that disrupts these very categories.

Is the pipe-tomahawk a unique object? Are there others like it, which we have slighted because of their very slippage of identity back and forth between contexts and historical actors? How broadly might we apply its lessons to other objects in other periods of cultural history? What is clear is that the pipe-tomahawk – in its own modest fashion – invites us to rethink the politics of cultural identity.

In concluding this essay, I would like to return to the question of how we theorize both individual and social identities in a world in which the boundaries and definitions of the nation-state can no longer contain (if they ever did) the emerging networks of voluntary affiliation, cross-national and global virtual communities, and strategic, constantly shifting alliances on the local, regional, and international levels. Older practices of art history are compatible with liberal constructions of multiculturalism, grounded in concepts of universal citizenship (or inclusive coverage), but that are nonetheless premised on assimilation and integration of difference into national identity.[25] Such liberal models of integration assume a one-directional flow of cultural influence. Liberal multiculturalism derives in turn from concepts of selfhood originating in the Enlightenment and premised on full autonomy, and on the presumption that one makes decisions and gathers knowledge about the world from a position of total neutrality – without the particularisms of social codes, conventions, traditions, habits, and rituals that serve to define – by contrast – ethnic »others«.[26] Enlightenment liberalism is enabled by beliefs in the authority of individual experience, and a vision of selfhood as monadic, autonomous, and co-equal. Without allegiances to anything beyond the self – to cultural traditions or collective responsibilities – choice indeed becomes free, non-contingent. But of course such an autonomous self is a fiction; liberal subjecthood is misguided, not only from a political standpoint (the subject within the social field), but also from the standpoint of postmodern theorizations of subjectivity as fundamentally relational and formed out of encounters with others.

In its most radical sense, however, multiculturalism – as numerous commentators have suggested – *assaults* the driving assumptions of Enlightenment liberalism. New, "improved" versions of multiculturalism align with more fluid conceptions of identity. The distinction is tagged by anthropologist James Clifford, who draws a polarity between »roots« and »routes«. Roots signify identities framed by fixed locations in space, and symbolized by the anthropological hut or dwelling at the center of the village. This place-centered version of identity is fixed upon a stable object of study that can be understood as existing within a particular ecology of social relations. Critical anthropology has increasingly substituted for this place-defined sense of identity an insistence on process, a continual coming-into-being through movement across space, along lines of travel that trace points of encounter. Paul Gilroy has helped open up a new phase of cultural studies around the concept of the »black Atlantic«.[27] We should bear in mind, however – despite the linkage between modernity and migration – that cultures traveled well before the modern era of transatlantic crossings, with its expansion of markets in both bodies and goods that accompanied the rise of capitalism and colonialism.[28] Clifford argues that conceptions of cultural purity came into focus precisely *in relation to* such forms of cultural hybridization. The very idea of contact zones came into currency in contrast to some putative moment of cultural stasis.[29]

Given the central historical role in cultural change played by colonization, migration, trade routes, displacement by war, famine, and climate, it is time to embrace the idea of the contact zone as not simply a peculiar space of encounter, but as a model of culture itself. Such a shift requires a different more fluid understanding of identity – both individual and cultural – as a coming-into-being that unfolds temporally. It also asks us to rethink the organicist conception of culture as something that grows from a root – or its related idea, from an interiorized selfhood – in order to emphasize instead a conception of culture as – to quote James Boon – »a multiply authored invention, a historical formation, an enactment, a political construct, a shifting paradox, an ongoing translation«, all formulations that emphasize process over essence; becoming over being.[30] Two questions emerge from this: how precisely do we fix an object of study in this moving world of continually evolving forms and identities? And who or what, in short, should be the object of study? Once we begin to detach our methods of inquiry from the notion of a grounded, rooted cultural self which produces objects as carriers of meaning, we may begin instead to focus more upon these processes of exchange.

If versions of multiculturalism most closely associated with identity politics have insisted – paradoxically – on fixed, insular cultural identities, contemporary scholarship in visual studies has begun to generate more case studies of the mobile, strategically flexible and adaptive character of material and expressive culture.[31] Post-colonial studies have given us a crucial understanding of how developments in the aesthetic and material realm take shape on a field of very uneven economic, political, and social power, producing strategies of resistance, appropriation, and adaptation. My contribution to this discussion, however, is to ask us to imagine a cultural space – however ephemeral and transitory – on which cultural encounters are not already determined by the politics of uneven power. That is the significance of the moment of exchange represented by the pipe-tomahawk: in its tense but productive interlocking of more or less equal parties, it instates a far more dynamic, decentered web of reciprocal influences flowing in several different directions simultaneously. We are coming increasingly to understand how objects create such spaces of intersubjective exchange – existing at the point of encounter between cultural subjects, but also acting as agents that transform those very subjectivities in an ongoing process. Within this oscillating field of intersubjective and intercultural encounter – evading, if only momentarily, fixed social scripts – new possibilities take shape, where familiar or tested forms of social experience give way to improvised roles and new possibilities of cultural growth mediated through objects. This model of intersubjectivity is implied in Native artist Jolene Rickard's statement that »I have had to learn all of the specifics of other cultures in order to move freely in the world«.[32] In place of a wheel with spokes – pathways leading to the hub of the centered national self – we have an energized field of exchanges between different cultural players, in which self and other reconstitute one another in the charmed circle of the object.

---

1 This shift is part of a broader postmodern turn in the humanities which include other developments relevant here, including a rethinking of the participant-observer model of anthropology, and of older psychological models of centered and stable subjectivity.

2 icholas Mirzoeff: *An Introduction to Visual Culture.* London/New York 1999, p. 13.

3 A representative sampling of recent books on the subject, along with those cited below, include Margaret Ditovitskaya: *Visual Culture: The Study of the Visual after the Cultural Turn*. Cambridge, MA, 2005; Deborah Cherry (ed.): *Art: History: Visual Culture*. Malden, MA, 2005; Michael Ann Holly and Keith Moxey (eds.): *Art History, Aesthetics, Visual Studies*. Williamstown, MA, 2002; Norman Bryson, Michael Ann Holly, and Keith Moxey (eds.): *Visual Culture: Images and Interpretations*. Hanover, N.H., 1994.

4 In visual culture theory, the term »transculture« has recently acquired currency to express the movement of objects across time and space and through circuits of cultural exchange. See Mirzoeff 1999 (as note 2), pp. 127–161.

5 See for instance Nikolaus Pevsner: *The Englishness of English Art: the Reith Lectures*. New York 1956. In his opening remarks, Pevsner stated that »the subject of a geography of art is national character as it expresses itself in art« (p. 11). Already by 1955, Pevsner felt compelled to defend his approach against charges that the growth of global communications and international science had rendered the stress on nationality obsolete. His answer was to lay claim to an enlarged definition of nationalism, capacious enough to embrace »seemingly opposed forms and principles … sympathies and antipathies …« (p. 11–12). Brushing lightly over »race« as a factor, Pevsner emphasized climate and certain historically persistent preferences stemming from the middle-class character of English society. For more, see Will Vaughan: »The Englishness of British Art« In: *Oxford Art Journal*, 13/1990, no. 2, p. 11–23.

6 Central to the concept of the intersubjective is the understanding that we know ourselves as subjects only in relation to others. See Kelly Oliver: »Identity, Difference, and Abjection« In Cynthia Willett (ed.): *Theorizing Multiculturalism: A Guide to the Current Debate*. Oxford, UK, 1998, pp. 168–186, especially p. 176. Related to this is the concept of the dialogic nature of subjecthood, which evolves not in terms of dialogue through two already constituted subjects, but as a fundamentally constitutive element of the subject »which can position itself as an ›identity‹ only in relation to what it lacks …« Stuart Hall: »Conclusion: The Multicultural Question« In: Barnor Hesse: *Un-settled Multiculturalisms: Diasporas, Entanglements, Transruptions*. London 2000, p. 230, drawing on the work of Charles Taylor: *Multiculturalism: Examining the Politics of Recognition* (1994). Intersubjectivity implies a critique of what Hall elsewhere calls »the self-sustaining subject at the centre of post-Cartesian western metaphysics«, a critique of which has been »comprehensively advanced« in the deconstructive discourses of recent decades. See Stuart Hall: »Introduction: Who Needs ›Identity‹?« In: Stuart Hall and Paul Du Gay (eds.): *Questions of Cultural Identity*. London 1996, p. 1. Of note here are also Marxist/Lukácsian/Frankfurt school understandings of bourgeois selfhood as itself dialectically constituted by social experience. All forms of subjectivity under capitalism – far from being autonomous, or a condensation of private experience – were imbricated with the social. Conditional on the structure of the social, subjectivity was, however – in such understandings – granted agency rather than being reduced to a mere reflection or effect of the social apparatus.

7 Jeremy Waldron: »Minority Cultures and the Cosmopolitan Alternative« In: Will Kymlicka (ed.): *The Rights of Minority Cultures*. New York 1995, p. 96, traces the rise of the concept of nationhood and that of the individual, to the same historical context.

8 See for instance Richard McLanathan: *The American Tradition in the Arts*. New York 1968, p. 4.

9 Read through the Oedipal narrative so central to Freudian psychoanalysis, this relationship between parent and child was inherently antagonistic. Freud reinforced older models of identity formation as agonistic, achieved through a break with the past, in some instances traumatic. The formation of national culture, both in relation to Europe and to internal divisions, has also been read through the lens of the Freudian family romance, as a form of symbolic patricide. For a classic instance, see George B. Forgie: *Patricide in the House Divided: A Psychological Interpretation of Lincoln and his Age*. New York 1979.

10 See Waldron 1995 (as note 7), p. 96.

11 Raymond Williams: *Keywords: A Vocabulary of Culture and Society*. New York 1976, p. 80.

12 This idea of the self as defined by ethical unity may be traced to Kant; see Waldron 1995 (as note 7), p. 94. See also James Clifford: *Routes: Travel and Translation in the Late Twentieth Century*. Cambridge, MA, 1997, p. 25.

13 David Theo Golberg: »Introduction« In: Goldberg (ed.): *Multiculturalism*. London 1994, paraphrased by Hall 2000 (as note 6), p. 210. See also Hall 1996 (as note 6), p. 3–4.
14 See Raymond Williams: *Culture and Society: 1780–1950*. New York 1958; and Beeke Sell Tower: *Envisioning America: Prints, Drawings, and Photographs by George Grosz and his Contemporaries, 1915–1933*. Cambridge, MA, 1990, pp. 38–39, on the distinction between Kultur and Zivilisation; also Hall 1996 (as note 6), p. 4–5 and passim.
15 The most ambitious attempt thus far is the co-authored volume *American Encounters: Art, History, and Cultural Identity*. Upper Saddle River, N.J., 2007.
16 On this point see Oliver 1998 (as note 6). Oliver argues that »neo-Hegelian theories« construct identity »through exclusion or abjection«; these include Mary Douglas, Judith Butler, and Julia Kristeva. Such theories, Oliver argues, are premised on a conflictual or oppositional model of identity in which difference is perceived as threatening to the ego. Kelly notes the application of these theories not only to individuals but to national and group identities in which rival or minority groups must be excluded as part of the policing of boundaries. Such analysis of identity formation as rooted in antagonism offers a psychoanalytic parallel to models of national identity formation in which difference (minority and colonized cultures) is abjected, with a resulting hierarchy of aesthetic values which postcolonial theory has decentered. In its place, Kelly draws on post-Freudian and post-Lacanian theorists such as Teresa Brennan to suggest that »the ego is neither self-contained nor self-generating, but rather the effect of an interplay of intersubjective psychic forces.« (Oliver 1998 (as note 6), p. 183). Such revisionist thinking bridges the division between psyche and body, grounding sociality – and by extension other forms of social exchange – in the earliest bodily experiences of the infant with its mother.
17 Edward Said: »The Politics of Knowledge« Republished in David H. Richter: *Falling Into Theory: Conflicting Views on Reading Literature*. Boston 2000, pp. 189–198.
18 Paul Gilroy: *Against Race: Imagining Political Culture beyond the Color Line*. Cambridge, MA, 2000, p. 6.
19 Hall 2000 (as note 6), p. 209.
20 Mirzoeff 1999 (as note 2), p. 26, in evoking these new pathways, uses the term »transculture« to encapsulate the recombinatory energies of cultural exchange.
21 The classical statement here is Gayatri Chakravorty Spivak: »Can the Subaltern Speak« In: Patrick Williams, Laura Chrisman: *Colonial Discourse and Post-Colonial Theory: A Reader*. New York 1994.
22 Richard White: *The Middle Ground: Indians, Empires, and Republics in the Great Lakes Region, 1650-1815*. Cambridge, NY, 1991.
23 *The Great Gatsby*. New York 1992 (first published in 1925), p. 189.
24 This object is reproduced in *American Encounters* (as note 15), p. 35. A special note of thanks to my colleague and collaborator Janet Berlo for all I have learned from her about Native arts during the period of encounter, and as importantly, about the lessons of cultural reciprocity to be learned from such study. The present essay draws directly on the rich exchanges among the team of authors who contributed to *American Encounters*.
25 See Hall 2000 (as note 6), p. 210. Goldberg 1994 (as note 13), p. 9 and passim, uses the term incorporation in contrast to integration/assimilation, to distinguish a post-liberal form of radical multiculturalism.
26 On the »foundational« nature of autonomy as a key concept in western philosophy, see Richard White: »Autonomy as Foundational« In Hugh J. Silverman (ed.): *Questioning Foundations: Truth/Subjectivity/Culture*. New York 1993, pp. 79–97.

27 Paul Gilroy: *The Black Atlantic: Modernity and Double Consciousness.* Cambridge, MA, 1993.

28 Aijaz Ahmad: »the cross fertilization of cultures has been endemic to all movements of people ... and all such movements in history have involved travel, contact, transmutation, hybridization of ideas, values and behavioural norms.« (1995; quote in Hall 2000 (as note 6), p. 226). And Arjun Appadurai has similarly insisted that »Natives, people confined to and by the places to which they belong, groups unsullied by contact with a larger world, have probably never existed.« (»Putting Hierarchy in its Place« In: *Cultural Anthropology* 3, no. 1, pp. 36–49.).

29 »Stasis and purity are asserted – creatively and violently – against historical forces of movement and contamination.« (Clifford 1997 [as note 12], p. 7).

30 James Boon: »Affinities and Extremes«, quoted in: Clifford 1997 (as note 12), p. 24.

31 David Hollinger for instance, identified an emergent »post-ethnic« model of cultural dynamics based on voluntary affiliation in place of essentializing assumptions; see: *Postethnic America: Beyond Multiculturalism.* New York, NY, 1995. Looking at history through a contemporary lens has opened up new understandings of how cultures took shape and changed in the past. Scholar of Latino art Tomas Ybarra-Frausto calls for an expanded American art from the so-called margins, in which scholars, archivists, and artists all work to establish points of contact between and among formerly discrete ethnic traditions. »Imagining a More Expansive Narrative of American Art« In: *American Art* 19, no. 3 (Fall 2005), p. 11.

32 Gerald McMaster (ed.): *Reservation X: The Power of the Place in Contemporary Aboriginal Art.* Seattle 1998, p. 128.

Peter Smith

Photography, Language and the Pictorial Turn

In this paper I wish to revisit some old arguments about pictures and writing and in so doing offer some reflections on current issues in photography theory and practice. I will note the degree to which post-conceptualist photography having sought either to privilege the picture, or alternatively to privilege written text, has brought into focus quite far-reaching issues about the work of art as a hybrid or mixed media form. One outcome of the tendency to ignore disciplinary and media boundaries reinforces a now widely accepted view that all signs signify in ways that transcend disciplinary boundaries and in ways that makes them equivalent and interchangeable semantic units. The democratic equivalence of all signs has provided theoretical legitimacy for artistic hybridization (I refer in particular to the hybrid form of the image-text) and the recent hegemony of the mixed media model of photographic practices. Within this perspective semiotics is seen as as a neutral metalanguage challenging not only the historical privilege of language but also the rhetoric of purity in the visual arts that has in the past sought earnestly to avoid the contamination of language. This paper does not quarrel with the political task of opposing cultural stratification and privilege in the conventional hierarchy of genres but does, however, question the assumed ontological equivalence of words and images.

Amongst those who now make a point of separating words and pictures I include the photographer Jeff Wall. Others continue to efface the disciplinary and institutional boundaries between picturing and writing. I include Allan Sekula in the latter group. The difference may not seem that crucial in view of the bewildering range of techniques and the commonplaceness of inter-artistic practices that have always existed. Nevertheless the debates that attach to the word/picture opposition still have a capacity to shed light on key issues affecting the way we think about contemporary art, not least because the image-text hybrid has always cast a shadow across the individual arts. It is perhaps worth noting (for the sake of argument) that one figure secures an identity in the realm of ›art‹ (Wall), whilst the other occupies an identity that seems a bit more in the world. Wall's avant-garde naturalism has a traditional look about it. It usually consists of large pictures with separate titles and the subject matter is often explicitly inscribed in the discourse of art. *The Story Teller* of 1986 for example (Fig. 1) recalls Manet's *Déjeuner sur l'Herbe.* Sekula's work, by contrast, is a »scripto-visual discourse«[1] which often challenges the institutional sites of art when located in the street or in a book. Wall's photographic works are designed for art galleries. They can of course also be seen in a book or a magazine (or on a screen) but that is not their primary site.

Some recent commentary has suggested that Wall is the conservative and Sekula is the radical in this comparison.[2] The pictorialism of Wall is viewed as nostalgic revival-

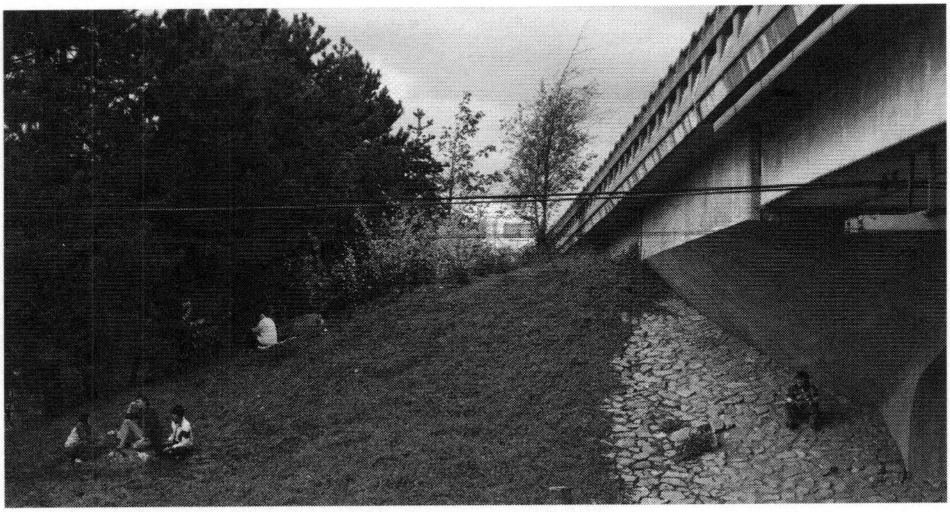

Fig. 1: Jeff Wall, The Storyteller, 1986 (courtesy of the artist)

ism (a reactionary turn). Sekula by contrast openly confronts the institututional separation of word and image and the theme of work (maritime labour for example) is itself conceptualised in the installation. For the critic Benjaminin H.D. Buchloh it is a reflexive practice that hovers between discourse and content.[3]

What I have just described is a quite straightforward ›argument‹ between two contemporary artists. The key difference in the polemic rest heavily on the injunction again medium specificity that has characterised so much late twentieth-century art. This is an injunction issued by postmodernist defenders of interdisciplinarity (like Victor Burgin and Sekula) who have counterposed a ›scripto-visualist‹ method against naturalism on the one hand and against the high modernist privileging of opticality as the basis for abstract art on the other. The position that favours language and hybridity has its roots in the first wave of conceptual art. It forms a major challenge to the isolation of pictures from other systems of communication and its proponents have argued forcefully that pictures are in any case always constrained by words. An example of this linguistic turn is to be found in the early work of Art and Language – a formation that emerged in England in the 1960s – whose work represented a sharp reaction against the anti-intellectualism of the post-war art world and a repudiation of the hegemonic role of art criticism. According to Art and Language the task for art was to »supplant ›experience‹ with ›reading‹«.[4]

By the mid-seventies the hegemonic role of language as primary material for conceptual art had given way to an increasing use of photography as a means of documenting performance and temporary installations, a strategy that sometimes juxtaposed writing, images and other forms. The use of photography (Burgin, Sekula, Hans Haacke, early Wall for example) was self-conscioulsy ›unaesthetic‹. It is worth noting how this affected artistic methodology: after a period of exclusive commitment to writing as art, language was no longer the master code. Artists like Burgin recognised that pictures might form the anchorage for words – this was in any case increasingly evident where banner headlines often competed with spectacular colour photographs in the tabloid press. There was an increasing recognition that in even the most language-centred modes of conceptual art pictures might also form a kind of anchorage for the written text.

It is possible to construe from this change a pictorial turn in the making. The rise of photography as a central practice in the avant-gardist sections of the contemporarary art world is connected to this. It was in any case an intermediary position for artists like Burgin. The so-called pictorial turn, however, appears in many forms. Photography had a certain appeal because of its currency as a functional and popular mode of communication. A recognition that photographs (like words) are constituent parts of complex signs systems thus undermines the difference between ›visual‹ and ›non-visual‹ communication. Burgin notes: »Simply because a message is, in substance, visual, it does not follow that all codes are visual. Visual and non-visual codes interpenetrate each other in very extensive and complex ways«.[5] In a critical reflection on this kind of revelation W.J.T. Mitchell has noted how art historians (in the Anglo-American world) suddenly woke up to the idea »that paintings, photographs, sculptural objects, and architectural monuments are fraught with ›textuality‹ and ›discourse‹«.[6] This belated ›discovery‹ for exponents of semiotic-influenced methods in the post-conceptual/art-photography schools of the twentieth-century *fin-de-siècle* was in fact to become an article of faith. Any counterveiling approach that admitted ›medium specificity‹ as an ontological pretender, any recognition that photographs might for example contain essential differences in a straight comparison with other types of signs, was out of the question since the conventionalist argument was now accepted as gospel truth. The authority of Christian Metz was called upon to finally dissolve the difference between word and image:

> »In truth, the notion of ›visual‹, in the totalitarian and monolithic sense that it has taken on in certain recent discussions, is a fantasy or ideology, and the *image* (at least in this sense) is something that does not exist.«[7]

The dominant linguistic turn thus moves stealithily into the semiotic turn and increasingly neutralises the word/image opposition. After 1968 it was motivated by a desire to break out of the academy of art and make use of language-based models of semiology in the deconstruction of commercial media culture. The imported New York School modernism that filled the English-speaking art journals of the period seemed to have little connection with social existence. As John Roberts has noted: »Greenbergian Modernism was vanquished through the theoretical return of the artwork as sign«.[8]

The blurring of boundaries between word and image, in the English context of the 1960s and '70s, represented a middling position between the linguistic and pictorial turning points in cultural politics. If the rupturing of disciplinary boundaries caused a major upheaval at this time – and there is evidence that it did[9] – it is nevertheless also true that these changes provided the background and inspiration for much of what was to follow. Amongst the many effects of ›interdisciplinarity‹ (including pedagogic cross-overs at university level) the coalescence of theory and practice was the most important. It spawned a mixing of media practices and an increasing heterogeneity in art practice including a wide and varied use of new media. By the 1980s photography in particular had become a primary medium in the visual arts. This in turn led to a massive increase

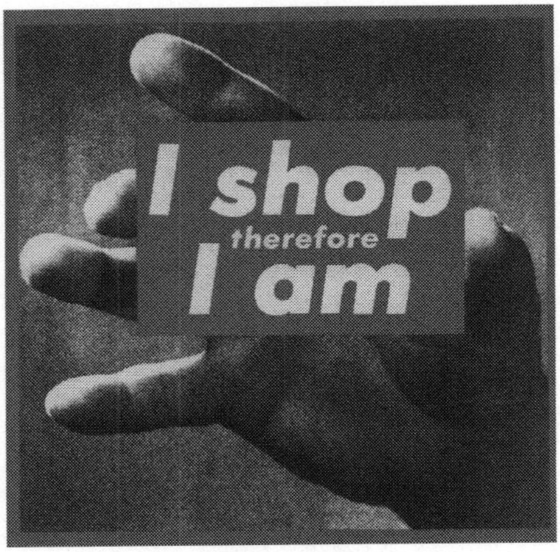

Fig. 2: Barbara Kruger, Untitled (I Shop Therefore I Am), 1987 (courtesy of the Mary Boone Gallery New York)

in political engagement amongst a generation of young artists influenced by identity politics and the semiotic guerrilla-warfare of the earlier generation of conceptualists. Indeed, this shift in intellectual and artistic fashion produced a new generation of non-specialist critics and multi-media practioners and a spate of new university courses devoted to interartistic and cross-curricular studies. This moment also produced the anomaly of a self-styled counter-hegemonic trend in the visual arts that quickly became fashionable and highly marketable. Artists such as Cindy Sherman, Barbara Kruger, and Richard Prince in the America – all working in the now dominant medium of photography – represented a new generation of artists whose consciousness-raising projects fitted in well with the glamour and exlusivity of the art/business world that supported it during the international art boom of the 1980s and beyond. Kruger's word play signals the skill of the copywriter and graphic artist in the philosophic pun: »I Shop Therefore I Am« (Fig. 2). The strength of this kind of work is the way rhetorical forms of wit and irony established a bridge between theoretical discourse and popular culture. It belongs to an honourable lineage of agitational graphic design. Despite its being for the most part restricted as a practice to the art world and its institutions (unlike the ›agit-prop‹ it quotes) Kruger's genre hybridity represented an attractive extension to the specialist discourse of political writing.

For the purposes of this essay I want especially to note that the interventionist and counter-hegemonic use of photography as a tool by second-generation conceptualists signals a gradual return to a mixed art practice. The motivation in this work (as I have argued) was essentially political. The full-blown return to pictures was, however, only partly driven by these motives. For example in the case of Jeff Wall the ›turn‹ to a pictorial paradigm was in fact a ›re-turn‹ driven by a rejection of pluralism and the hybrid forms of conceptual and post-conceptual art.[10] This position is defended by Wall as a reaction against a recuperated vanguardism. It is, however, worth noting that the upsurge in commercial and public support for progressive art in this period co-incided with the return of the image as a key factor in post-modernist aesthetics. As I have noted the linguistic turn was a transgressive move into criticism and philosophy and, as with the critic Clement Greenberg in pre-war America, a rejection of commodity culture. Insofar as the linguistic sign and the visual sign were deemed to serve similar functions, the intellectual and political functions of photography and the image-text were ideologically consistent with the original turn to the written word as an optional artistic métier. This explains why the return of the image in the 1970s represents not so much a self-conscious rejection of the language-based model (there was no sudden change of direction) but a desire to extend the self-reflexive critique of art toward an expanded field that increasingly encompassed a critical assault on commercial culture.

The work of Burgin in particular remained strongly rooted in a logocentric espistemology.

A more nuanced account of the pictorial turn is rooted in older philosophical debates about pictures and words. The underlying thematic in this debate centres on medium specificity or more broadly what Mitchell calls »the immanent vernaculars of representation.«[11] Let us note how Burgin in particular has struggled to position his own trans-disciplinary practice in opposition to »specificity« and the »traditional« divide between words and pictures.[12] From quite early in his career as a photographer Burgin has sought to distance his own work from the »single image aesthetic«.[13] This notwithstanding, the ›phantasmic‹ element in his mature work clearly demonstrates an awareness of the image as something that elevates sensory experience as a basis for knowledge. In this sense his photographs seem to prioritise the world as foundation for the production of consciousness. His work is thus reflexively concerned with this process. In some ways this may look a bit like a realist epistemology. His writing, however, seems to consistently refuse the specificity pictures even whilst he exploits their ›natural‹ effects. »I want to stress the image not as illusion but as *text* [his emphasis]« he says, and »Mental processes exchange images for words and words for images. *It's not a matter of translation* [my emphasis]«.[14] In other words the ontological sameness of verbal and visual signs is underlined. Photography for Burgin thus became a pragmatic extension of his theoretical work as he was increasingly drawn to ›visual culture‹ as a site for critical sabotage and deconstruction.

In 1976 Burgin designed and fly-posted a street poster, *What Does Possession Mean to You?* The juxapostion of image and text in this poster demonstrates a cut-and-paste technique symptomatic of the growing trend in the postmodern avante-garde for use of ›quotation‹ and intertextuality. The poster literally uses quotation (»7% of Our Population Own 84% of the Wealth« is from *The Economist*), but also ›quotes‹ a type of visual rhetoric in the image of a young couple as symbols of intersecting gender and wealth mythologies in advertising.

More importantly the poster demonstrates Burgin's interest in mediation itself. The work is explicitly political in its choice of material but a deeper meaning attaches to the deconstructive politics of representation. As with Burgin's later work this poster typifies a kind of ›knowing‹ critique of the sign, a strategy in which the simulation of images becomes routine. It is a reflexive methodology in which the attempt to find a neutral matalanguage of represention is always in danger of losing its connection with what Jessica Evans has called »external ›societal‹ logic«.[15] Alex Potts is another sceptic on this matter when he describes the dangers of infinite regression in the »wanton chase from sign to signs«, and »endless semiosis«.[16] The concern here is about a polysemic world of spectacle that no longer requires an »outside, a referent or a general public«.[17] The determined opposition to ›naïve realism‹ relies on a kind of quotation aesthetics in which all images are coded versions of other images. If the belief in the indexicality of the photographic message is held in suspension , or denied as it often is these days,[18] it is treated like all other signs – that is as a constituent part a purely symbolic order in which meaning is ever deferred. When the sign carries an ideological value it is »not the reflection of real social relations but the reflection of the social imaginary of its subject. The image of an image, it is deprived of all real denotation«.[19]

It is important to recognise how mediation sets off a procession of signals that seem to transcend objective reality. There is, nevertheless, a sense in which we can say that photographs have a complex and negotiable relation with conventional reading and in any case are always a relay for something outside signification. The comparison with language is instructive in this regard since the photograph in contrast is ineluctably connected to its referent in a way that language is not. At the very least we can say that the insistence on the importance of the process of signification as an exclusive realm of connotation seems to leave out something that never really goes away in even the most dogmatic anti-realist theory.

Mitchell sets his sights on what he describes as the over-confident denouncement of the ›natural‹ and ›non-conventional‹ status of the photograph,[20] in comments that relate to Burgin's rigid conventionalism. Whilst Mitchell accepts that »›language‹ in some form usually enters the experience of viewing photography«,[21] the suggestion that photographs are (as Burgin expressed it) »invaded by language« seems (to Mitchell) to be not only over-stretching the metaphor but tantamount to suggesting an affinity between photography and language. To say that in certain ways, in particular circumstances, a photograph may be »invaded« by language is one thing. Who would deny it? The anchorage of a picture's meaning in language (and vice versa) is well known. »Invaded by«, in this example, is not, however, the same as »identical with«.[22] For Mitchell the metaphor should certainly be more carefully gauged to the problematic of the picture/word opposition. What we are bound to say (following Mitchell) is that the »invasion« – rather than dissolving difference – might in fact produce opposition and resistance. There might in other words be »some value at stake in such a resistance, some real motive« as Mitchell notes, »for a defence of the non-linguistic character of the photograph«.[23]

The critical framework for a re-evaluation of the »non-linguistic« status of photography (pace Mitchell) derives from Roland Barthes's *Camera Lucida* (1981). This post-semiotic Barthes revisits an early provocation: the photographic image as *»a message without a code«*,[24] a way of thinking that points towards the need for a re-evaluation of the photographic image. As Mitchell notes there is »one connotation always present in the photograph … it is a pure denotation; that is what it is to recognise it as a photograph rather than some other sort of image«.[25] Mitchell thus comments on a description of a hypothetical wedding snap:

> »Conversely the denotation of a photograph, what we take it to represent, is never free from what we take it to mean … Connotation goes all the way down to the roots of the photograph, to the motives for its production, to the selection of its subject matter, to the choice of angles and lighting. Similarly, ›pure denotation‹ reaches all the way up to the most ›readable‹ features of the photograph: the photograph is ›read‹ *as if it were* the trace of an event, ›relic‹ of an occasion as laden with aura and mystery as the bride's garter or her fading bouquet.«[26]

What is at stake here has importance for the way photographs are seen. Insofar as there is such as thing as medium specificity we might consider the way documentary photography in particular, in some of its forms, connects the photographer and audience with what John Roberts has called the »dialogic and communicative functions of photography«.[27]

The recent interest in medium specificity and the return to the question of the ontology of the photographic image (see Baetens and Gelder)[28] establishes a new connection between the earlier modernist engagement with the reportorial and socio-cultural functions of photography. This marks a return to an engagment with the peculiarity of the photograph and its unique capacity to mediate between the experience of modernity and the perceived need to act as witness to that experience. The denotative power of the photograph is key to an understanding of this.

Barthes's emphasis on the paradoxical nature of the photograph serves to remind us that the photograph always has two messages: one without a code (the analogical) and one that performs a rhetorical function. The first is denotative and the second is connotative. For Mitchell this poses a significant sense of difference between the two modes of being. One must be »neutral« and »objective« and the other is invested with meaning. There exists a sense of resistance between the two. The existence of these two levels suggests something like the distinction between photography and language. Barthes argues that the denoted and the connoted message are not in collusion (they are actually resistant to each other) but the latter (the coded message of connotation) »develops on the basis of a *message without a code*«.[29] The parasitical relation of the coded message in this case (the case of the photo-text) suggests that the value of photography lies in its apparent freedom from values – that is in the suspended ›reality‹ of its pro-filmic moment. Mitchell has shown how this paradox of coded versus uncoded message production suggests a way of thinking about the imbrication of photography and language. There is an argument that it is precisely this sense of difference between the writing and photography that gives substance to the photo-essay.

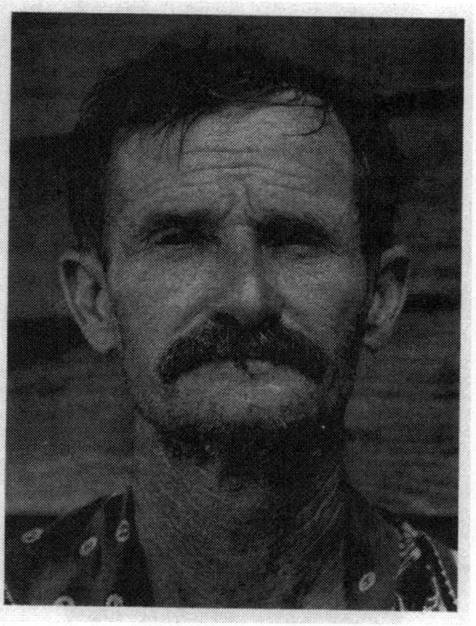

Fig. 3: Walker Evans, Let Us Now Praise Famous Men, 1939

Mitchell recognizes a certain power in the abrasive urban and regional subject matter of documentary photographers in late nineteenth-century and 1930s depression period America. He specifically refers to the pioneering photo-essay of Jacob Riis, *How the Other Half Lives* (1890) and the collaborative work of the writer James Agee and the photographer Walkers Evans's *Let Us Now Praise Famous Men*, of 1939 (Fig. 3). According to Mitchell the power of these images derive in part from their shock value. But there is something else – something more than shock – which is the sense of resistance between image and text. Mitchell notes how the shift from reading to seeing is perhaps awkward. It is, nevertheless, this awkwardness that can be used in a reflexive and self critical way.

»[...] to make the instrumentality of both writing and photography and their interactions serve the highest interests of "the cause" [the left-wing idealism of the project] by subjecting it to criticism while advancing its banner«.[30]

Mitchell's point is that separation of image and text – as two distinct narratives – in the book establishes a certain tension between the two things. In the case of Agee and Evans's book in particular the refusal to anchor the images with a self-explanatory or rationalising text allowed the two discourses to meet tangentially in a way that allows a partial but deliberately incomplete attempt to document its subject. The design of the book leaves gaps in the narrative, inserts false names, resists the temptation of journalistic closure and objectification of the subject matter. But despite sensitivity to formal considerations it is rooted in something that keeps the reader's attention. You might say the procession of signifiers has an end point, a basis in fact that conspires with the illusionistic trappings of the imagery. The meaning is elusive but it retains a level of epistemological power that is arguably missing in postmodernist obsessions with the »shifting networks of symbolic forms.«[31] Mitchell shows that *Let Us Now Praise Famous Men* is an attempt at a truthful statement that draws attention to its own instrumentality as much as it does to the subject matter. The images are not merely illustrative, and Agee claimed that the images and the text are »co-qual, mutually independent, and collaborative«.[32] Mitchell is in fact keen to dispel the danger of the sentimentalising narrativity of the photo-essay and notes that some of the best examples are not merely consciousness raising but disrupt the passage from reading to seeing and make the text interactive and challenging.

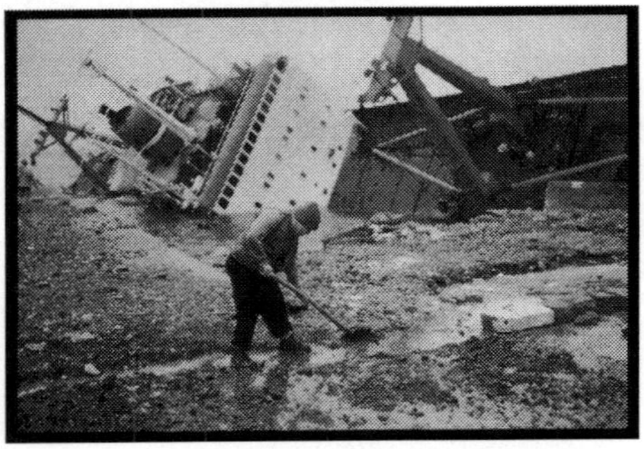

Fig. 4: Allan Sekula, Shipwreck and Workers, Part of Titanic's Wake, 1998/2000 (courtesy of Christopher Grimes Gallery Santa Monica, CA)

The historical examples analysed by Mitchell invite comparison with the recent work of Allan Sekula and I would like to draw attention to his attempt to breathe life into the unfashionable and demonised genre of documentary, and in particular *his* use of the photo-essay. In 2005 Sekula exhibited a monumental photographic series entitled *Shipwreck and Workers* (Fig. 4) in two outdoor locations that invite comparisons (obvious differences notwithstanding) with *Let Us Now Praise Famous Men*.

What connects Sekula with the tradition of humanist documentary photography is his willingness to struggle with the theme of work. As with earlier photo-essays Sekula shows a respect for the ›naïve realism‹ of the photograph. In some key examples this is a tradition that celebrates work rather than consumption and has important connections with democratic and idealist struggles for social and political change. Sekula's practice also represents an attempt to pursue a working method that continues to address the separation between the labour of the artist and the critic. In a statement that echoes James Agee's thinking in the 1930s Sekula continues to develop the type of mixed media practice that, in the words of Van Gelder, »aspires to abolish the the discursive schism between the the critical essay and the artwork«.[33] Sekula observes:

»[A]s soon as you create a relay between text and image, you undermine any purist claims for either text or image. Neither element is foundational. The image is no longer the truth upon which the text is a commentary or subjective gloss, nor is the text a pinning down of a truth that is otherwise elusive in the image«.[34]

In the case of Sekula we can see a contemporary attempt to demonstrate the dialectical nature of the photo-essay in which language and photography interact as they might do in the many other hybrid media forms that we take for granted in our daily lives. Burgin's insistence that pictures are almost never seen on their own is correct. This does not, however, mean that they are the same as writing, and we should recognise that the case for medium hybridity (no longer controversial anyway) might in fact – when taken too far – undermine important media differences. The question of whether the image-text is an inescapable fact of post-medium life is still matter for conjecture. At a time when new technology appears to have digitally blended all signs there is in the photo-essay an object lesson for current practice in the visual arts. It seems to offer a format that combines the radical interventionist strategies of two quite disparate artistic formations: the humanist projects of early-twentieth century documentary photography with the anti-aesthetic imperatives of radical conceptualism. There is, moreover, the example of Sekula's major projects (including *Fish Story* of 1995) which intermingle empirical research and critical comment with a certain resistance to curatorship and the aesthetic appropriation of the photograph. Sekula seems to show a respect for lineages that reach back to the demotic traditions of earlier photographic exhibitions in which archival projects formed a basis for engagement with class oppression, social fracture and the regimes of industrialised labour. The revival of the photo-essay and the re-habilitated practices of the photo-document may in some limited way halt the trafficking of popular culture as art. Insofar as the photo-essay exploits media difference it offers a confrontation between the way things are and the way things look.

It is significant that Sekula is scornful of the return to pictorialism in the work of Jeff Wall.[35] The failure of Wall, in this perspective, is that it negates the critical aspirations of conceptual art and returns to the aesthetically conservative ideology of the »single picture aesthetic«. In conclusion it should be noted that both Sekula and Mitchell have in their different ways argued for the value of the image-text as a means for sustaining a popular hybrid format that extends beyond the museum and art gallery and continues to exploit the critical interaction of writing and pictures. Sekula is following the critical legacy of the 1930s in a way that finds a dynamic role for photography and retains a link with the social world. It is also significant, however, that Sekula, like Agee and Evans, avoids the conventions of captions and narrative structure so that, as Mitchell observes (in his assessment of *Let Us Now Praise Famous Men*) the separation of image and text is not »simply a formal characteristic but an ethical strategy, a way of preventing easy access to the world they represent«.[36] As noted above this relates to the attempt to block a sentimentalised or objectifying view of the worker (in *Shipwrecked* and *Fish Story*). As with Agee and Evans's book there is no obvious way to read these installations. The disruption of conventional sequencing of images and text negates the production of fixed meanings. When Mitchell says that »our labor as beholders is as divided as that of Agee and Evans«[37] the same might be said of our response to Sekula's work. The linguistic message is a foil which reminds us that the picture is a different thing – it is an emanation of a ›past reality‹ that makes us want to think more deeply about the photograph's resistance to language. Despite the challenging nature of these projects we may note also an important shift in emphasis away from the politics of representation to a greater recognition of values that attach to the objects and experiences represented.

---

1 The phrase is used by Victor Burgin in Tony Godfrey: »Sex, Text, Politics: An Interview with Victor Burgin« In: *Block* 7, 1982, p. 9.

2 See comment by Sekula cited in Hilde Van Gelder: »A Matter of Cleaning Up: Treating History in the Work of Allan Sekula and Jeff Wall« In: *History of Photography*, Vol. 31, Number 1, Spring 2007, passim.

3 See Benjamin H.D. Buchloh: »Photography Between Discourse and Document« In: Allan Sekula: *Fish Story*. Rotterdam/Düsseldorf. Nd, pp. 189–200.

4 Cited in Simon Morley: *Writing on the Wall: Word and Image in Modern Art*. London 2003, p. 146.

5 »Photographic Practice and Art Theory« In: Victor Burgin (ed.): *Thinking Photography*. London 1982, p. 83.

6 W.J.T. Mitchell: *Picture Theory*. Chicago 1994, p. 14.

7 The quotation is cited approvingly by Burgin 1982 (as note 5), p. 83.

8 John Roberts: *The Art of Interruption*. Manchester 1998, p. 147.

9 The editorial comment in *Block* 7, 1982 makes this point: »More than most other practitioners in the visual arts, he [Burgin] has indicated the relevance of textual analysis to the still image and the possibilities for a genuinely subversive art practice. Problems of gallery space and the lack of serious critical interest have led Burgin, like a number of other British artists, to exhibit primarily in Europe and America.«

10 Wall has observed: »My work has been criticised for lacking interruption [...]. But, already by the middle of the 1970s, I felt that the ›Godardian‹ look of this art had become so formulaic and institutionalized [...]. See »Interview: Arielle Pelenc in Dialogue with Jeff Wall« In: Thierry de Duve et al: *Jeff Wall*. London 1996, p. 11.

11 Mitchell 1994 (as note 6), fn. 10, p. 14.

12 Medium specificity is condemned by Burgin as (amongst other things) a symptom of patriarchal authority. See his *The End of Art Theory: Criticism and and Postmodernity*. Houndsmill, Basingstoke, Hampshire and London 1986, p. 47.

13 The phrase is cited by Van Gelder 2007 (as note 2), p. 73.

14 Godfrey 1982 (as note 1), p. 8.

15 »Victor Burgin's Polysemic Dreamcoat« In: John Roberts (ed.): *Art Has No History: The Making and Unmaking of Modern Art*. London/New York 1994, p. 208.

16 Alex Potts: »Sign« In: Robert S. Nelson and Richard Shiff (eds.), *Critical Terms for Art History*. Chicago 1996, p. 19.

17 Evans »Victor Burgin's Polysemic Dreamcoat« (as note 15), p. 219.

18 See Joel Snyder's scepticism on indexicality and the photograph in James Elkins (ed.): *Photographic Theory*. New York/London 2007, pp. 369–400.

19 A. Badiou and F. Balmes: *De l' Ideologie*. Paris 1976, p. 30. Cited in Kevin McConnell, Kevin Robins: »Marxist Cultural Theory« In: Simon Clarke, Terry Lovell, Kevin McConnell, Kevin Roberts, and Victor Jeleniewski Seidler (eds.): *One-Dimensional Marxism: Althusser and the Politics of Culture*. London 1980, p. 166.

20 Mitchell 1994 (as note 6), p. 282.

21 Ibid., p. 282.

22 See Burgin 1986, p. 51. The military notion of photographs being »invaded« by language signals his intellectual connection with the tradition that has produced a pervasive »denigration of vision in twentieth-century French thought«. Burgin's iconophobia is rooted in this tradition. See Martin Jay: *Downcast Eyes: The Denigration of Vision in Twentieth-Century French Thought*. Berkeley/Los Angeles 1994.

23 Mitchell 1994 (as note 6), p. 283.

24 The well-known phrase is from Roland Barthes's essay: »The Photographic Message« In: Roland Barthes: *Image, Music, Text*. Trans., Stephen Heath. London 1977.

25 Mitchell 1994 (as note 6), p. 284.

26 Ibid., pp. 284–285

27 Roberts 1998 (as note 8), p. 4.

28 See Jan Baetens and Hilde Van Gelder: »Editorial« In: *History of Photography*, Vol. 31, No. 1, Spring 2007, pp. 1–2.

29 Mitchell 1994 (as note 6), p. 284.

30 Ibid., p. 288.

31 The phrase is used by Burgin in his essay: »Perverse Space« In: Beatriz Colomina (ed.): *Sexuality and Space*. New York 1992, p. 236.

32 Mitchell 1994 (as note 6), p. 290.

33 Van Gelder 2007 (as note 2), p. 73

34 Cited by Van Gelder 2007 (as note 2), p. 73.

35 Ibid., p. 74.

36 Mitchell 1994 (as note 6), p. 295.

37 Ibid., p. 300.

Maggie Gray

»The fantasy bribe«: Comics and Punk

In this paper I argue that the study of visual culture has inherited a latent paradigm that situates it firmly on one side of what has been called the impasse between critical theory and cultural studies. This impasse has been described by Dave Beech and John Roberts as follows: »there is no shared ground between seeing mass culture as the site of popular resistance to structures of authority and the view that mass culture is one the main structures by which individuals are alienated from their humanity and interests«.[1] Contemporary discourse around visual culture iterates much of late cultural studies redemptive model of consumption particularly in its conceptualisation of »everyday experience«.[2] This paper proposes that to transcend this impasse it is productive to return to the debates of the late 1970s that attempted to rethink the nature of the mass cultural commodity, and in particular to Frederic Jameson's article »Reification and Utopia in Mass Culture«. These assessments retain the critical charge of the Frankfurt School analysis and reinstate production as a determinant factor while allowing for negationist strategies through mass culture. It is only such an alternative explanatory model that can adequately address practices that attempt an unqualified refusal and critique of the given proscribed cultural sphere such as punk and Alan Moore's »Roscoe Moscow« comic strip.

It is perhaps useful to briefly retrace how this impasse emerged. Critical theory's approach to mass culture obviously derives primarily from the culture industry thesis of Theodor Adorno and Max Horkheimer. This theory had an important impact on academic analysis of mass culture, particularly in terms of the expansion of the field of cultural inquiry in the 1960s and 1970s to include previously neglected forms.[3] However, the analysis of mass cultural forms as objects of manipulation addressing the false needs of passive consumers, coupled with a privileging of modernist practice as an autonomous and authentic space, was also strongly criticized in scholarly circles. In the United States, there emerged from American Studies in the 1960s the opposed concept of popular culture, which attempted to redress the balance by addressing consumption and audience rather than production and distribution, »stressing the idea of an active production of meanings« on the part of the consumer.[4] Popular culture studies, however, merely inverted a caricatured Frankfurt School analysis, ignoring questions of social function with regard to concepts of ideology and the commodity and instead espoused popular culture as authentic and democratic. In effect this new discipline promoted a facile populism that equated such forms with »the voice of the people« and »the voice of democracy«.[5]

In the U.K. the poles of debate were structured somewhat differently around the opposition between structuralism and culturalism.[6] Arguments were correspondingly more nuanced and complex with figures such as Stuart Hall avoiding the crude populism of the U.S. variant while restoring a limited sense of agency and activity on the side of the recipient. However, it is important to distinguish between the period of Hall's directorship of the Birmingham Centre for Contemporary Cultural Studies (CCCS), in which cultural practices were situated in relation to a wider determining totality of hegemonic power and the limitations of resistance within the cultural sphere were acknowledged, and the later institutionalised period. In the context of the entrenchment of cultural studies as an academic field, early work on the potentially transgressive uses of mass cultural artefacts by subcultures ultimately led to a voracious accumulation of dissident interpretations of mass cultural phenomena that neglected »the absolutely essential relations of cultural power – of domination and subordination« that figures such as Hall had originally insisted upon.[7]

These two rival sets of antinomies of autonomous high art versus instrumentalised mass culture or elitist high art versus democratic or radical popular culture have continued to dog academic debate,[8] and following the trajectory from popular culture studies to cultural studies have now apparently cropped up, although again in more nuanced form, in the new discourses around visual culture, visual studies or Bildwissenschaft. Such discourses, once again appealing to this »kind of camp thinking«, have tended to be formulated in opposition to traditional art history and its field of inquiry: the prevalent notion being, as Horst Bredekamp puts it, that »visual studies is [...] everything that the narrowest definition of art history is not«.[9] A less coherently defined field even than cultural studies, visual culture, in its wide range of variants, shares with its predecessor an expanded range of objects of study, reacting against the perceived inherent hierarchies of art history; and situating such objects in everyday life and an anthropological model of culture.[10] Influenced by semiotics and post-structuralism, it also emphasises reception and the multiple subjective exegesis of variegated users; but concentrates on models of visual perception, in reaction against the fetishisation of the text in the linguistic turn that originally spawned such schools of thought.[11] In particular by continuing late cultural studies emphasis on subjective models of reception and redemptive consumption at the expense of consideration of the materiality of the object and its production, visual culture is ultimately affirmative, allowing for no resistant strategies or transformative practices beyond what Roberts terms a »micrology of dissent«.[12]

Returning to Jameson and the debates of the 1970s that attempted to transcend this two-camp mentality can thus perhaps provide an alternative model for thinking about mass culture, that itself aligned with the radical auto-critique articulated through mass cultural forms of that time such as punk. Jameson's essay included two key propositions. The first is that theories of mass culture have defined their object against high culture in an ahistorical and undialectical manner, based on problematic binaries of value. As well as ignoring how historically popular forms have gone up the »cultural escalator« in Hall's terms,[13] such theoretical models also neglect to acknowledge that both high and mass culture are »objectively related and dialectically interdependent phenomena [...] twin and inseparable forms of the fission in aesthetic practice under late capitalism«.[14] In this way Jameson actually builds on a more adequate reading of

Adorno, and his assertion that high art and mass culture are »torn halves of an integral freedom, to which however they do not add up«.[15]

Related to this first proposition is Jameson's critique of the »sociologists of manipulation« and the vulgar interpretation of the culture industry thesis that dismisses culture as sheer ideological manipulation. As a way of thinking about the ideological function of mass culture without resorting to a model based on false consciousness Jameson employs a revised model of the Freudian concept of repression as a mechanism »which strategically arouses fantasy content within careful symbolic containment structures which defuse it«.[16] Thus in order to sublimate, manage or repress social and political anxieties and fantasies, mass cultural works have to address and give expression to such fears and desires: »works of mass culture cannot be ideological without at one and the same time being implicitly or explicitly Utopian as well: they cannot manipulate unless they offer some genuine shred of content as a fantasy bribe to the public about to be so manipulated«.[17] With this model, reminiscent of the work of Ernst Bloch, Jameson cuts a path through the competing characterisations of cultural forms as either wholly corrupt or wholly authentic by asserting that they are structurally contradictory, a site of tension between antagonistic social interests which are only magically resolved.[18] As Rita Barnard asserts, this position transcends the standoff between »optimistic populist theories celebrating mass culture as a new vernacular and pessimistic totalitarian theories, denouncing mass culture as manipulation and propaganda«.[19] Michael Denning has noted the alignment of Jameson's analysis with that of Stuart Hall and his assertion that in mass culture »alongside the false appeals, the foreshortenings, the trivialisation and shortcircuits, there are also elements of recognition and identification, something approaching a recreation of recognisable experiences and attitudes to which people are responding«.[20]

However, the question that arises from this claim for the sublimating function of the mass cultural commodity is: what scope is there for transformative and critical practice to negate, transcend or frustrate this function, especially if we accept Denning's assertion that »mass culture has won: there is nothing else«? Visual culture in its accommodation to the given would seem to deny the possibility of such practices confining resistance or transgression to mere private consumer choices. Jameson himself asserts that any such practice must go beyond merely »studding [...] individual artistic discourse with class and political signals« and points to cultural production that draws on »the collective experience of marginal pockets of the social life of the world system« such as British working-class rock.[21] Punk, I would argue, represented an attempt to both undermine and exploit the contradictory nature of mass culture in a way that was indeed antagonistic rather than accommodating to existent cultural configurations, and pointed beyond them to transformed relationships between production and reception.[22] It is therefore problematic to subsume it under pluralist notions of atomised dissent that ultimately valorise actual existing »popular culture« in an uncritical manner, as so much discourse around visual culture implicitly or explicitly does.[23]

One of the key ways in which punk defined itself was in opposition to rock and its perceived ideology of authenticity that ultimately reinforced the Romantic mystification of the cultural commodity as inhering some use value.[24] Punk instead returned to rock's degraded other Pop, and its supposed inauthenticity or artifice.[25] This self-awareness of its own implication in a system of commodified mass culture was made apparent for

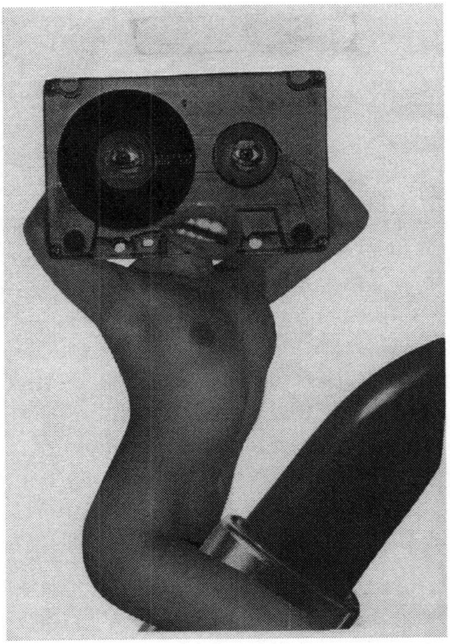

Fig. 1: Linder, Untitled, 1978, Image courtesy of Stuart Shave/Modern Art

example in the punk visuals of Jamie Reid and Linder, who »appropriated [...] materials from the trash populism of tabloid culture and downmarket advertising.«[26] (Fig. 1) A correlative to the rejection of rock authenticity was the refusal of rock technical virtuosity as manifested in long and intricate guitar solos. Punk songs, by contrast, were stripped-down, uncomplicated and short, promoting a deskilling in line with the DIY attitude that was another of its key features.[27] Alongside this anti-professionalism was the denunciation of the reified distinction between performer and audience at punk gigs. Punk, in these ways, radically questioned form, demystifying and de-romanticising the conventions of performance and musicianship, and undermining the rock illusion of being situated in an authentic space outside of the system of commodity exchange. In the wake of the assimilation of rock and the counter-culture more broadly into the commercial mainstream, punk's oppositionality rested not only on the articulation of a critique of authoritarian capitalist society but a simultaneous attempt to resist recuperation by exposing the very alienating mechanism of commodified culture rather than attempting to circumvent it. Intimately tied to the political and social context in which it emerged, commonly characterised as a time of polarisation which marked the end of consensus politics, punk was seen to address issues of social deprivation, unemployment and authoritarian repression but did so negatively, enacting such conflict and thereby rendering the harmonious and imaginary resolution of such issues through mass culture problematic.

The Sex Pistols perhaps represent the most concrete embodiment of what Jon Savage calls this »finely tuned mixture of the authentic and the constructed«.[28] Malcolm McLaren's theoretical promotion of the band drew from Dadaist and anti-art practices, Situationist ideas about the realisation and supersession of art, and from contemporary analyses of youth cultures by the CCCS and others. McLaren performed the role of the sixties bohemian promoter and entrepreneur but presented himself as an all-powerful manipulator in such a way that exposed the exploitative role of his opportunist rock predecessors. Indeed, in Julien Temple's film *The Great Rock 'n' Roll Swindle* (1979), McLaren narrates the entire Sex Pistols project and punk itself as an orchestrated effort to rip off the music industry and manipulate the media.[29] While remaining a controversial account, the film reveals the politics of McLaren's intervention as the construction of a situation that would expose, as Robert Garnett puts it, the »illusory pleasures and fraudulent myths of the popular culture industry itself«.[30] This was supposedly achieved by producing a band that, as Simon Frith describes, »drew attention to its own construction [in such a way] that the usually smooth, hidden gears of commerce were always on

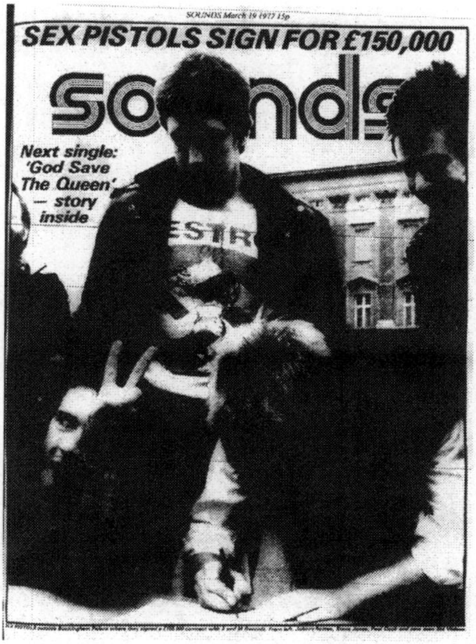

Fig. 2: Sounds cover, March 19th 1977

noisy display«.[31] What I am trying to suggest is that punk, because of its refusal of harmonious integration of its simultaneous expression of social desires and ironic critique of the very mass cultural form in which it expressed them, worked with a sophisticated analysis of mass culture akin to Jameson's dialectical model.

The »Roscoe Moscow, Who Killed Rock 'n' Roll?« strip that Alan Moore contributed to music weekly *Sounds* from March 1979 to June 1980 interrogated similar questions of artifice and authenticity in mass culture. (Fig. 2) Alan Moore worked for the paper under the assumed name Curt Vile due to the fact that he was still claiming unemployment benefits, a pseudonym which resonated with wider punk and post-punk use of fake names such as Jonny Rotten and Poly Styrene. However, in contrast to the ratty line style of much punk cartooning, Moore's artwork, with its fanatical stippling style, bore the strong influence of sixties underground comix, and particularly the work of figures such as Robert Crumb and S. Clay Wilson. Despite the stylistic disparity between Moore's work and that in punk fanzines, his strips shared their visceral frenetic energy and rejection of the slick professionalism of the mainstream.[32]

Roscoe Moscow depicted the efforts of its eponymous protagonist, described by Moore himself as »an alcoholic, sexually inadequate neurotic who can't hold down a job and dresses like a private eye as part of a pathetic attempt at self respect«, to track down the killer of Rock 'n' Roll.[33] During his investigation Moscow encounters loosely-veiled and often merciless parodies of proto-punk and punk icons such as Iggy Pop and Malcolm McLaren. By virtue of the fact that the strip was published in the context of a weekly magazine Moore also used the comic to comment satirically on political issues that concerned its readership, for instance the rise of the National Front and the intensified threat of nuclear war.

Alongside punk references, Moore importantly also engaged with a questioning of comics formal conventions and construction that echoed punk's self-critical transgressions of commodified musical forms. This was achieved through an ironic self-referentiality that contravened conventional storytelling and the suspension of disbelief, transgressing the boundaries between author and reader, and calling attention to the strip's constructed existence as fiction. For example, Moscow and other characters frequently revealed an awareness of their existence as characters in a comic strip, Moscow in one episode pronouncing, in reference to his future antagonist Sinister Gloves, »then of course there wuz the minor mystery o' the geek with the mickey mouse gloves who turned up in the last panel of every third episode and whose very existence I was totally unaware of«.[34] (Fig. 3) The constant exposure of the strips artificiality, defying

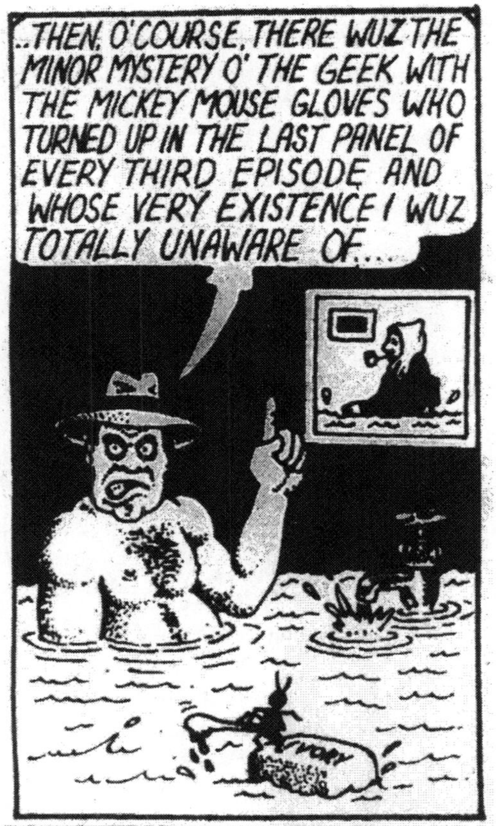

Fig. 3: Curt Vile (Alan Moore), Roscoe Moscow, Who Killed Rock 'n' Roll?, Episode 30 »Washing the Detective!!« Sounds, 27th October 1979, © Alan Moore

naturalistic comics' conventions, consistently rendered the relationship between the characters, reader and author unstable and subverted the reader's expectations. Further, it consistently threatened to rupture the illusion of direct, unmediated access to either the author's »authentic« expression or a meaningful homogenous narrative. Thus although Moore's strip implicated itself in punk's critique of social norms through its vulgarity and testified to the capacity for mass culture to articulate an antagonistic politics, its form was consistently hyperbolic, corrosive, ironic and deflationary, resistant to any kind of harmonious integration or positive affirmation.

This implicit negotiation of the dialectical contradiction of mass culture is also explicitly worked through in the climax of the Roscoe Moscow strip, which reveals the history of the project to kill Rock 'n' Roll as an orchestrated attempt by the heads of all nations to assassinate rock and roll icons and thus »demoralise the rebellious force of youth«.[35] Ultimately it was discovered »that it was easier to buy rockstars than eliminate them«: the accompanying panel shows Moore himself crying about Mick Jagger, as »Street Fighting Man« comes out of the speakers in the background.[36] However the project was threatened in the mid-seventies by punk: »for some reason, youth fought back!! There was a massive resurgence of godless anarchy, hatred of authority and all the evils we thought we'd eradicated«.[37] (Fig. 4) Moore thus posits popular music as a potential oppositional threat to the established order but counterbalances this with its potential co-optation by the market.

Yet Moore's analysis is more nuanced than a simple account of a process of inherently resistant or authentic youth culture being recuperated. In the subsequent episode the project to murder Rock 'n' Roll is put alongside a deliberate political program to create destitution, repression, and boredom that is recognisable as the experience of early Thatcherism. Gloves recounts how he and his co-conspirators »have slowly tightened the screws on the people of Britain« through an artificial economic crisis and crippling inflation, deliberate and degrading mass unemployment and resultant strike action, police collaboration with extreme right-wing groups, and sexual repression through a media onslaught, the only remaining form of escape from which was Rock 'n' Roll.[38] Moore thus complicates his analysis by conceptualising mass culture, as Jameson does, as both expressive of utopian desires and simultaneously a mechanism for their management: to remove mass culture as a safety valve would lead to the need to realise such desires through revolutionary action. The conclusion is, however, fatalistic, in that the foreseen result of the destruction of sublimating commodified culture is actually fascism, an apocalyptic outcome that reveals much of the nihilistic political character of the late seventies and the urgency of contemporary anti-fascist struggles. (Fig. 5)

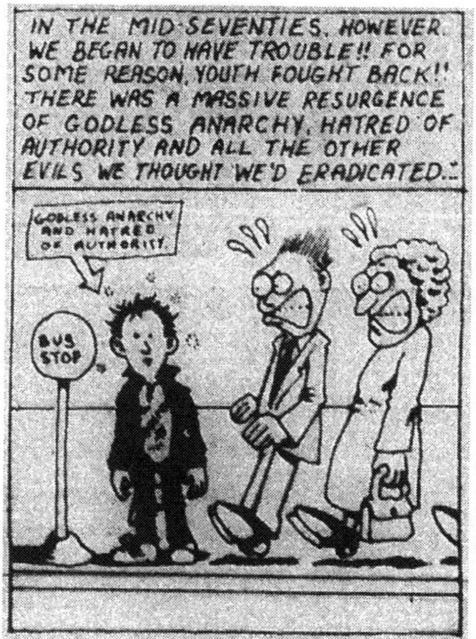

Fig. 4: Curt Vile (Alan Moore), Roscoe Moscow, Who Killed Rock 'n' Roll?, Episode 53 »Working for the Clampdown« Sounds, 10th May 1980, © Alan Moore

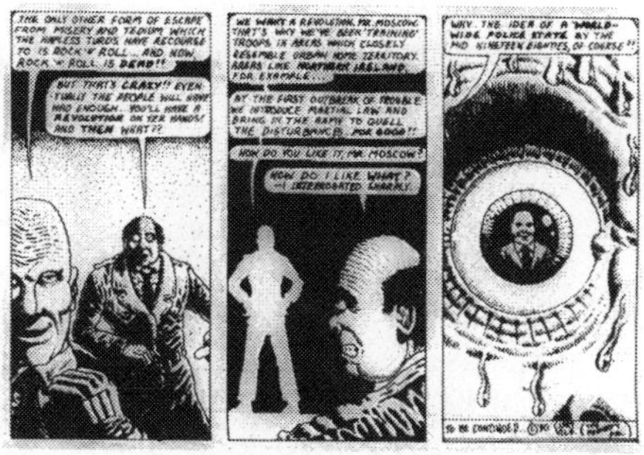

Fig. 5: Curt Vile (Alan Moore), Roscoe Moscow. Who Killed Rock 'n' Roll?, Episode 54 »State of the Nation!« Sounds, 17th May 1980, © Alan Moore

Moore's strip – and punk more broadly – thus revealed an awareness of the contradiction at the heart of the mass cultural commodity, the fantasy bribe identified by Jameson. The response of such practices was an attempt to negate that sublimating function by consistently exposing it. Both appealed to the potentially transformative desires of an antagonistic cultural politics, the demands for collectivity, self-determination and unbridled pleasure that lay behind a visceral critique of authoritarian society and iconoclasm of repressive social values. But this extended to an auto-iconoclasm that undermined the capacity to express or realise such desires in any authentic and unmediated manner within the existing confines of mass culture. This refusal of sublimation or magical resolution ironically ultimately returns us to Adorno's definition of the successful work of art as »one which expresses the idea of harmony negatively by embodying the contradictions, pure and uncompromised, in its innermost structure«,[39] a critique of both mass culture and the system that structures it, as Greil Marcus asserts, »exploding out a spot no one in the Frankfurt School had ever recognized: mass culture's pop cult heart«.[40] It is only an account of mass culture that addresses the determinant impact of production and commodification, and how social desires and anxieties are repressed and displaced in the realm of consumption and everyday life that can admit mass cultural practices that refuse and antagonise this very mechanism and point beyond it. Visual culture by rehashing late cultural studies' optimistic and uncritical celebration of the popular, by effacing production, ideology, materiality and commodification, is in actuality pessimistic and conciliatory – offering only diffuse, disassociated and privatised strategies of making do.

---

1 Dave Beech, John Roberts: *The Philistine Controversy*. London/New York 2002, p. 148.

2 For example note Nicholas Mirzoeff's assertion: »Just as cultural studies has sought to understand the ways in which people create meaning from the consumption of mass culture, so does visual culture prioritize the everyday experience of the visual«. Nicholas Mirzoeff: »What is Visual Culture?« In: *The Visual Culture Reader*. London/New York 1998, p. 7.

3 Despite being first published in 1947, Adorno and Horkheimer's *Dialectic of Enlightenment* made an impact primarily following its definitive German publication in 1969 and its first English translation which appeared in 1972.

4 infried Fluck: »Popular Culture as a Mode of Socialization: A Theory about the Social Functions of Popular Cultural Forms« In: *The Journal of Popular Culture*, vol. 21, Issue 4, March 1988, p. 31.

5 Ray B. Browne: »Popular Culture as the New Humanities« In: *The Journal of Popular Culture*, vol. 17, Issue 4, March 1984, p. 1.

6 Michael Denning: »The End of Mass Culture« In: *International Labor and Working Class History*, no. 37, Spring 1990, p. 4.

7 Stuart Hall: »Notes on Deconstructing the Popular« In: R. Samuel (ed.): *People's History and Socialist Theory*, London 1981, p. 232. It is useful to note for example John Clarke's notion of »magical resolution« in relation to the limitations of subcultural style. See John Clarke: »Style« In: *Resistance through Rituals: Youth Subcultures in Post-War Britain*. Abingdon 2005, pp. 175–191. Later works in cultural studies were more heavily influenced by figures such as Michel de Certeau and poststructuralists and hence the emergence of diffused notions of resistance, a redemptive model of consumption and a shift from issues of power to plurality and diversity. See John Roberts: *Philosophizing the Everyday, Revolutionary Praxis and the Fate of Cultural Theory*. London 2006, pp. 86–97.

8 As Andreas Huyssen asserts, despite postmodernist claims that the distinction between »high« and »low« has been effaced, this has often merely manifested in a simple reversal of the old Greenbergian hierarchy. See Andreas Huyssen: »High/Low in an Expanded Field« In: *Modernism/Modernity*, vol. 3, no. 9, 2002, pp. 363–374.

9 Horst Bredekamp: »A Neglected Tradition? Art History as Bildwissenschaft« In: *Critical Inquiry*, vol. 29, no. 3, Spring 2003, pp. 418–428.

10 The source of much of the attractiveness of visual culture studies, but also of much debate within the field, is its inter-, post- or trans-disciplinarity. The lack of consensus particularly regarding the object of study (images, visuality, vision, the visual?) means that it is difficult to define as a theoretical practice.

11 It is interesting to consider the academic reception of comics in this regard – the emergence of the legitimised form of the ›graphic novel‹ coincided to a certain degree with the linguistic turn and led to a focus on comics' narrative structures and possibilities. The advent of visual studies is concomitant with a shift of focus to the visual element in much comics scholarship but an approach towards the medium from a visual culture perspective is hampered by the fact that is still essentially a form of print media (much visual culture prioritises new media).

More importantly, just as the ›world-as-a-text‹ paradigm neglected comics' visual component, its replacement by a ›world-as-a-picture‹ paradigm threatens to efface its crucial narrative distinction, especially from the aspects of visual culture that isolate and hierarchise the visual.

12 Roberts 2006 (as note 7), p. 96. In fact through the dematerialisation and disembodiment of the image, visual culture often moves further away from production and facture than cultural studies. In some cases images become fetishised to such an extent that they appear autogenetic and free-floating, happily propagating and exchanging themselves and criss-crossing geographical and cultural borders with ease. The extent to which such agency is denied to the consumers and producers of both images and their material carriers is often ignored.

1 As both Jameson and Hall note the distinctions between high and popular are historically situated and fluid – the most common exemplifier being works of figures such as Shakespeare or Dickens, ›popular‹ in their historical context but subsequently elevated in status. Hall 1981 (as note 7), p. 234.

14 Frederic Jameson: »Reification and Utopia in Mass Culture« In: *Social Text*, no. 1, Winter 1979, pp. 133–134.

15 Theodor Adorno: »Adorno on Benjamin« In: Ronald Taylor (trans. ed.): *Aesthetics and Politics: Debates Between Bloch, Lukács, Brecht, Benjamin, Adorno*. London 1980, p. 122.

16 Jameson 1979 (as note 14), p. 141.

17 Ibid., p. 144.

18 Bloch emphasised the anticipatory, emancipatory and utopian elements not only of mass culture but daydreams, everyday life and political ideologies, a surplus of unrealised desires beyond legitimising and mystifying ideological functions. See Ernst Bloch: *The Principle of Hope*, three volumes, Cambridge, MA 1986.

19 Rita Barnard: *The Great Depression and the Culture of Abundance: Kenneth Fearing, Nathaniel West and Mass Culture in the 1930s*. New York 1995, p. 5.

20 Hall 1981 (as note 7), p. 233.

21 Jameson 1979 (as note 14), p. 140.

22 Punk is a much contested concept around which there have emerged several competing definitions, myths and orthodoxies. I am unable here to provide more than what may appear sweeping generalisations that do not take into account the diverse and divergent elements of punk ranging from anarcho-punk to neo-Nazi punk. It is not my contention that punk was essentially radical or revolutionary, but that particularly in its opposition to a recuperated and reified form of rock it broadly represented a critique of mass culture from within.

23 Griselda Pollock highlights this tendency in visual culture when she notes that without »critical contestation of what is at stake in ideological investments in high culture and the global capital investment in popular culture« the result is a »move from high culture-Art History to popular culture-Visual Culture« that is »utterly regressive«. Griselda Pollock: »Responses to Mieke Bal's ›Visual Essentialism and the Object of Visual Culture‹ (2003): Visual Culture and its Discontents: Joining the Debate« In: *Journal of Visual Culture*, vol. 2, no. 2, 2003, p. 259.

24 Terry Bloomfield: »Resisting Songs: Negative Dialectics in Pop« In: *Popular Music*, vol. 12, no. 1, January 1993, pp. 13–31.

25 Simon Frith: »Rock and the Politics of Memory« In: *Social Text*, no. 9/10, The 60s without apology, Spring/Summer 1984, p. 62.

26 Robert Garnett: »Too Low to be Low, Art pop and the Sex Pistols« In: Roger Sabin (ed.): *Punk Rock: So What? The Cultural Legacy of Punk*, London/New York 1999, p. 23.

27 This attitude was famously encapsulated in the illustration in punkzine *Sideburns* from December 1976, which stated »This is a chord. This is another. This is a third. Now form a band«. See Jon Savage: *England's Dreaming, Sex Pistols and Punk Rock*. London 2005, p. 280.
28 Ibid., p. 163.
29 McLaren stars in the film as »The Embezzler«. The film is divided into Lessons including »How to Manufacture Your Group« and »How to Steal as Much Money as Possible From the Record Company of Your Choice«.
30 Garnett 1999 (as note 26), p. 22.
31 Simon Frith and Howard Horne: *Art into Pop*. London/New York 1987, pp. 132–133.
32 See Guy Lawley: »›I like Hate and I hate everything else‹. The influence of punk on comics« In: Sabin 1999 (see note 26), pp. 100–119.
33 Curt Vile (Alan Moore): »Curt Replies response to reader Derek Hitchcock's letter« In: *Sounds*, May 17th 1980, p. 63.
34 Curt Vile (Alan Moore): »Roscoe Moscow, Who Killed Rock 'n' Roll?« Episode 30 »Washing the Detective!!« In: *Sounds*, 27th October 1979, p. 46, panel 6.
35 Curt Vile (Alan Moore) »Roscoe Moscow, Who Killed Rock 'n' Roll?« Episode 53 »Working for the Clampdown« In: *Sounds*, 10th May 1980, p. 44.
36 Ibid., p. 44, panel 5.
37 Ibid., p. 44, panel 12.
38 Curt Vile (Alan Moore): »Roscoe Moscow. Who Killed Rock 'n' Roll?« Episode 54 »State of the Nation!« In: *Sounds*, 17th May 1980, p. 25.
39 Theodor Adorno: *Prisms*. London 1967, p. 274.
40 Marcus 2001 (as note 23), p. 70.

Asko Lehmuskallio

Culture and Mass-Mediated Pictures: A Processual View

Introduction

Visual culture studies and image studies (Bildwissenschaften) have shown that images mediate our knowledge of the world as well as our social relations – specifically relations with other people and objects and our relation to our possible pasts. But while the visual, its role in theory and everyday life has received increasing attention, the concept of ›culture‹ has remained surprisingly vague. In introductions to and discussions on the emerging field of visual culture/image studies, it has been emphasized that it is important to break out of the constraints of Arnoldian high-culture,[1] but it seems that in many studies the concept of ›culture‹ is still associated with people living in close proximity to one another and sharing a whole way of life. ›Western culture‹ especially is a frequent trope that is used to differentiate a set of images and image practices from non-Western image practices, implying a borderline between ›the West and the Rest‹. This implied borderline insinuates that culture would be itself inscribed into images and media.[2] On the other hand, many of these studies have shown that images call for their own practices and that images travel, from media to media and locality to locality, thus gaining ›lives of their own‹. In introducing Hans Belting's triangular interrelation between the image, body and medium, Bakewell's suggestion to consider humanmade images as image acts and combining these thoughts with the call in social sciences to a re-focus on practices, I would like to suggest following a practice-related approach to culture that does not connect cultures to one particular location but rather to a logic of self-organization.[3] In reflecting on culture, this shifts the focus from ideas to embodied, materially mediated arrays of specific practices[4] that are, at least partially, translocal. Translocality means in this context a filtered (re-)embedding of deterritorialized practices.[5] Translocal practices are not ›the same‹ in different locales, but have enough traits in common that a person coming from a specific context might orient her-/himself in it; Augés non-places – airports, trains and highways – are a good example for such locales for translocal practices. This paper does not intend to define what culture is, but rather to orient questions regarding the cultural to specific practices, which are empirically analyzable in interactions with people, media and images that flow, albeit disjunctively.[6]

Culture: a Problematic Noun

It seems that there is a certain agreement that we are living in a globalized world in which commodities, people, technologies, ideas and money move from specific places to others – even though there is discordance on when this process started and how our present differs from previous epochs. Following Marc Augé I assume that our here and now, especially in cities, differs from other times on the basis of the overabundance of events, spatial overabundance and the individualization of references.[7] Assuming that people living spatially close to each other also share a whole way of life has become somewhat problematic; people share some cultural practices with each other, but differ in a wide array of other depending on age, income, gender, ethnicity, religiosity, political views, class and identification with specific (imagined) and actually experienced communities. The mediated information that we focus our attention on is also everything but homogenous. Due to advances in information and communication technologies, everyday communication is becoming ever more mediated. This implies a transformation of the idea of the social, since an affiliation to specific groups has to be at the same time attributed and imagined.[8] The individual experiences ever more his/her belonging to specific (imagined) communities through media events and media rituals.[9]

The noun ›culture‹ is easily associated with a sort of internalized substance, a set of shared ideas, beliefs and abstractly specified rules or norms that govern people, allegedly making their behavior and thinking predictable. Thus the word culture is mainly used, as Abu-Lughod notes, in order to construct similarities and differences, dualisms between ›us‹ and ›them‹, serving as a central component for distancing and othering. A whole set of writers have tried to show how using the concept of culture to designate socially coherent groups sharing whole ways of life actually tends to homogenize very heterogeneous people and creates problematic naturalized boundaries.[10] Culture has been an explanatory principle[11] that does not hold up to contemporary empirical observations. This is why some authors have gone so far as to suggest dismissing the noun culture, either by shifting focus to its adjectival form ›cultural‹[12] or by refocusing attention, e.g. on configurations of power, education and wealth[13] or on events, acts, people and processes.[14]

With the increasing movement of commodities, people, technologies, ideas and money, a wide array of international standards and advertised ways of acting, specific cultural elements and whole practices have become dislocated and can be found dispersed in surprising places. Francisco Osorio discusses this phenomenon in reflecting the uses of television. »(…I)n every (society) (…) in which television is present, people most often use the television set to watch television. This may seem obvious, but it is not. No society worships the television set. No society builds a ceremonial place for the television set inside or outside of the house (…) or (…) uses the television set to build fences, for example.«[15] Thus pictorial media structure ways of looking, practices of looking.[16] The material dimension of cultural practices, such as of watching television, does not determine the performative and discursive dimensions – but it surely seems to have an effect on them.[17]

Cultural dissemination »does not require physical proximity or a specific type of gemeinschaft ties, only social interaction, however (mass-)mediated and casual this may be – just seeing, hearing, or reading of one another may suffice for mutual imitation«.[18] Many translocally shared cultural practices are nevertheless everyday behavior that we do not assign too much meaning to; taking the bus, sitting on a chair, watching a movie, walking on a street or taking snapshot photographs. Bourdieu has famously noted: »It is because subjects do not, strictly speaking, know what they are doing that what they do has more meaning than they know.«[19]

Practices

Hörning stresses the dual nature of practices. On the one hand, they constitute a set of routine interaction patterns, a shared doing that is considered to be normal. This focus on practices might show how deep-seated specific hegemonic practices are. On the other hand, in situational practices individuals might also manage to use their ultimately indeterminate character for their own purposes. This implies not only a tolerance for other kind of practices that are lived out in different locales; it also raises the question of how we actually deal in our lives with other ways of doing.[20]

Following Fredrik Barth, »all views are singular and positioned« and no one can give a definite account of ›culture‹.[21] Individuals differ in their experience of the world and the practices they have learned or have access to, thus living in distinct worlds. Individual learning of practices is a neverending process of social adaptation guided by the desire to construct mutually compatible associations with e.g. the speech-sounds that one hears and constructs.[22] Interactions are organized in social settings around shared practical understandings and thus have organizational and communicational value. The focus in analysis changes from culture-as-being to culture-as-process, of practices used to order our interactions in the world – with »embodied capacities such as know-how, skills, tacit understanding, and dispositions.«[23] In living practices out, power relations and social disparities come to the fore. They are not only contested and different between individuals or specific groups of people but also heterogeneous, uncoordinated and possibly incommensurable during the lifetime of an individual.

Already one shared practice suffices for mutual interaction. An Afghan who joined his family in Finland a few months ago, is a good example of this. Although he had never been outside of Afghanistan before, he was shortly after his arrival already playing chess with the Finnish husband of one of my colleagues. They shared a similar cultural technique and were able to engage in a shared practice.

Image Practices: Image-Body-Medium and the Practice Turn

Images call for their own cultural practices. Following Knorr Cetina, these might increasingly take the form of object-centered sociality, an »orientation towards objects as sources of the self, of relational intimacy, of shared subjectivity and of social integration.«[24] Images are made using specific techniques in order to fit explicit formats and they have their places, where they are taken to, kept, collected and looked at. These practices involve embodied subjects that have developed techniques of the body that only make sense with and in front of images – elsewhere they would, as Schulz and Mersmann point out, be deemed deviant behavior.[25] Examples include sitting in front of a silver screen while waiting for a movie to begin, or gathering around a photo album to look at the pictures from last year's vacation.

Hans Belting has formulated an outline that focuses explicitly on image practices, and it seems helpful in analyzing these practices.[26] His model consists of a triangular interrelation between the image, the body and the medium. *Images* are in Belting's terminology both pictures hanging on walls and mental representations, but images only come into being if bodies regard them. Bodies have to serve both themselves as a medium where images are regarded, as well as orient themselves towards other media that bring pictures into being in the first place. »[*E]ndogene* images however react also to *exogene* images which tend to take the ruling part in this cooperation. Images neither exist only on the wall (or in the TV) nor only in our heads. They cannot be extricated from a continuous exercise of interaction which has left so many traces in the history of artefacts.«[27]

The *medium* again is understood as a »vector, agent, *dispositif*, [...] or support, host and tool of images.«[28] Images, in this understanding, are themselves not media, but use media in order to become visible in the first place. They migrate between different media and are thus not bound to any specific carrier, although the media they use in turn form the visual appearance of the images. The *body* itself is understood as a medium of its own that is able to re-present images and separate endogenous from exogenous images and has the capability to construct new artificial images that might be regarded by other living bodies. A body might serve as well as a medium for exogenous images, such as make-up, masks, clothing, tattoos and gestures.

Belting's model is highly dynamic and opposes a rigid dualism between internal and external representations. Any changes in either images, bodies or media effect the other interrelated concepts; thus his model is in itself process-related and can be used to study individuals and how we make sense of the world around us. Belting emphasizes that this is not a semiological analysis, since images, unlike the written word, do not have a specific code that links them with their model. Susanne Langer has made a similar distinction between presentational and discursive forms, arguing that pictorial representations are symbolic expressions, just as language is, but of a different kind than language.[29] And Liza Bakewell has termed these symbolic expressions image acts. (Humanmade) »[i]mages, rather than re-present reality and therefore be largely descriptive, are more accurately categorized as actions.«[30]

Not only do we look at pictures and interpret them in various ways, ordering them in our webs of meaning according to hegemonic, oppositional or negotiated readings[31], pictures themselves order us and our situational behavior.[32] Daniel Miller points out that the micro-routines of daily life socialize us so that we order things in specific ways and are again ordered by the things themselves which we use for our micro-routines.[33] Like Miller, a wide range of practice theorists stress that human activity is centrally organized around embodied, materially mediated arrays of specific practices.[34] This calls for a re-focus on doing, on the active ingredients of social life.[35] Thus bodies and discursive activities are constituted within practices; they do not reside mainly in the head of actors as ideas or outside of them in material constellations. For individuals to be able to live practices out, the techniques in order to do so have to be learned, as must the shared conventions structuring these practices.

Mass-Mediated Pictures: Contemporary Changes and Lives of Their Own

Mass-media, consisting mainly of newspapers, radio, cinema, television and the Internet, has made it possible to communicate with a broad range of people without the people having to gather at a specific place to venerate materially mediated representations, known from many religious and political cults. It has also made large-scale asynchronous communication possible, although the broadcasting of live events was and continues to be an important function of radio and television. With the advent of new communicational forms supported by recent developments in information and communication technologies, constructing and publishing content have become practices available to people with access to the technical devices needed and the competence and desire to do so. Especially people identifying with specific subcultures and politically active groups have been important pioneers of this trend, using radio, video, the copy and the fax machine in order to distribute their materialized interpretations either within small social networks or as broadly as possible.[36]

Mass-mediated images are an important source for the imagination, which according to Appadurai is always a social practice. Images and imaginations are not bound to geographical areas such as the ›West‹ or ›Africa‹; rather, they are transmitted translocally. Following Mersmann, image practices are not born and produced in a no-man's land, and the images needed for these practices »are not moving around without purpose – as it is often stressed in the context of the globalization debate. Images are moving forces, image transmissions also include the transference of power.«[37] Thus the social lives of images are always connected to human beings working behind, with and for these images. Or, as Régis Debray puts it, the external memory of a picture has to be activated by people who carry the knowledge, an internal memory, used to decipher the external one.[38] The techniques needed to participate in practices such as reading a newspaper, watching television or going to the movies have had to be learned and maintained by reproducing them.

Abu-Lughod notes in her study on the effects of television on Upper Egyptian peasants that taking mass-mediated pictures seriously – in her case television – »forces us to think about ›culture‹ not so much as a system of meaning or even a way of life but as something whose elements are produced, censored, paid for, and broadcast across a nation, even across national boundaries.«[39] Hence, the power implicit in the nature of mass-mediated cultural artifacts in the service of a wide range of interests has to be taken seriously. The special challenge in trying to analyze some of these cultural forms is that broadcasted material transmitted by newspapers, radio, movies, television or the Internet does not meet simple or obvious communities and are always only a part of people's complex lives.[40] Already 15 years ago, Daniel Miller wrote: »In the contemporary world, the ethnographer who travels to highland New Guinea or goes to study shamans in Brazil is likely to have the (...) experience of finding people who will ask questions about the latest shift in popular music styles or the characters of a soap opera on national television.«[41]

Partially, the similarities in cultural practices in different regions can be attributed to the rather asymmetrical patterns of interaction that traditional mass-media supports. Since mass-mediated content is more often received than created, the differences in reception are not necessarily that great, although people certainly relate the content to personal and shared associations. Reading the newspaper is, like watching television, clearly a cultural practice that is similar around the world. It is for most users a form of quasi-mediated interaction, meaning that they do not partake in creating the actual content of what they read every day. Rather they need to learn specific techniques of the body in order to be able to turn the pages or decide in which direction to read.

Although practices are on the one hand repetitive ways of dealing with the world, reproductions of former ways of doing that help us in adapting to our environment without having to constantly think about how to put one foot before the other when walking or how to use a fork while eating, they are as well inclined to change; doing something differently is always an option.[42]

Sounding the Idols: *New York Times 09/02–09/03*

Mitchell has suggested that a way to react to the plethora of images that surround us in our daily lives, from advertisements to surveillance cameras and screens showing us being watched, which suggest specific ways of embodied action, and might discipline our docile bodies, would be to develop »a certain tactical hesitation in the impulse to critical iconoclasm, a curatorial and hermeneutic reflex, a sounding rather than a smashing of the offending image.«[43]

Pia Lindman shows in her visual analysis of the coverage of embodied suffering in a newspaper how not only media but images specifically seem to create us. Lindman transforms the cultural practice of reading the newspaper into a study of how mass-mediated pictures inscribe themselves in our bodies, to perhaps later find an intermediated embodiment when suffering. Lindman's example is interesting because she shows that difference, hybridity and complexity is not only to be found in far away places, but also at home – in the very center of the so called West. Lindman was in New York on September 11th, 2001, when two airplanes crashed deliberately into the two towers of the World Trade Center. She experienced the incident as horrendous and it awoke personal feelings of fear and loss. Similarly, Lindman was touched by the spontaneous personal and collective mourning that seemed to be omnipresent in the urban landscape of New York. This helped her in handling the feelings that the powerful incident had awoken. Nevertheless, she was indignant to see the mass media seize the representations of grief and amplify them by distributing them to a wide variety of breakfast tables, cafés, airport lounges and newspaper stands around the world for the purpose of justifying a war. Lindman asked herself: »[w]ho has the right to define how Americans, Palestinians, Israelis, or any other individuals affected by terrorism should grieve and who has the right to make those gestures of grievance public and official?«[44]

Answering the question seemed futile, but she started a visual analysis, deconstructing the ways in which loss, suffering and grievance are made public using pictures in newspapers. She wanted to explore how mass-mediated pictures suggest how individuals might give form to their emotions, a correct way of embodiment. In her view, gestures express human relationships based on affect. Following Goffman, Lindman explains: »affect is the reciprocal relationship between a person and his social environment and is based on social conventions.«[45]

Lindman started to collect pictures from the New York Times between 2002 and 2003, including embodied gestures associated with grief, suffering and death taken from a wide range of geopolitical locales. She traced the gestures with a pencil on vellum paper and used these drawings as her instructions when re-enacting the gestures in front of a video camera. She concentrated in her physical gestures only on the bodily positions depicted in the drawings, not investing in emotions or in acting the gestures out in any way. Lindman took video stills, which she again printed out and traced with a pencil on vellum paper (Fig. 1, 2). The videos and the second drawings were then exhibited, and she has performed the embodied acts at a wide range of public monuments, without reference to their original context, thereby connoting our everyday in-

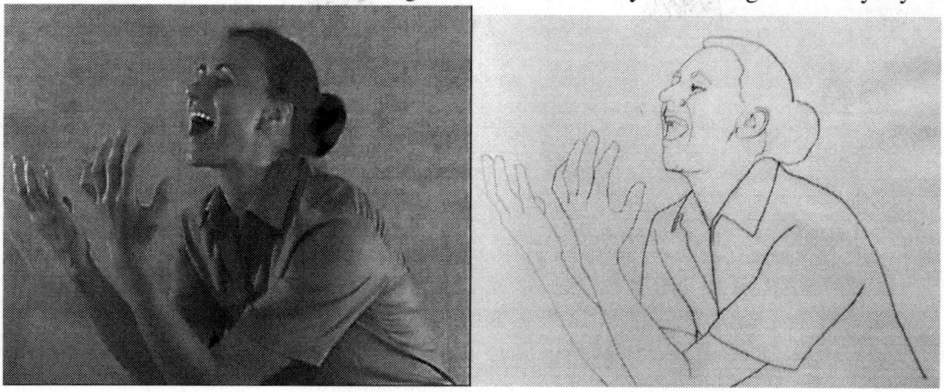

Fig. 1, 2: Pia Lindman, New York Times 09/02–09/03, 2002–2003. A video still of re-enacting gestures depicted in newspaper photographs in front of a video camera and a pencil drawing on vellum paper made from the video still

teraction with specific images. In her delicate research on the coverage of embodied suffering, of emotions finding their forms in affects, she aims »to illuminate some of the relationships between a photograph, its mediation and the idea of original content, in this instance emotional human reactions to terrorism.«[46] Her search for specific gestures brings her close to the work of Aby Warburg, which he did, in his own words, as a cultural seismograph. Obviously the gestures she found were not depicted for the first time when they were printed on the pages of the New York Times; they have a long cultural history in the history of imaging.

Instead of just being a response to specific ways of transmitting and fostering ideological practices and embodiments of discourses, Lindman's drawings had their own agency. Lindman explains:

> »[w]hat I had not foreseen, however, was how the simple pencil line drawings of myself became almost like empty containers, depositums, creating room for emotional investment by the viewer, something I perceive all but lost by the browsing of one's daily newspaper over breakfast, or better yet, the flow of multiple images and crawling texts on today's hyper-mediated television or computer screen.«[47]

Lindman altered the translocal cultural practice of reading the newspaper. Seeing pictures of very private mourning practices disseminated publicly, she responded to them with her visual analysis, which did not reduce visual materials to texts but took them seriously as a presentational form – using images as her tools of symbolic expression. She did not intend to substitute reading the newspaper with a new practice, but widened the spectrum of action associated with it.

In Lindman's case none of the original photographers of the first pictures could have imagined the trajectories that their pictures, or parts of them, would take. Chappatte's cartoon addresses this question in an eloquent way (Fig. 3). The pictured draughtsman is surprised when the images he just finished drawing come to life. As their producer, the draughtsman seems unable to control them. They start to move by themselves, their movements have unforeseen effects. Original pictures might become themselves images, which are reproduced in different contexts, on different materials, become active parts in social constellations and might even be embodied on living subjects. In each instance the picture is used as a part of argumentational strategies, although many might suggest that pictures carry a surplus value beyond this simple trait.

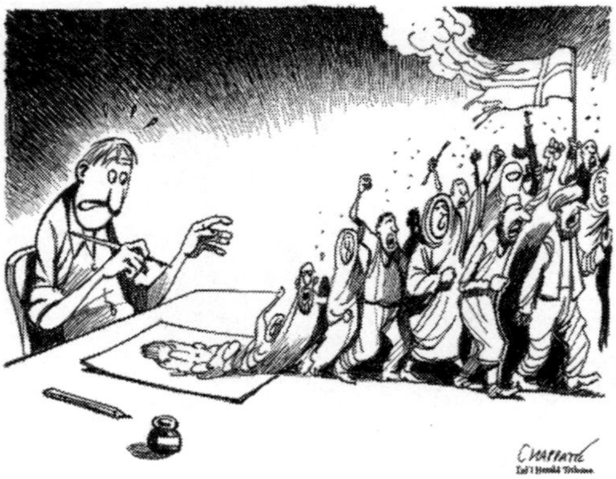

Fig. 3: © Chappatte, Cartoon War, 2006, www.globecartoon.com. Chappatte drew this cartoon as a response to the upheavals that took place after caricatures of the prophet Mohammed were published in the right-wing Danish newspaper Jyllandsposten.

Mitchell argues that pictures are actually alive, not so much because they are so objectively but because human beings act as if they were.[48] Lindman, in capturing the gestures depicted in newspaper photographs of violent events, seems only to bring to the fore what all of us are confronted with. The power of images is that they seem to ›hail‹ a reaction, they call for specific practices. Mitchell defines their power via three categories used to describe religious paraphernalia, the idol, the totem and the fetish. He points out that the idea of the enlightened subject is nothing more than a projection of an ideal. In favoring the concept of the totem as an instrument for analysis, Mitchell asks: »[d]o we create images or do they create us? [...] Totems are made things, artificial images. But they take on an independent life. They seem to create themselves, and to create the social formations that they signify.«[49] Thus, images do suggest specific practices at the cost of others. Lindman highlights this with her visual analysis and suggests new kinds of actions related to this practice. The amount of work behind these practices and the ones she criticizes is immense. Doing differently is never easy and it might well remain a singular act.

Lindman's way of doing differently, her transformation of a socially deeply rooted bourgeoisie practice into a visual refection on the effects of visually mediated affects, is in itself extraordinary. It does not inform us of the actual ways in which ordinary people read and use newspaper photographs nor does it show necessarily what effects these photographs have on us. It is, rather, a highly sophisticated analysis and subsequent image act of a person who has had the possibility to reflect on the ways in which mass-mediated images ›hail‹ us: how they suggest specific behavioral modes and invite us to participate in specific ways of being. Lindman shows with her work that cultural appropriation has to be seen as a creative process that does not merely reproduce copies of previous practices; it always includes the possibility to implement traditional ways of doing things differently. Here her work echoes Bruce Kapferer, who notes that people are not cultural dopes following blindly a cultural meta-structure imposed on their lives.

Thus the caricature previously shown oversimplifies at first sight a bundle of topics related to what it depicts. But having in mind the format for publication being a caricature, it actually seems to question the notion of pictures gaining their own independent lives. Rather it seems to address the fact that after the small, rather right-wing Danish newspaper Jyllands Posten asked different people to draw caricatures depicting the prophet Mohammad and published them, nobody seemed to notice. The people who later expressed that image act to have been an insult against their religious feelings, are not the ones who read the newspaper. ›Concerned journalists‹ had to take the pictures and visit Danish mosques to find imams who evidently were insulted of this kind of behaviour. From here the pictures were carried on with a delegation to Arabic countries to trigger support for a protest against them. It took five months for what Western media dubbed ›instant reactions to the insult‹. This means that images emerge in specific environments from which they unfold their effects, societal functions and possible meanings, but only in cooperation with people.[50]

Conclusions

I have tried to argue that the still common understanding of culture as a complex whole of the way of life of people living close to one another does not correspond to contemporary empirical observations found in anthropological literature on culture and globalization. It does not take modern heterogeneous ways of living into account. Neither does it take the processual or dynamic dimensions of culture into account. I have proposed instead to apply to practice theorists, who maintain that culture is instead to be thought of as coming to the fore in specific practices that have a material, performative and discursive dimension. These are obviously not freely selectable, but clustered in specific circumstances regulating social communication and access to societal decision-making. Nevertheless, this view makes it more difficult to talk about geographically bound practices, although certainly not all practices compete everywhere equally for attention and acceptance.

Changes in mass-media have made image practices more complex. Access to similar cultural materials is possible from remote regions, via newspapers, radio, cinema, television and the Internet. Although the meanings that people attach to specific media content might differ fundamentally, similarities in the material base and embodied practices are noteworthy. These are only visible, if we do not focus mainly on representations but on the ways in which experience is mediated situationally. Pia Lindman shows with her work that cultural practices do not dictate responses to them but might be used as stepping stones for criticism. Importantly, she practices a way of visual analysis that does not reduce images to texts but uses images as argumentational tools. Similarly she shows how transmitted cultural practices always meet existing practices and are open to adjustments and radical changes – not only in far away places but also in the so called West.

This does not imply that cultural differences do not exist – on the contrary, cultural differences then become visible ›at home‹ as well. Pondering on one's assumptions about with whom one actually shares common techniques and practices might give way for an opening that facilitates new common practices across geographical locales. The focus on practices makes it clear that they could just as well be organized differently – with different associations, materials and embodied interactions. Culture is in this understanding not to be equated with identity, society or community but rather as a set of resources that have to be worked for by each individual in order to be able to use them. This individual work is necessarily partial and incomplete and thus accounts already in itself for the distinct worlds that we live in. It is a never-ending process of adjusting one's knowledge to one's social and object-filled worlds.

Acknowledgments

Foremost I would like to thank Jutta Held for her enthusiasm in critical scientific work, which she has been able to share to her younger colleagues. Remembrance in her will certainly prevail. I would also like to thank Norbert Schneider who has done significant work in completing the current issue of *Kunst und Politik* which Jutta Held once started. This text has been improved by the thoughtful comments of Peter J. Bräunlein, Sakari Tamminen, Jaana Näsänen and Vilma Lehtinen. Pia Lindman and Chappatte/ Globecartoon have kindly granted me the right to reproduce their pictures.

---

1 Matthew Arnold: *Culture and Anarchy*. http://www.gutenberg.org/etext/4212 2003 (accessed 3.1.2008).

2 Examples for this approach can be found in Ian Heywood: *Interpreting Visual Culture: Explorations in the Hermeneutics of the Visual*. London/New York 1999; Richard Howells: *Visual Culture: An Introduction*. Oxford 2003; Matthew Rampley: »Visual Culture and the Meanings of Culture« In: Matthew Rampley (Hg.): *Exploring Visual Culture: Definitions, Concepts, Contexts*. Edinburgh 2005, p. 5–17. E.g. Rampley speaks of ›contemporary Western society‹, although stating that cultures are dynamic. Viktoria Schmidt-Linsenhoff has discussed this issue regarding the postcolonial turn and critical art history in Viktoria Schmidt-Linsenhoff: »Kunst und kulturelle Differenz oder: Warum hat die kritische Kunstgeschichte in Deutschland den postcolonial turn ausgelassen?« In: *Kunst und Politik. Jahrbuch der Guernica-Gesellschaft*, Vol. 4, 2002, p. 7–16.

3 Irit Rogoff makes here a distinction between a culture of singularity and a culture of specificity. Irit Rogoff: »Translating the Image – Cross Cultural Contemporary Art. A Research Project at Goldsmiths College/London« In: *Kunst und Politik. Jahrbuch der Guernica-Gesellschaft*, Vol. 4, 2002, p. 113–116.

4 Cf. Theodore R. Schatzki: »Introduction: practice theory« In: Theodore R. Schatzki, Karin Knorr-Cetina, Eike von Savigny (Hg.): *The Practice Turn in Contemporary Theory*. London/New York 2001, p. 1–14.

5 Cf. Julia Reuter: »Postkoloniales Doing Culture. Oder: Kultur als translokale Praxis« In: Karl H. Hörning, Julia Reuter (Hg.): *Doing Culture. Neue Positionen zum Verhältnis von Kultur und sozialer Praxis*. Bielefeld 2004, p. 239–255. She calls these translocal practices ›translokale soziale Praktiken‹.

6 Cf. Arjun Appadurai: »Grassroots Globalization and the Research Imagination« In: *Public Culture. Society for Transnational Cultural Studies*, Vol. 12, 2000, No. 1, p. 1–19.

7 Marc Augé: *Orte und Nicht-Orte. Vorüberlegungen zu einer Ethnologie der Einsamkeit*. Frankfurt/M. 1994.

8 Cf. John B. Thompson: *The Media and Modernity. A Social Theory of the Media*. Cambridge/Stanford 1995; Debra Grodin, Thomas Lindlof: *Constructing the Self in a Mediated World*. Thousand Oaks 1996.

9 Cf. Daniel Dayan, Elihu Katz: *Media Events. The Live Broadcasting of History*. Cambridge/London 1992; Eric W. Rothenbuhler: *Ritual Communication: From Everyday Con-*

versation to Mediated Ceremony. Thousand Oaks 1998; Nick Couldry: *Media Rituals. A Critical Approach.* London/New York 2003.

10 Edward W. Said: *Orientalism. Western Conceptions of the Orient. With a new Afterword.* London 1995; Lila Abu-Lughod: »Writing against culture« In: Richard G. Fox (Hg.): *Recapturing anthropology: Working in the present.* Santa Fe 1991, p. 137–162; Lila Abu-Lughod: »The Interpretation of Culture(s) after Television« In: *Representations*, Vol. 59, 1997, Special Issue: The Fate of ›Culture‹: Geertz and Beyond, p. 109–134; Arjun Appadurai: *Modernity at Large. Cultural Dimensions of Globalization.* Minneapolis 1996; James Clifford: »On Collecting Art and Culture« In: James Clifford (Hg.): *The Predicament of Culture. Twentieth-Century Ethnography, Literature, and Art.* Cambridge 1988, p. 215–251; Jack Goody: »Culture and its Boundaries: A European View« In: Robert Borofsky (Hg.): *Assessing Cultural Anthropology.* New York 1994, p. 250–260; just to name a few.

11 Gregory Bateson: »A Theory of Play and Fantasy« In: Gregory Bateson: *Steps to an ecology of mind. With a new foreword by Mary Catherine Bateson.* London/Chicago 2000 (1972), p. 177–193.

12 E.g. Robert Borofsky: »Rethinking the Cultural« In: Robert Borofsky (Hg.): *Assessing Cultural Anthropology.* New York 1994, p. 243–249; Alan Barnard, Jonathan Spencer: »Culture« In: Alan Barnard, Jonathan Spencer (Hg.): *Encyclopedia of Social and Cultural Anthropology.* London 1996, p. 136–143; Appadurai 1996 (as note 10).

13 Abu-Lughod in Christoph Brumann, Lila Abu-Lughod, E. L. Cerroni-Long, Roy D'Andrade, Andre Gingrich, Ulf Hannerz and Andreas Wimmer: »Writing for Culture. Why a Succesful Concept Should Not Be Discarded [and Comments and Reply]« In: *Current Anthropology*, Vol. 40, 1999, Supplement: Special Issue: Culture. A Second Chance?, p. 15.

14 Fredrik Barth: »A Personal View of Present Tasks and Priorities in Cultural and Social Anthropology « In: Robert Borofsky (Hg.): *Assessing Cultural Anthropology.* New York et. al 1994, p. 358. For a good overview of these debates, with further references, see Brumann et. al 1999 (as note 13) and for a more general overview on ›culture‹ and its history Michael M.J. Fischer: »Culture and Cultural Analysis as Experimental Systems« In: *Cultural Anthropology*, Vol. 22, 2007, No. 1, p. 1–65. Brumann himself ›writes for culture‹ similarly trying to criticize Herderian conceptions of culture. Using the noun seems to me to carry too many seeds for misunderstanding and thus I prefer to talk of cultural action consisting of situated practices that may consist of a broad array of shared practices that make interaction possible in the first place.

15 Francisco Osorio: »Proposal for Mass Media Anthropology« In: Eric W. Rothenbuhler, Mihai Coman (Hg.): *Media Anthropology.* Thousand Oaks/London/New Delhi 2005, p. 43–44; although one might argue that watching television bears many ritualistic elements including para-social interaction with superhuman beings. Similar to Osorio Richard Chalfen has noticed peculiar similarities in the ways in which people have used film cameras in order to take private snapshot photographs. Not only are the occasions for taking snapshot photographs similar in different families in the U.S., living far away from each other, but also who is pictured and how they are pictured. Chalfen has to posit the research question at the end of his study: »If we find that similarities outnumber trivial differences for all groups studied, we should be prepared to take the construct of Kodak culture even further. Speculation and consideration must be given to the fact that inexpensive camera equipment, produced for nonprofessional use in contexts of home-mode communication, carries with it some form of ›operating instructions‹ – instructions that somehow provide a model for appropriate behavior

on a cross-cultural basis.« Richard Chalfen: *Snapshot Versions of Life*. Bowling Green, Ohio 1987, p. 163–164.

16 Marita Sturken, Lisa Cartwright: *Practices of Looking. An Introduction to Visual Culture*. Oxford/New York 2001.

17 The discursive, performative and material are dimensions borrowed from Peter Braun. He uses them to analyze medial practices (mediale Praxis) and medial apparatuses (derived from Baudry). Peter Braun: *Mediale Mimesis. Licht- und Schattenspiele bei Adelbert von Chamisso und Justinus Kerner*. München 2007, p. 81.

18 Brumann et. al 1999 (as note 13), p. S23.

19 Pierre Bourdieu: *Outline of a Theory of Practice*. Cambridge 1977, p. 79.

20 Appadurai writes »that there is a growing disjuncture between the globalization of knowledge and the knowledge of globalization. (…) [G]lobalization as an uneven economic process creates a fragmented and uneven distribution of just those resources for learning, teaching, and cultural criticism that are most vital for the formation of democratic research communities that could produce a global view of globalization. That is, globalization resists the possibility of just those forms of collaboration that might make it easier to understand or criticise.« Appadurai 2000 (as note 6), p. 4.

21 Barth 1994 (as note 14), p. 357–358.

22 Cf. Ernst von Glasersfeld: *Radikaler Konstruktivismus. Ideen, Ergebnisse, Probleme*. Frankfurt/M. 1997.

23 Schatzki 2001 (as note 4), p. 7.

24 Karin Knorr-Cetina: »Sociality with Objects: Social Relations in Postsocial Knowledge Societies« In: *Theory, Culture & Society*, Vol. 14, 1997, No. 4, p. 9. She discusses this in relation to the intertwinement of individualization and objectualization.

25 Birgit Mersmann, Martin Schulz (Hg.): *Kulturen des Bildes*. München 2006, p. 13.

26 Hans Belting: *Bild-Anthropologie. Entwürfe für eine Bildwissenschaft*. München 2001; Hans Belting: »Image, Medium, Body: A New Approach to Iconology« In: *Critical Inquiry*, Vol. 31, 2005, No. 2, p. 302-319.

27 Ibid., p. 9.

28 Ibid., p. 10.

29 Susanne Langer: *Philosophy in a New Key. A Study in the Symbolism of Reason, Rite, and Art*. Cambridge 1979, p. 79–102. Peter Bräunlein suggests to focus on Langer and Belting when studying image practices and image acts, Peter J. Bräunlein: »Bildakte. Religionswissenschaft im Dialog mit einer neuen Bildwissenschaft« In: Brigitte Luchesi, Kocku von Stuckrad (Hg.): *Religion im kulturellen Diskurs. Festschrift für Hans G. Kippenberg zu seinem 65. Geburtstag*. Berlin 2004, p. 195–231.

30 Liza Bakewell: »Image Acts« In: *American Anthropologist*, Vol. 100, 1998, No. 1, p. 22.

31 Stuart Hall: »Encoding, Decoding« In: Simon During (ed.): *The Cultural Studies Reader*. London/New York 1999, p. 501–517.

32 Mersmann, Schulz 2006 (as note 25).

33 Daniel Miller: »Artefacts and the Meaning of Things« In: Tim Ingold (ed.): *Companion encyclopedia of anthropology*. London/New York 1994, p. 396–419. The situative use of artifacts for cultural practices has been explored especially by Edward Hutchins: »Material anchors for conceptual blends« In: *Journal of Pragmatics*, Vol. 37, 2005, p. 1555–1577. He shows how cognitive duties are offloaded to material objects, and these again serve as material anchors making more complex thinking easier.

34 Theodore R. Schatzki, Karin Knorr-Cetina, Eike von Savigny (Hg.): *The practice turn in contemporary theory.* New York 2001. See for further thoughts as well Andreas Reckwitz: »Grundelemente einer Theorie sozialer Praktiken« In: *Zeitschrift für Soziologie*, Vol. Aug. 2003, No. 4, p. 282–301; Karl H. Hörning, Julia Reuter (ed.): *Doing Culture. Neue Positionen zum Verhältnis von Kultur und sozialer Praxis.* Bielefeld 2004.

35 There are manifold approaches to practices in social sciences, which explains also the diverse positions taken by the authors in Schatzki et. al 2001 (as note 34) and Hörning and Reuter 2004 (as note 34). What they do have in common is a focus on embodied practices and material configurations as integral structuring mechanisms of human life.

36 See e.g. Asko Lehmuskallio: »Constructing Perceptual Shifts: Notes on Culture Jamming as a Political Tool« In: Johanna Sumiala-Seppänen, Matteo Stocchetti (Hg.): *Images and Communities. The Visual Construction of the Social.* Helsinki 2007, p. 199–228, on culture jamming and Faye Ginsburg: »Culture/Media: A (Mild) Polemic« In: *Anthropology Today*, Vol. 10, 1994, No. 2, p. 5–15, on indigenous media production.

37 Birgit Mersmann: »Bildkulturwissenschaft als Kulturbildwissenschaft? Von der Notwendigkeit eines inter- und transkulturellen Iconic Turn« In: *Zeitschrift für Ästhetik und Allgemeine Kunstwissenschaft*, Vol. 49, 2004, No. 1, p. 91–109.

38 Régis Debray: *Einführung in die Mediologie.* Bern/Stuttgart/Wien 2003.

39 Abu-Lughod 1997 (as note 10), p. 121.

40 Ibid., p. 112.

41 Miller 1994 (as note 33), p. 405.

42 Karl H. Hörning, Julia Reuter: »Doing Culture: Kultur als Praxis« In: Karl H. Hörning, Julia Reuter (ed.): *Doing Culture. Neue Positionen zum Verhältnis von Kultur und sozialer Praxis.* Bielefeld 2004, p. 9–18; Reckwitz 2003 (as note 34). Since practices are never reproduced identically, they themselves change as well, which explains the adaptability of practices to different situations while being perceived as remaining the same. Doing differently again may have many reasons: feeling uncomfortable, because other people act differently, reflecting on current behavior, because current practices do not lead to wished results when acting in specific interaction contexts, or if one wants to broaden or narrow one's room for maneuver.

43 W.J.T. Mitchell: *What Do Pictures Want? The Lives and Loves of Images.* Chicago/London 2005, p. 191.

44 Pia Lindman: »The New York Times, Monuments, Art and Affect: Re-enactments in greyscale« In: Graham Coulter-Smith, Maurice Owen (Hg.): *Art in the Age of Terrorism.* London 2005, p. 84. Her work has been discussed as well by Kriss Ravetto-Biagioli: »The Visual Grammar of Suffering. Pia Lindman and the Performance of Grief« In: *PAJ. A Journal of Performance and Art*, Vol. 28, 2006, No. 3 (PAJ 84), p. 77–92.

45 Ibid., p. 83.

46 Ibid., p. 87.

47 Lindman 2005 (as note 44), p. 88.

48 Mitchell 2005 (as note 43). Alfred Gell has shown how in specific interaction constellations different entities have different agency. Mitchell's point would reflect a constellation where Gell attributes agency to the index (that is to the materialized picture). Alfred Gell: *Art and Agency. An Anthropological Theory.* Oxford et. al 1998.

49 Ibid., p. 105.

50 Cf. for a similar argument regarding the publication and distribution of the notorious Abu Ghraib photographs André Gunthert: »Digital Imaging goes to war. The Abu Ghraib photographs« In: *Photographies*, Vol. 1, 2008, No. March, p. 103–112.

Hille Koskela

The Performative Geography of Webcams

Visual meets virtual

In the early utopian predictions, the Internet was perceived as *an identity modification tool*. It was believed that the virtual realm would enable people to hide or change identities and claim to be who ever they had dreamt of being. It was somewhat naively assumed that essential parts of the physical life could be replaced. In the virtual world, »misrepresentations of self« were understood to be opportunities rather than morally precarious actions.[1] Furthermore, the Internet was believed to create an arena for *new interactive democracy*.[2] There was a serious discussion about digital cities and virtual agoras which were predicted to work as new kind of public spheres and ultimately democratic interactive service portals.[3] As Bernard describes the early optimistic hopes, the Internet would create »a seamless place where we can all coexist and be treated equally«.[4]

Both the new identities and the new public spheres were conceptualised as being *detached from the visual*. Individuals would be liberated from their visual appearances, and cities would be functional without material or visual content. Currently, however, the Internet is one of the most important channels through which visual images are presented and circulated. There are more and more sites were *webcams* provide live visual representations of material »real people« and »real places«. This can be argued to have two opposite consequences. On one hand, people gain agency in the production and circulation of images. On the other hand, image production supports voluntary mutual control and moralism.

There is a huge range of webcams presenting various public, semi-public and private spaces. Since the »humble coffee pot«[5] – the first webcam ever, installed in the Cambridge University campus – the phenomenon has literally exploded. One can click into a collection of urban and rural landscapes from all over the world, construction sites, zoos and wildlife reserves, beaches and ski resorts, malls, airports, taxi cars driving around, restaurants and night clubs, hair dressers saloons, house pets, family living rooms or bedrooms etc.[6] To describe the variety of these cameras, and to make sense of different motivations behind them, I have roughly grouped them into five categories. The categories, of course, are partly overlapping but, nevertheless, this rough taxonomy helps to grasp the phenomenon. First, there are webcams which show *points of interest* – kind of »innocent« representations of places and phenomena such as famous landmarks, scenic landscapes or on-land and under-water nature. Second, there are *functional* webcams with which one can check weather conditions, traffic flows, queues in airports, crowds in shopping malls etc. Third, many webcams are *interactive*. It is possible to observe places of interest, pan and zoom with the camera and search for acquainted people or scan archives of the past moments on a particular site. Fourth, there are *subcultural* webcams some of which are clearly voyeuristic while others sustain semi-private social relations and subcultures ranging from gay communities to religious parishes. And fifth, there are *commercial* webcams which charge the viewers. Most of these are in one way or the other related to dating or sexual relations, some being directly pornographic.

The categories play with the public-private distinction. Functional webcams show mostly public spaces, but points of interest combine public spaces with private qualities, such as people walking on the street. Interactive webcams can engage both the viewers behind the camera and the audience in front of it. The latter function may mean posing to the cameras or sending messages with them, the former enables the public to pan and zoom the cameras with their own computers. Subcultural and commercial webcams often show private spaces but some of them relate to semi-public or public spaces of clubbing or sex related entertainment. Webcam based art projects – as I shall discuss in this paper – provide creative readings of the typologies, hence, showing unpredictable connections between the viewer and what is wathced as well as giving new cultural meanings to elsewhere established functions.

The illusory power of representation

A topic which is of utmost importance here, is what Frohne calls »the fetishization of real time and live-effects«.[7] One of the key explanations for the popularity of many current forms of visual representation, ranging from interactive crime programs to reality TV in general, and from thereon to webcams, is »the promise of reality«.[8] Reality, however, is a tricky concept and »the illusory power of representation«[9] brings up the complicated question of »truth«. Even so, creating an *impression of truth* is often essential. Pinck writes about »the skycam« – a news helicopter reporting crime to television.[10] He identifies stylistic measures which are used in order to create an impression of reality: instability of the image, action and movement of both the targets and the optical source itself, as well as proximity.

There is a historical continuum of what has been perceived as a »proof for truth«. In late 19th century, photography was somewhat uncritically perceived as proof. Photography »contributed to a modern regime of truth: the camera would reveal the world in a new way«.[11] Since late 20th century it has been clear that photographs can be manipulated, characters erased, and that pictures are not evidently true. Pinck argues that TV subsequently took the place of photography and »we are only likely to believe what we see on TV«[12]. Presently, however, the truth value of television has been faltered. Reality TV shows have not contributed to giving the TV impression of being more real – on the contrary.[13] When the fiction has increasingly become »indistinguishable from reality«[14], ever more proof is needed that anything appears true.

In the slippery field of selective representations, surveillance camera material has remained quite solid, and surveillance videos have somehow taken over the place of television.[15] Surveillance footage audience is »expected to relate to the footage as self-evident description of the events recorded«[16]. The old »flickering piece of black-and-white footage«[17] and »casual framing, haphazard composition, uncontrolled lighting, slice-of-life facticity«[18] have sustained their roles as icons of surveillance imaginary. These types of images are easily perceived as being »without any possibility of error«[19]. Even so, as Balshaw and Kennedy point out, »the operations of the eye are not only biological and formal, but also cultural and psychological«[20]. Eventually, surveillance »does not find knowledge, but creates it«[21]. Not a single everyday text can be interpreted in a universally coherent way, but different audiences provide different readings of it. Bogard argues that information which is gathered is increasingly integrated into *simulated* models of reality, and hence »sight and foresight, actual and virtual begin to merge«[22].

Webcams are, indeed, an everyday example of actuality and virtuality merging together. Two properties make them interesting for the public: their *realtimeness* and their *realplaceness*. Without these two qualities their images would be nothing but pictures among others. The very idea of webcams – or at least the idea they endeavour to keep up – is that the viewer is able to see what happens »right there at that particular moment«. The realtimeness of webcams supports the idea originality, making places memorable and imageable. Local time yields to real time. Local presence and »telepresence«[23] melt into each other, forming a new experience of place.[24] Local place yields to (any) real place.

However, quite often the images are conceptually fuzzy and it is hard to interpret; to distinguish »reality« from staging. In the end, we only see what a webcam agrees to show us. It organises and structures things in its own specific way, a way that claims to be essentially realistic.[25] Cities which present their most clichéd landscapes[26] and individuals who to turn their whole lives into a pose[27] blur the difference between existing and presenting. The *banality* of the images is ambivalent. On one hand, when watching »nothing happening« it is hard to believe that what one sees is »really real«. On the other hand, it is precisely the banality which renders the images of webcams reliable.[28]

Performative/Geography

Let me next examine the two key words in the title of this article: performativity and geography. The whole idea of webcams, simply thinking, is *performance*. They are performing places and performing people. New technologies enable the public to represent the everyday and provide them with the possibility of self-expression in global media. There are endless possibilities to download videotaped material and to streams of images onto the Internet.[29] The public is able to create »shows« without »outside editors, directors, or producers to decide who gets how much airtime«[30].

The visual representations of public urban space contribute to »transforming the landscape of cities into new *imagescapes*«[31]. Webcams, as well as films or photographs, »provide selective representations of the city and shape the metaphors, narratives and syntax which are widely used to describe the experience of urban living«[32]. Most often, the iconography of »citycams« reminiscent the 19th century dioramas and panoramas, in which »the real city« was never actually displayed but »the city's image became the spectacle itself«[33]. Citycams produce an extremely plain image of cities, presenting places that attract tourists, market squares, harbours, or downtown pedestrian areas. Hence, they eulogise clichéd, most apparent landscapes, producing »a particular *re-*

framing of urban reality«[34]. The choice »may look haphazard but most often is actually quite tendentious«[35].

Private webcams, on the other hand, seem to open up radically new subjectivities.[36] In contrast of being targets of the ever-increasing surveillance by the authorities, people play an active role in the production of images.[37] The deliberate exposure of the self,[38] in the era of intensified surveillance, can be perceived as radical. Nevertheless, webcams play their role in proving that people wish to have agency. When »the camera moves from a recording instrument to an integral aspect of the subjects' lives«[39], exposing oneself is connected to identity formation. As Zizek argues, »today, anxiety seems to arise from the prospect of NOT being exposed to the Other's gaze all the time, so that the subject needs the camera's gaze as a kind of ontological guarantee of his/her being«[40]. Or, in Frohne's words, contemporary fear is »that of being withdrawn completely from the gaze of the others«[41] and there is »compulsive desire to attain telepresence, to verify and validate one's own existence«[42]. Performativity is a crucial concept here. It makes a clear distinction to the Foucauldian understanding of surveillance according to which being seen relates with being disciplined. Performativity makes it possible to »separate surveillance from representational self-evidence«[43]. It brings additional, yet complicated, credit to *exposure*.

Geography, widely speaking, relates to webcams at least in three different ways. First, they form a mundane, every-day visual version of »time-space-compression«. The term can be described a processes which accelerates the experience of time, simultaneously reducing the significance of distance.[44] Most often it refers to technologies of communication that elide spatial and temporal distances. Webcams provide a possibility for *virtual travel*[45]. Travelling around the world, using webcams in different places in every continent, enables a quick wheel chair travel. At first sight, the landscapes may seem trivial and dull. Nevertheless, live real-time video streams give the viewer a strong feeling of »being there«. One can go around the globe with a swift speed. Webcams are »blurring of our perception of different levels of reality«[46].

Second, webcams relate closely to *urban politics*. Some of them promote the images of cities being an increasingly important place marketing tool. When competition intensifies and cities must market themselves »their ›imageability‹ becomes the new selling point«[47] At the same time, webcams contribute to the politics of purification. Times Square in New York is perhaps the most famous example of »purified space«. New York's zero-tolerance policy has been applied for exclusion of the marginal groups from public urban space. This exclusion has changed the nature of the square, it becoming a business led, theme park like »disneyfied« space.[48] Times Square has sixteen interactive real-time citycams, which show general views as well as more detailed pictures of people passing by.[49] The politics of purification and webcam presentation go hand in hand.[50] The cameras complement the development in urban space. Purification was an essential prerequisite of the installation of the cameras. A square with homeless people, prostitutes and drug users around is not a place glorious enough to be world-widely presented. Nevertheless, since the square is now widely presented, it is ever more important to keep it impressive and pure. In this sense, webcams justify surveillance and social control. The representation of this place on the Internet via information and communication technologies, contributes to the production of space on the urban street level realm.

Third, many webcams – in contrast to those over Times Square – participate in the critical discussion about the *dichotomy of public and private space*. They provide new readings of public space pointing out how, essentially, it should be a place where anyone has a right to come without being excluded. They criticise the emerging restrictions in public space, as well as the privatisation of it. Furthermore, many webcams undermine the binary opposition of public/private by turning the most private spaces into public. They are glaring examples of the complex mobilities which are going on between and across public and private spaces, being enabled by the proliferation of information and communication technologies. This topic deserves a closer examination, and I shall now discuss it with examples from the webcam art scene.

Eyes of Laura, and some others …

Presently, the use of webcams by artists is quite widespread. Internet based art is no longer exceptional avant-garde but, rather, a loose and dispersed genre of conceptual practices. Art projects are a fruitful way of discussing the issues surrounding webcam presentation because they focus on several substantial aspects of seeing and being seen, while simultaneously, purposefully blurring the difference between »real« and »fictional« images. Hence, they succeed in going behind the discussion about »truth«, nevertheless, bringing up important questions of the dangers, possibilities and complicated ethics of webcam exposure. Furthermore, many of them set visual images into a political context. I've chosen to present four projects here: *Empire 24/7* by Wolfgang Staehle, *Demonstrate* by Ken Goldberg and his colleagues, *Eyes of Laura* by Janet Cardiff and *Homecammer* by Cheryl Sourkes. In order to elaborate the critical discussion these projects foster, and to explain how they deal with the public/private dichotomy, I shall start the description by public space and proceed towards semi-public and private space.

Wolfgang Staehle is a German born video artist currently based in New York.[51] He has produced series of live online video streams. Lastly, his works were presented in the *Closed Circuit: Video and New Media at the Metropolitan* exhibition in the Metropolitan Museum of Art, New York, in 2007. First one of Staehle's on-line video projects was *Empire 24/7*, a continuous recording of the top one-third of the Empire State Building that was broadcast live over the Internet (Fig. 1). Staehle used a video camera pointed out of an office building window, capturing a continuous image of the Empire State Building. The expression 24/7 in the name of the installation refers to availability of access. The work was first shown at *net_condition* exhibition at ZKM, Karlsruhe in 1999.

Within the art scene, this work which consists of mundane real time images has been described as an hommage to Andy Warhol. It clearly leans conceptually on Warhol's eight-hour film *Empire* from 1964. Staehle himself states that he has been »interested in what happens when nothing happens« and aims to »perceive things in their authenticity«[52]. It can also be interpreted as transcending technology into an update of the landscape genre, and »playing with the sublime«[53]. From outside the art discussion, Staehle's work seems scenic and picturesque. It presents its target as beautiful object of the gaze – a piece of public space seen from bird's eye perspective, an iconic object, a famous building. Compared, for example, to the forever streaming, flashing and rushing pictures from the Times Square, Staehle's images are extravagantly static. The work

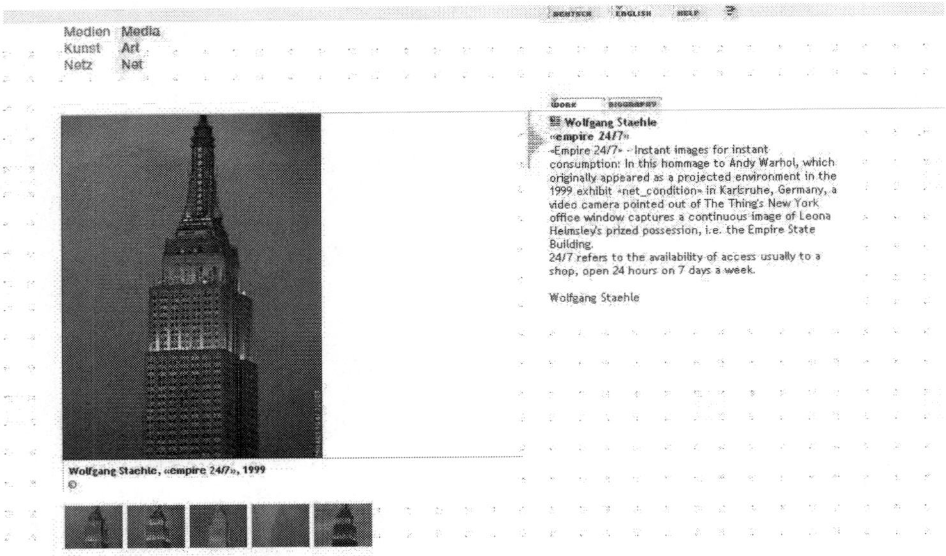

Fig. 1: Wolfgang Staehle, Empire 24/7, 1999, www.medienkunstnetz.de/works/empire24-7

leaves its viewer passive. Furthermore, *Empire 24/7* is intentionally apolitical. It does not make any statement, but provides exactly the kind of »innocent representation« I described in the beginning of the paper. It forms a critical re-reading of those cameras which show points of interest without any other function. The banality of the piece, however, does not seem to render it reliable. Rather, spectacle, simulation, virtual reality and urban reality can be seen as »collapsing into each other«[54]. Authenticity both disappears and appears in its virtualisation.

Ken Goldberg, born in Nigeria, is currently a professor of engineering at University of California Berkeley, specialised in the fields of robotics and automation.[55] Apart from being active in the academic world, Goldberg is also a well-known artist, producing installations that make use of various robotic technologies. His works aim to discuss corporeality within the increasingly digitised culture. One of the latest exhibitions where his installations were presented was »Fastforward: Robots« in Palazzo delle Arti, Napoli, Italy, in 2007. *Demonstrate* was a project published in 2004 by Goldberg and eleven of his colleagues, commissioned by the Whitney Museum, New York (Fig. 2). It consisted of a state-of-the-art robotic webcamera over UC Berkeley's Sproul Plaza, accessible on the Internet to anyone for six weeks. Participants could remote control the camera, zoom in and out, and view any activity in the Plaza, as well as send textual comments. The archive or the project offers, as the artists themselves claim, »a portrait of public space as viewed from the public in cyberspace«[56].

The project was purposefully timed to coincide with the 40th Anniversary of the »Free Speech Movement« at the very birthplace of the movement. The Free Speech Movement was a radical student movement that changed the political atmosphere at universities across the US, and provided a model for future student activism. Hence,

Demonstrate – unlike *Empire 24/7* – was inherently political. As an art work, it remained less established, less widely circulated and (even) more ephemeral than

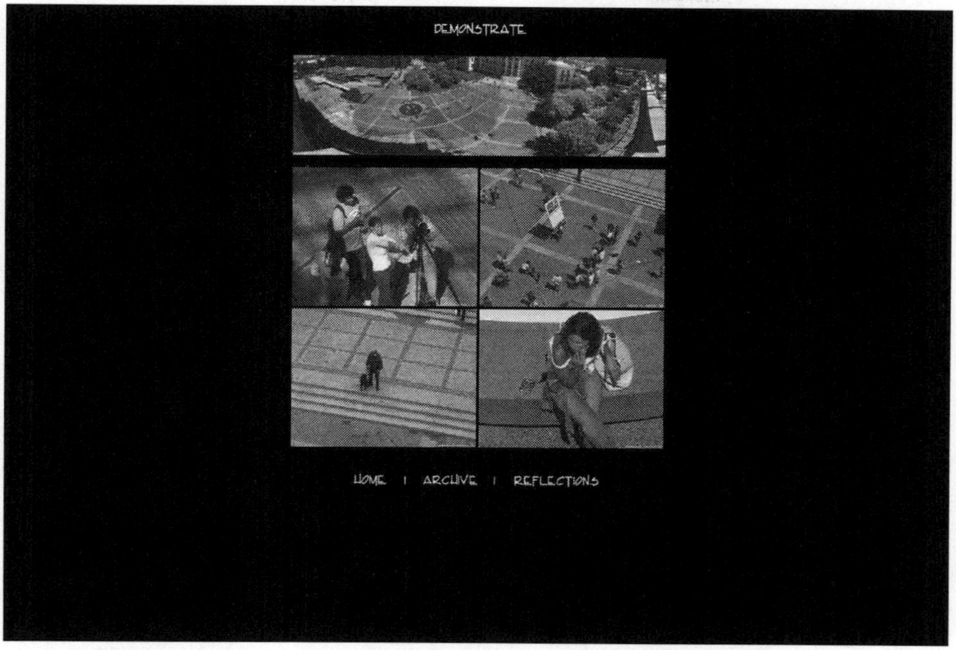

Fi. 2: Ken Goldberg, Demonstrate, 2004, demonstrate.berkeley.edu/signin.htm

Staehle's work, and its value clearly resides in its political statement. It directly participates in the discussion about the publicness of public space. It makes use of the functionality of webcams and brings their interactivity to the art scene. *Demonstrate* can be read as an anti-statement for the current trends – as was evident in Times Square – of using webcams for purification, commodification, zero-tolerance policies and exclusion of marginal groups. In visualising the concept of public space, giving »the right to observe« to those who conventionally remain solely »observed«, the work also contributed to surveillance critique. Furthermore, it brought the Internet to its very origins by providing – momentarily – an on-line, materially based arena for interactive democracy, communication and free expression. The project cleverly showed that »the bureaucratic-institutional tactics of surveillance«[57] or the »individual's total surrender to the media's regime of the gaze«[58] are not the only future options. The civic world strikes back in creative ways.

Janet Cardiff is a Canadian artist who has specialised in installations, audio art and films.[59] She is famous for her interactive »audio walks« – sonic virtual journeys, using recorded voices and sounds delivered via headset – which have taken place for example in London and New York. In 2001 Cardiff and her collaborator George Bures Miller won an award at the Venice Biennale with their interactive film *Paradise Institute*. As Cardiff's previous works, the online piece *Eyes of Laura* depends on the active participation of the viewer (Fig. 3.). It relies on the interactive role which the cameras enable.

The name of Cardiff's work (as Staehle's) echoes a past film, namely, Irvin Kershner's 1978 murder-mystery *Eyes of Laura Mars*. The site, with commission of the Vancouver Art Gallery, is a publicly open virtual blog for a fictional bored security guard »Laura«

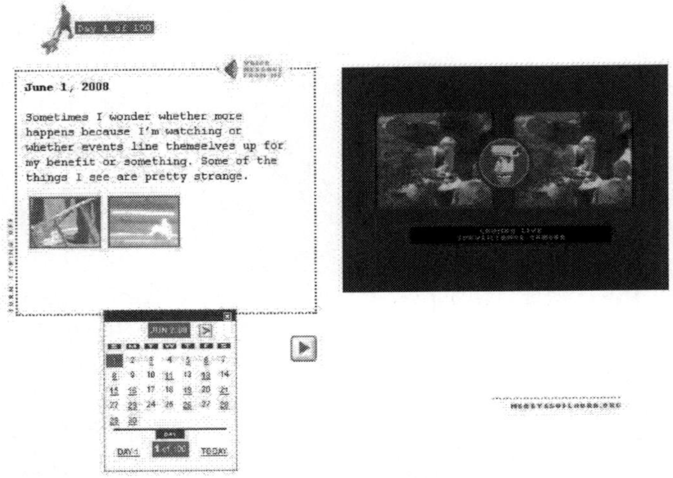

Fig. 3: Janet Cardiff, Eyes of Laura, www.eyesoflaura.org/index3.php

who works at art gallery monitoring surveillance footage. Laura posts on-line a diary, pictures and audio clips, videotapes showing segments of what she sees around her, and also lets the viewer to control the security cameras.

The idea of *Eyes of Laura* is a constructed reality, based on surveillance imagery. Seemingly, the blog is a narrative about watching through the character of Laura. Nevertheless, the video clips presented are not purely illustrative, but raise questions concerning images and interpretation. Pointing at the complex politics of interpretation, the blog succeeds in reminding the audience that images are conceptually fuzzy. As *Demonstrate*, the blog provides anyone with the possibility of acting as the controller – playing with surveillance. The difference is that on this website the audience views a fictional semi-public space, not a truly existing public space. This fictional observer's view is political, indeed, but it's also messy. It is the image-mediated epistemology that wakes the viewers up to ask in what ways their own ideas superimpose the stories they want create surrounding the images seen. Within the conventional surveillance context, »every camera functions within a field of power and prejudice structured by visual markers«[60]. The »semiotics of suspicion«[61] explain why the blog is so fascinating. Furthermore, the site points out how watching and being watched structure around reveries of voyeurism and exhibitionism.[62] Public scrutiny, indeed, is pleasurable activity – entertainment[63] – and the audience is easily ready to participate in this »banal voyeurism«. Last but not least, it must be pointed out that Laura's (fictional) character reminds the viewer of Allen's point I presented in the beginning: surveillance »creates« knowledge. Eventually, there is no truth to be grasped.[64]

Cheryl Sourkes is a Canadian artist who has specialised in photography, especially through new technologies.[65] Her work deals with the real world versus the virtual world, and discusses the ways we perceive and understand what we see around us. Sourkes creates artwork using »fleeting and transitory« images generated by webcams,

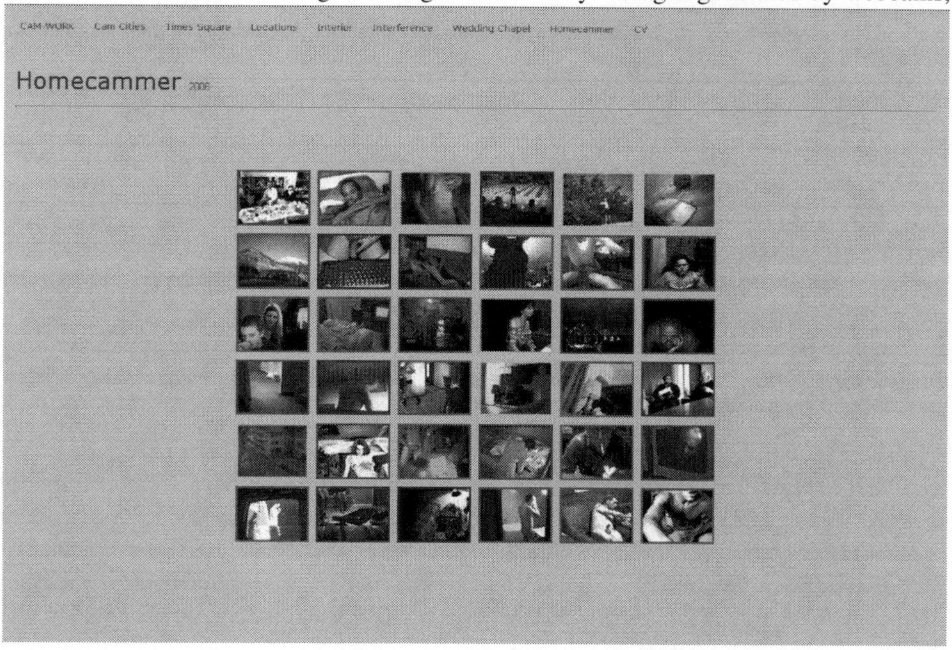

Fig. 4: Cheryl Sourkes, Homecammer, www.cherylsourkes.com/homecammer.htm

digitally mastering, reformatting and transforming them into still images or videos. Her recent exhibition *Live Free Webcams* in Peak Gallery, Toronto, Ontario, in 2007 presented some of the picture I will discuss here. *Homecammer* on Sourkes' website, shows a collection of stills taken from webcams of ordinary people formatted for gallery exhibitions between 2000–2007 (Fig. 4). The 36 pictures, presented in alphabetical order by their titles, show numerous situations: views from windows, interiors, but mostly people doing various everyday things such as eating, smoking, lying in bed, playing games, watching TV, computing, or displaying sex.

By joining real with imaginary and fiction with non-fiction, Sourkes raises questions about time and space, public and private, and our understanding of the virtual world and social sphere. Once the exposures are recontextualized, they turn into indeterminate hybrids, being more substantial and, simultaneously, more ambivalent than at their source.[66] While the images are ostensibly as banal as any webcam images, with a conscientious look, their banality mystically disappears and gives way to new meanings. By remaining outside any mainstream political or commercial interests, the work succeeds in discussing the subcultural nature of webcams. As *Eyes of Laura*, *Homecammer* presents a critical comment on surveillance, yet, in a very different sense. As Goddard states, in these images »surveillance seems to be absorbed by those being surveyed as if it were sunshine on their skins«[67].

Undeniably, Sourkes strikes home in stating that she is documenting *a paradigm shift.*[68] Surveillance no longer succeeds in working as a scare tactic. Nevertheless, surveillance – in traditional sense – does not play such a substantial role in the world of webcams that might be imagined. *Homecammer* is a story about surveillance, but at the same time, it points out how people can live *with* surveillance (i.e. others' gaze) and be liberated from the *shame* generally connected to it. Despite of the images being somehow random, there is certain theatricality in them. A viewer can sense that the subjects are constantly aware of the possibility of being seen, yet, comfortable with the idea – either enjoying the presence of the camera, or finding it indifferent. Indeed, all of the figures shown seem to be entirely innocent of wrongdoing in any sense.[69] Sexual display appears to play a central role in the images, and the targets surely associate themselves with a certain degree of exhibitionism. This display, however, also twists into an issue of voyeuristic interpretation: a critical viewer undoubtedly discovers that »under the eyes of the cameras all sorts of activity becomes reinterpreted as sexual«[70]. The interpretation resides in the eye of the beholder.

A brief wrap-up

Visual images have clearly become an established part of the Internet. Webcams are part of the virtual realm but are also able to give new meanings to real places, adding them new layers of interpretations.[71] They build a peculiar, fascinating bridge between the world of technology and the tangible world. One interesting consequences of dispersed scrutiny is that the moral binary opposition »good/bad« seems to be breaking.[72] This is evident in amateur webcam presentations as well as webcam art work. The differences between the authorities and the public, outsiders and insiders, the controlled and the controllers, have faded. While, »the idea of privacy as a possession we need to protect is deeply embedded in our culture«[73], in the increased sharing of images »the boundary between private action and public presentation becomes more and more fluid«[74]. Representations – as well as their interpretations – »traffic between physical and mental space«[75].

Webcams can be interpreted as a way of creating people capable of resisting the traditional readings of embodiment.[76] People seek to be subjects rather than objects, and in doing this they »reclaim the copyright of their own lives«[77]. By revealing parts of their intimate lives, people are also liberated from shame and the ›need‹ to hide, which leads to something I have called »empowering exhibitionism«[78]. Revealing can be conceptualised as a political act – a way of resisting the objectifying nature of surveillance. Furthermore, webcams provide new readings of public space, either by creating new aesthetic expressions of the material world, or by participating the contested debates about it. As I have show, *the political geographies of webcams* range from supporting the mainstream urban politics to creating arenas for critical expressions and alternative democracies. Webcam art works have a »counter-hegemonic engagement with surveillance practice«[79]. They all – each in a different way – make use of the slipperiness of images. Unlike simple virtual wheel chair travels, they make it clear that it is possible to play with surveillance and to perform to it.

1 See: Margaret Wertheim: »The Pearly Gates of Cyberspace« In: Nan Ellin (ed.): *The Architecture of Fear*. New York 1997, pp. 295–302. Rosie Higgins, Estella Rushhaija & Angela Medhurst: »Technowhores« In: Cutting Edge (eds.): *Desire by Design: Body, Territories and New Technologies*. London 1999, pp. 111–122. Lynn D. Roberts & Malcolm R. Parks: »The Social Geography of Gender-Switching in Virtual Environments on the Internet« In: Eileen Green & Alison Adams (eds.): *Virtual Gender: Technology, Consumption and Identity Matters*. London 2001, pp. 265–285.

2 See: Mike Featherstone & Roger Burrows: »Cultures of Technological Embodiment: An Introduction.« In: Mike Featherstone & Roger Burrows (eds.): *Cyberspace/Cyberbodies/Cyberpunk*. London 1995, pp. 1–19. Leslie Regan Shade: »Is there free speech on the Net? Censorship in the global information inrfastructure.« In: Rob Shields (ed.): *Cultures of Internet. Virtual Spaces, Real Histories, Living Bodies*. London 1996. pp. 11–32.

3 See: Mike Crang: »Public Space, Urban Space, Electronic Space. Would the Real City Please Stand Up?« In: *Urban Studies*, 37/2000, No. 2, pp. 301–317.

4 Catherine Bernard: »Bodies and Digital Utopia« In: *Art Journal*, 59/2000, No. 4, p. 29.

5 Thomas J. Campanella: »Webcameras and the Telepresent Landscape« In: Stephen Graham (ed.): *The Cybercities Reader*. London 2004, p. 58.

6 For a further discussion see: Hille Koskela: »The Other Side of Surveillance. Webcams, Power and Agency« In: David Lyon (ed.): *Theorizing Surveillance: The Panopticon and Beyond.* Cullompton 2006, pp. 163–181. Hille Koskela: »Webcams, TV Shows and Mobile Phones. Empowering Exhibitionism« In: *Surveillance and Society*, 2/2004, No. 2/3, pp. 199–215. camcentral.com/listings.php?task=menu&item=category. www.earthcam.com/.

7 Ursula Frohne: »›Screen Tests‹. Media, Narcissism, Theatricality, and the Internalised Observer« In: Thomas Y. Levin, Ursula Frohne & Peter Weibel (eds.): *CTRL[SPACE]: Rhetorics of Surveillance from Bentham to Big Brother.* Karlsruhe 2002, p. 256.

8 Nic Groombridge: »Crime control or crime culture TV?« In: *Surveillance and Society*, 1/2002, p. 38.

9 Maria Balshaw & Liam Kennedy: »Introduction: Urban Space and Representation« In: Maria Balshaw & Liam Kennedy (eds.): *Urban Space and Representation.* London 2000, p. 3.

10 Pascal Pinck: »From Sofa to the Crime Scene. Skycam, Local News and the Televisual City« In: Balshaw & Kennedy 2000 (as note 9), p. 64.

11 John Macgregor Wise: »An Immense and Unexpected Field of Action. Webcams, Surveillance and Everyday Life« In: *Cultural Studies*, 18/2004, No. 2/3, p. 424.

12 Pinck 2000 (as note 10), p. 64.

13 See: Gareth Palmer: »Video Vigilantes and the Work of Shame« In: *Jump Cut 48*, Winter 2006.

14 Slavoj Zizek: »Big Brother, or, the Triumph of the Gaze Over the Eye.« In: Levin, Frohne & Weibel 2002 (as note 7), p. 226.

15 See: Hille Koskela: »Hijacking Surveillance? The New Moral Landscapes of Amateur Photographing« In: Katja Franko Aas, Helene Oppen Gundhus & Heidi Mork Lomell (eds.): *Technologies of (In)security: The Surveillance of Everyday Life.* London 2008.

16 John McGrath: *Loving Big Brother: Performance, Privacy and Surveillance Space.* London 2004, p. 52.

17 Aaron Doyle: »An Alternative Current in Surveillance and Control: Broadcasting Surveillance Footage of Crimes« In: Kevin D. Haggerty & Richard V. Ericson (eds.): *The New Politics of Surveillance and Visibility*. Toronto 2006, p. 199.

18 Geoffry Batchen: »Guilty pleasures.« In: Levin, Frohne & Weibel 2002 (as note 7), p. 458.
19 Carole Rivière: »Mobile Camera Phones: A New Form of ›Being Together‹ in Daily Interpersonal Communication.« In: Rich Ling & Per Egil Pedersen (eds.): *Mobile Communications: Re-negotiation of the Social Sphere.* Surrey 2005, p. 182.
20 Balshaw & Kennedy 2000 (as note 9), p. 8.
21 M. Allen: »›See you in the City!‹ Perth's Citiplace and the Space of Surveillance« In: Katherine Gibson and Sophie Watson (eds.): *Metropolis Now: Planning and the Urban in Contemporary Australia.* Australia 1994, p. 144.
22 William Bogard: *The Simulation of Surveillance.* Cambridge 1996, p. 66.
23 Paul Virilio: »The visual crash« In: Levin, Frohne & Weibel 2002 (as note 7), p. 109.
24 Koskela 2006 (as note 6), p. 169.
25 See: Louis-José Lestocart & Charles Penwarden: »Aporie sur l'Enfermement« In: *Art Press* 303, July/August 2004, pp. 38–42.
26 See: Koskela 2006 (as note 6).
27 See: Batchen 2002 (as note 18).
28 See: Ilpo Koskinen: »Managing Banality in Mobile Multimedia« In: Raul Pertierra (ed.): *The Social Construction and Usage of Communication Technologies: European and Asian Experiences.* Manila 2007, pp. 48–60.
29 Laura Huey, Kevin Walby & Aaron Doyle: »Cop Watching in the Downtown Eastside. Exploring the Use of (Counter)Surveillance as a Tool of Resistance« In: Torin Monahan (ed.): *Surveillance and Security. Technological Politics and Power in Everyday Life.* New York 2006, p. 154.
30 Brooke A. Knight: »Watch me! Webcams and the Public Exposure of Private Lives« In: *Art Journal*, 59/2000, No.4, p. 24.
31 M. Christine Boyer: »Twice-told stories: the double erasure of Times Square.« In: Iain Borden, Joe Kerr, Jane Rendell & Alicia Pivaro (eds.): *The Unknown City: Contesting Architecture and Social Space.* Cambridge 2001, p. 36.
32 Balshaw & Kennedy 2000 (as note 9), p. 4.
33 M. Christine Boyer: »Cities for Sale: Merchandising History at South Street Seaport.« In: Michael Sorkin (eb.): *Variations on a Theme Park: The New American City and the End of Public Space.* New York 1992, p. 186.
34 Ibid. p. 187, italics added.
35 Koskela 2006 (as note 6), p. 168.
36 See: Krissi M. Jimroglou: »A Camera with a View: JenniCAM, Visual Representations and Cyborg Subjectivity.« In: Eileen Green & Alison Adam (eds.): *Virtual Gender: Technology, Consumption and Identity.* London 2001, pp. 286–301.
37 See: Koskela 2004 (as note 6).
38 E.g. Knight 2000 (as note 30).
39 Ibid., p. 24.
40 Zizek 2002 (as note 14), p. 225.
41 Frohne 2002 (as note 7), p. 275.
42 Ibid. p. 256.
43 McGrath 2004 (as note 16), p. 14.
44 See: David Harvey: *The Condition of Postmodernity: An Enquiry into the Origins of Cultural Change.* Oxford 1989.
45 www.webcamworld.com
46 Bernard 2000 (as note 4), p. 27.

47 Boyer 1992 (as note 33), p. 193.
48 John Bell: »Times Square. Public Space Disneyfied« In: *The Drama Review* 42/1998, No.1, pp. 25–33.
49 www.earthcam.com/usa/newyork/timessquare
50 For a more detailed discussion see: Koskela 2006 (as note 6).
51 www.wolfgangstaehle.info/, see also www.postmedia.net/e-flux/staehle.htm, www.wolfgangstaehle.info/templatePages/biblmView.php?id=6&view=text
52 Quoted in Karen Rosenberg: »The Accidental Historian.« In: *New York News & Features*, September 6th, 2004. nymag.com/nymetro/news/people/columns/intelligencer/9796/
53 Ibid.
54 Tiziana Terranova: »Demonstrating the Globe: Virtual Action in the Network Society.« In: David Holmes (ed.): *Virtual Globalization. Virtual Spaces/Tourist Spaces*. London 2001, p. 130.
55 goldberg.berkeley.edu/index-flash.html, see also www.ieor.berkeley.edu/~goldberg/art/, cwis.usc.edu/users/goldberg/art.html
56 Demonstrate 2008, Project description. demonstrate.berkeley.edu/project.php
57 Frohne 2002 (as note 7), p. 257.
58 Ibid.
59 the-artists.org/artist/Janet_Cardiff.html, see also www.artfocus.com/JanetCardiff.html, www.eyesoflaura.org, www.virtualmuseum.ca/Exhibitions/Photos/html/en/mk-essay.html
60 McGrath 2004 (as note 16), p. 22.
61 Frohne 2002 (as note 7), p. 269.
62 See: Philip Tabor: »I am a Videocam.« In: Ian Borden, Joe Kerr, Jane Rendell & Alicia Pivaro (eds.): *The Unknown City. Contesting Architecture and Social Space*. Cambridge 2001, pp. 122–137.
63 See: Kevin D. Haggerty: »Tear down the Walls: On Demolishing the Panopticon.« In: David Lyon (ed.): *Theorizing Surveillance: The Panopticon and Beyond*. Cullompton 2006, pp. 23–45.
64 See: Allen 1994 (as note 21).
65 ww.cherylsourkes.com, see also www.gallery.ca/cybermuse/showcases/meet/artist_e.jsp?artistid=5169, www.digitalmediatree.com/sallymckay/pageback/37321/
66 See: Cheryl Sourkes 2008, Cam work. http://www.cherylsourkes.com/
67 Peter Goddard: »Candid cameras« In: Toronto Star, Saturday, April 14, 2007. www.peakgallery.com/reviews/reviews_2007/07_sourkes_rev.htm
68 See: Ibid.
69 See: Ibid.
70 McGrath 2004 (as note 16), p. 73.
71 See: Campanella 2004 (as note 5), pp. 57–63.
72 See: Koskela 2008 (as note 15).
73 McGrath 2004 (as note 16), p. 56.
74 Frohne 2002 (as note 7): 256.
75 Balshaw & Kennedy 2000 (as note 9), p. 3.
76 See: Jimroglou 2001 (as note 36).
77 Koskela 2004 (as note 6), p. 206.
78 Ibid.
79 McGrath 2004 (as note 16), p. 217.

Markus Buschhaus

In großer Nähe so fern. Warum es ›nicht-künstlerische Bilder‹ nur in der Kunstwissenschaft geben kann

»The difficulty is to learn how to be iconophilic for one form of visual culture without being iconoclastic for the others.«[1]

1. Schattenboxen in der Fachzeitschrift? Annäherungen an ein Trugbild

»Art History and Images That Are Not Art« ist der Titel eines Aufsatzes, den der Kunstwissenschaftler James Elkins im Jahre 1995 in der Fachzeitschrift *The Art Bulletin* veröffentlichte.[2] Auf den ersten, vielleicht unbedarften Blick scheint das Thema, welches Elkins mit diesem Titel veranschlagt, sicherlich überraschend. Zwar ist es keine Überraschung, dass ein Kunstwissenschaftler in einer Kunstzeitschrift über Kunstgeschichte bzw. Kunstwissenschaft[3] und über Bilder schreibt. Jedoch geht es hier um Bilder, die, durchaus mit einem gewissen Nachdruck, eben keine Kunst sein sollen. Auf den zweiten, vielleicht weniger unbedarften Blick wird zu entgegnen sein, Kunstwissenschaftler hätten sich in der Kunstwissenschaft schon immer auch mit Bildern beschäftigt, die halt keine Kunst seien und dennoch ganz selbstverständlich in das Aufgabenfeld der Kunstwissenschaft fielen. Insofern könne das von Elkins offenkundig in Angriff genommene Thema nicht wirklich überraschen, ganz im Gegenteil, es laufe Gefahr, sich auf einen Allgemeinplatz zu berufen. Dies könne man bloß den Unbedarften als neuen Blickwinkel, als überraschende Sichtweise verkaufen, keinesfalls aber jenen, welche die Regeln der Kunst kennen und sie seit langem schon beispielhaft beherrschen. Im Folgenden soll der Versuch unternommen werden, zwischen beiden Standpunkten zu vermitteln, indem beiden widersprochen wird: Weder nämlich beschäftigt sich die Kunstwissenschaft ganz selbstverständlich mit solchen, wie es bei Elkins heißt, »nonart images«[4], noch ist eine solche Beschäftigung grundsätzlich und unter allen Umständen auszuschließen.

Bereits im Titel seines Beitrages kennzeichnet Elkins einige der Koordinaten, welche gerade auch für kontrovers diskutierte Bildwissenschaften in den letzten Jahren von Belang gewesen sind. Dazu zählen: der Einsatz verschiedener Disziplinen und Wissenschaften sowie deren Rolle im Rahmen einer wie auch immer gearteten bildwissenschaftlichen Herausforderung; die Notwendigkeit der Erarbeitung, Vertiefung und Überprüfung von Bildbegriffen, gehe diese nun induktiv oder deduktiv vonstatten; die Klärung der Kunstfrage, welche sich aus ganz unterschiedlichen Beweggründen immer wieder aufdrängt oder aber gezielt ins Spiel gebracht wird, um fragwürdige oder berechtigte Ansprüche zu untermauern; schließlich auch der Bereich des Historischen, welcher ganz wesentlich auf eine Bestimmung des Verhältnisses zwischen alten, scheinbar überkommenen, und neuen, scheinbar voraussetzungslosen Bildern und Bildwelten hinausläuft. Keineswegs auf die Gegenstandsebene beschränkt, sondern durchaus nachdrücklich auch auf das Selbstverständnis der am bildwissenschaftlich motivierten Diskurs beteiligten Disziplinen zielend, bewegt sich dieser Problembereich entlang historiografisch empfindlicher Begriffe wie Tradition, Innovation und Revolution.

Vor diesem Hintergrund macht es sich vorliegender Beitrag zur Aufgabe, die Bedeutung nachzuzeichnen, welche die ›nonart images‹ oder »nicht-künstlerischen Bilder«[5] für die Kunstwissenschaft in zeitgenössischen Diskussionen um bildwissenschaftlich motivierte Forschung haben. Dabei interessiert es weder, dass die Kunstwissenschaft ganz unbestritten kompetent über ›künstlerische Bilder‹ zu sprechen in der Lage ist, noch spielt es eine Rolle, ob und wo sie dies tut. Und es interessiert auch kaum, wie mit ›nicht-künstlerischen Bildern‹ eigentlich umzugehen sei, noch steht im Vordergrund, was unter Bildwissenschaften überhaupt verhandelt werden könnte. Hingegen interessiert es ganz wesentlich, mittels welcher Strategien der Ausweitung und Ausgrenzung einige Kunstwissenschaftler sich gegenwärtig nicht nur am bildwissenschaftlichen Diskurs beteiligen, sondern diesen, zumal in Hinblick auf ›nicht-künstlerische Bilder‹, zu monopolisieren versuchen. Erkenntnisleitend ist dabei die These, dass die programmatisch in Anspruch genommene Nähe zu ›nicht-künstlerischen‹ Bildwelten gegenwärtig wohl nicht nur methodologisch verspielt, sondern auch forschungspolitisch missbraucht wird.

2. Die Bilder und ihre Künste: ein Abriss

»Die Ausweitung des Bilddiskurses erfordert eine Fülle neuer und präziser Distinktionen«[6], heißt es in einem Beitrag Gottfried Boehms, der sich ausdrücklich bildwissenschaftlich mit Bildern in den Wissenschaften und der Medizin befasst. Ohne Zweifel hat der hier programmatisch in Aussicht gestellte ›Bilddiskurs‹ – für welchen das Etikett ›Bildwissenschaft‹ eine institutionelle Heimat disziplinären Zuschnittes verspricht – eine nahezu unbegrenzte Vielfalt an Bildbegriffen zu Tage gefördert. Diese Vielfalt ist teilweise disziplinären Traditionen verpflichtet, teilweise beruht sie auf genuin interdisziplinären Entwürfen, teilweise speist sie sich aus transdisziplinären Übergriffen, und teilweise läuft sie auf eine vermeintlich oder tatsächlich universale Bilddisziplin hinaus. Diese Bildbegriffe sind keineswegs unbedarft, ganz unabhängig davon, ob sie sich im Einzelfall, also für die jeweilige Fragestellung, als günstig oder ungünstig erweisen, und auch unabhängig davon, ob sie sich komplementär oder alternativ zueinander verhalten.

So lassen sich, um nur einige wenige Beispiele des weit gefächerten und tief gestaffelten Bilddiskurses zu nennen, Bilder aus medientechnischer[7] oder phänomenologischer[8], aus semiotischer[9], historischer[10] oder bildkultureller[11] Motivation in den Blick nehmen und zur Sprache bringen. Offenkundig ist es vor allem das letzte Feld, welches Elkins in seinem Aufsatz »Art History and Images That Are Not Art« bestellt, wenn er neben den schon erwähnten ›nonart images‹ auch ›religious images‹, ›scientific images‹ und freilich ›art images‹ heranzieht.[12] Entsprechend legt diese Rede von ›nonart images‹ – oder anderenorts von ›nicht-künstlerischen Bildern‹ – zunächst einmal eine

Trennung von Bild- und Kunstbegriff nahe, wie sie sich sowohl systematisch als auch historisch ausweisen lässt.

Systematisch gilt einerseits, dass sich Kunst nicht ausschließlich, nicht einmal notwendig überhaupt bildhaft manifestiert[13]; und andererseits, dass eben nicht jedes Bild als Kunst in den Blick geraten muss.[14] Zwischen diesen beiden Feststellungen entfaltet sich, zumal in der zweiten Hälfte des letzten Jahrhunderts, eine einigermaßen unübersichtliche, historisch und historiografisch arg umkämpfte Grauzone, die an dieser Stelle nur benannt, ganz sicher aber nicht erläutert werden kann. Damit gemeint sind die widersprüchlichen Diskussionen etwa um den Kunststatus der Fotografie. Diese stellten vor dem Hintergrund einer heute offensichtlichen Verwechslung von Kunst- und Bildbegriff vor die Entscheidung, entweder kein fotografisches Bild, unter welchen Umständen auch immer, als Kunst, was auch immer das im Einzelnen sei, durchgehen zu lassen, oder aber, nachgerade andersherum, ein jedes fotografisches Bild, aus welchem Grund auch immer aufgenommen und wo auch immer vorgefunden, als Kunst zu verhandeln.[15]

Einer bestimmten Spielart der Bildforschung jedenfalls gerät die Einsicht in die »Dichotomie in der Kunst- und in der Bildgeschichte«[16] zum eigentlichen Beweggrund, überhaupt von ›Bildwissenschaft‹ zu sprechen. Dass dies nicht nur, wie oben angerissen, systematisch, sondern auch historisch nachvollziehbar ist, verdeutlichen die Titel zweier einschlägiger Publikationen, nämlich *Bild und Kult. Eine Geschichte des Bildes vor dem Zeitalter der Kunst* von Hans Belting aus dem Jahre 1990 und *Vom Bild zum Kunstsystem* von Beat Wyss aus dem Jahre 2006. ›Nonart images‹ liegen insgesamt also nicht nur wesentlich zahlreicher vor, sondern sie sind auch historisch deutlich älter. Historisch gefällige Beispiele für ›nonart images‹ finden sich seit jeher in den mannigfaltigen Bildwelten des Mittelalters, unter welche nach Elkins die ›religious images‹ fallen, wenngleich sie kaum ausschließlich dort zu verbuchen sind.[17] Aktuell gefällige Beispiele für ›nonart images‹ liefern nicht nur, aber vor allem jene gleichfalls mannigfaltigen Bildwelten, in welchen Elkins die ›scientific images‹ unterbringt. Nicht zuletzt deshalb heißt es etwa bei Boehm: »Wissenschaftliche Bilder sind integraler Bestandteil einer Bildgeschichte bzw. einer Bildwissenschaft.«[18]

Diesem Umstand haben zuletzt zahlreiche Forschungsarbeiten Rechnung getragen, die sich mit *Bildwelten des Wissens*[19], mit *Bilderwissen*[20], mit *Bildern des Wissens*[21] und mit *Wissenschaftlicher Visualisierung*[22] beschäftigt und dabei gar einen »Wechsel vom text- zum bildvermittelten Wissen«[23] oder eine »›Piktorialisierung‹ der Naturwissenschaften«[24] ausgemacht haben. All diesen Beiträgen ist die Frage nach der Funktion von Bildern für die Produktion und Organisation von Wissen gemein; und all diese Beiträge teilen die Ansicht, dass an Bildern und durch Bilder verhandelt werden kann, was buchstäblich nicht zu wissen ist und ausdrücklich bestenfalls erst gewusst werden wird. Insofern kann mittlerweile mit einiger Berechtigung behauptet werden, dass diese sogenannten ›wissenschaftlichen Bilder‹ – welche bei Elkins als ›scientific images‹ zu den ›nonart images‹ zählen – ein äußerst fruchtbares Forschungsfeld für Bildfragen aller Art geworden sind. Entsprechend lassen sich zentrale Probleme bildwissenschaftlich motivierter Diskussionen an ihnen ablesen.

3. Vor den zwei Kulturen: die Angst vor bildkultureller Vielfalt

Im durchaus programmatischen Vorwort des ersten Bandes der *Bildwelten des Wissens*, einem *Kunsthistorischen Jahrbuch für Bildkritik*, heißt es:

> »Für Bilder, die in einer umfassenden Kultur einer Arbeit am Wissen betrachtet werden, hat sich die Theorie von den zwei Kulturen, Natur- vs. Geisteswissenschaft, als überaus hinderlich erwiesen.«[25]

Es spielt gerade deshalb eine außerordentliche Rolle, ob Bilder – hier mit aller Vorsicht formuliert – als ›wissenschaftliche‹ oder ›religiöse‹ oder ›künstlerische‹ in den Blick genommen und zur Sprache gebracht werden, weil Bild, wie Manfred Faßler erklärt, unhintergehbar »kulturelle Handlung«[26] ist.

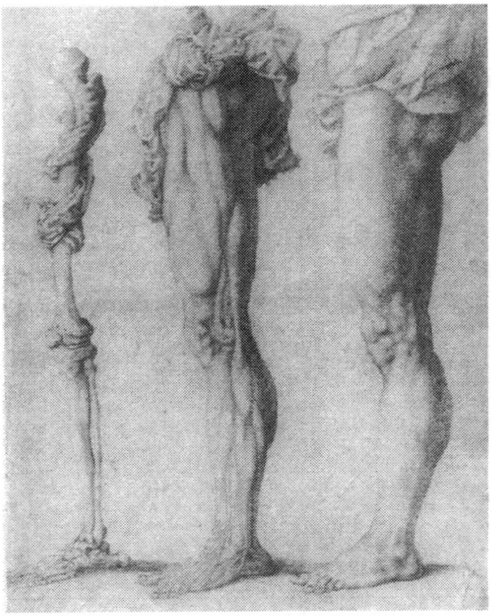

Abb. 1: Alessandro Allori, Beinstudie, 1560er Jahre

Insofern ist die offenkundige Kritik an C. P. Snows kontrovers diskutierter Zwei-Kulturen-These aus dem Jahre 1959 einigermaßen aufschlussreich. In der Tat macht Snow eine Trennung zwischen naturwissenschaftlicher und künstlerisch-philosophischer Wissenskultur aus, womit er aber, und dies wird oft oder gerne übersehen, gleichsam eine Denkfigur einführt, welche es erlaubt, die Naturwissenschaften gerade nicht als ein für alle Mal in sich geschlossenes, unabhängiges System zu begreifen.[27] So werden bestimmte Methoden, Strategien und vor allem Praktiken der sogenannten ›hard sciences‹ überhaupt erst als kulturell bedeutsam und vor allem als vergleichbar mit philosophischen, literarischen oder künstlerischen Positionen ausgewiesen. Auf welcher Ebene ein solcher Vergleich, gerade hinsichtlich der Bilderfrage, sinnvoll sein mag – auf der Ebene der Produktion, auf der Ebene des Produktes oder auf der Ebene des Gebrauchs dieses Produktes – sei hier zunächst dahingestellt und später noch einmal aufgegriffen.

Deutlich ist jedenfalls, dass eine gegenwärtige, etwa kulturwissenschaftlich ambitionierte Berücksichtigung von Snows These der zwei Kulturen ganz sicher nicht darauf hinauslaufen sollte, aus den zwei Kulturen wieder eine einzige Kultur zu machen, wie es in den *Bildwelten des Wissens*, womöglich ohne Kenntnis der Schriften Snows, getan wird.[28] Genau andersherum müsste es darum gehen, den Kulturbegriff breiter zu fächern und gleichzeitig tiefer zu staffeln,[29] dies freilich immer unter Berücksichtigung des Umstandes, dass Kulturen in Bewegung sind. Leider scheint gerade die kunstwissenschaftliche Auseinandersetzung mit Bilderfragen kaum dazu angelegt, diese Arbeit zu leisten. Denn ein Blick auf eine Vielzahl der Beiträge, welche sich mit sogenannten ›nicht-künstlerischen Bildern‹ und ›nonart images‹ beschäftigen, zeigt genau im Gegenteil, dass hier, wie Peter Geimer kritisch, aber zutreffend anmerkt, »Harmoniediskurse«

im Rahmen eines »humanistischen Versöhnungsprogramms«[30] am Werk sind. Als unverdrüsslich beschworene Bezugsgröße derartiger Rede erscheint jene Renaissance, in welcher Künste und Wissenschaften angeblich noch eins gewesen sind, was sich in ganz außergewöhnlicher Weise in der frühneuzeitlichen Anatomie und ihrer Zusammenarbeit zwischen Anatomen und Künstlern zeige.[31] Aus diesem vermeintlich goldenen Zeitalter der Künste und Wissenschaften wird dann im nächsten Atemzug gerne ein hoffnungsvolles Programm für die Zukunft formuliert, welches häufig deckungsgleich ist mit der in den *Bildwelten des Wissens* angedachten ›umfassenden Kultur einer Arbeit am Wissen‹.

Diese gibt es gegenwärtig nicht, und es wird sie auch nicht geben – und es hat sie, zumal in der frühneuzeitlichen Anatomie, auch nicht gegeben. Dies jedenfalls wird deutlich, wenn man Anatomie und Kunst des 16. Jahrhunderts vor dem Hintergrund ihres jeweiligen Bildhaushaltes betrachtet und sie dabei weder gegeneinander ausspielt, wie es etwa Theodor Hetzer in seiner *Geschichte des Bildes* tut[32], noch miteinander verwechselt, wie es Erwin Panofsky unterläuft[33]. Denkt man Anatomie und Kunst in der Frühen Neuzeit hingegen miteinander auseinander, kann man, gerade bei Berücksichtigung ihrer jeweilig wesentlich bildmedialen Verfasstheit, auch der Ausformung einer professionellen und einer Künstleranatomie, welche spätestens in der zweiten Hälfte des 16. Jahrhunderts vollzogen ist, Rechnung tragen.[34] (Abb. 1, 2)

»Bild«, so stellt Faßler fest, »ist kein Ruheraum der Kultur«[35] – wobei gleichermaßen im Umkehrschluss gilt, dass eine Kultur eben auch keinen Ruheraum für Bilder bietet. Kulturen, so ließe sich sagen, fordern Bilder, und Bilder fordern Kulturen heraus. Genau das hat eine bildwissenschaftliche Auseinandersetzung mit sogenannten ›nicht-künstlerischen Bildern‹ und ›nonart images‹ nicht nur auszuhalten, sondern auch sichtbar zu machen, sei es historiografisch, sei es systematisch. Entsprechend richtet sich etwa *Kulturen des Bildes* »gegen eine global verstandene Bildkultur und ein monokulturelles Bilddenken, das Bilder aus ihren Kontexten herausschneidet, um reine Bildlichkeit extrapolieren zu können. [...] ›Kulturen des Bildes‹ – dieser programmatisch gesetzte Titel zielt auf die Verknüpfung, Verschmelzung und Auseinandersetzung unterschiedlicher Kulturen im Bild ab. [...] In diesem Zuschnitt gibt sich die Frage nach den ›Kulturen des Bildes‹ als eine kulturwissenschaftliche Fragestellung zu erkennen: Wo Kultur zunehmend als bildvermittelte in den Blick gerät, da verändert sich auch die Sicht auf Bilder.«[36]

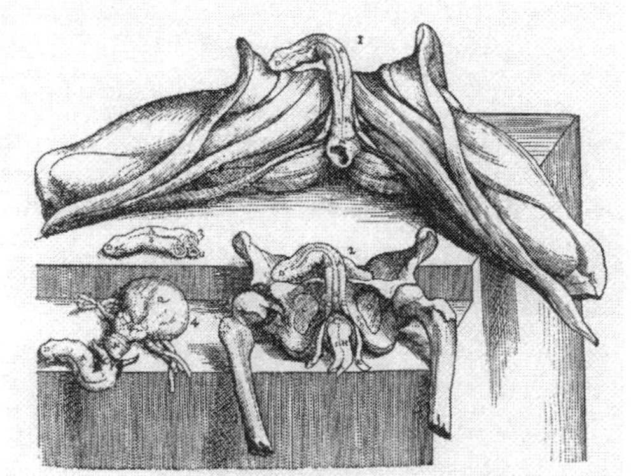

Abb. 2: Bildtafel aus De humani corporis fabrica *von Andreas Vesalius, 1543*

4. Glanz und Elend der Kunstwissenschaft als Bildwissenschaft

Bilderstreit: ›starke‹ und ›schwache‹ Bildlichkeit

Wenn Bilder also in einem unmittelbaren Verhältnis stehen zu den Kulturen, von denen sie aufgeführt werden und welche sie gleichsam selbst mit gestalten, dann liegt es nahe, Bilder unter anderem auch als Botschafter von Kulturen aufzufassen – durchaus unabhängig davon, ob die betroffenen Kulturen ihren Bildhaushalt in diesem Sinne verstanden wissen wollen oder nicht. Dies spielt auch eine Rolle für Begriffsbildungen wie ›nonart images‹ und ›nicht-künstlerische Bilder‹, welche zwar bildkulturell motiviert sind, aber statt denjenigen Kulturen, die damit adressiert werden sollen, den eigenen Standpunkt zu benennen scheinen. Dieser Standpunkt gibt sich, zunächst einmal, als einer zu erkennen, der künstlerische Bilder als das Maß nimmt, anhand dessen andere Bilder – eben: ›nicht-künstlerische Bilder‹ – auf welche Art und Weise und aus welchem Grund auch immer zu messen sind. Damit wird, ob beabsichtigt oder nicht, zumindest eine Unhintergehbarkeit künstlerischer Bildbegriffe – oder genauer: jener Bilder, die als Kunst verhandelt werden können – angedeutet. Dieser Umstand sei hier als ästhetizistisch-phänomenologisches Missverständnis gekennzeichnet.

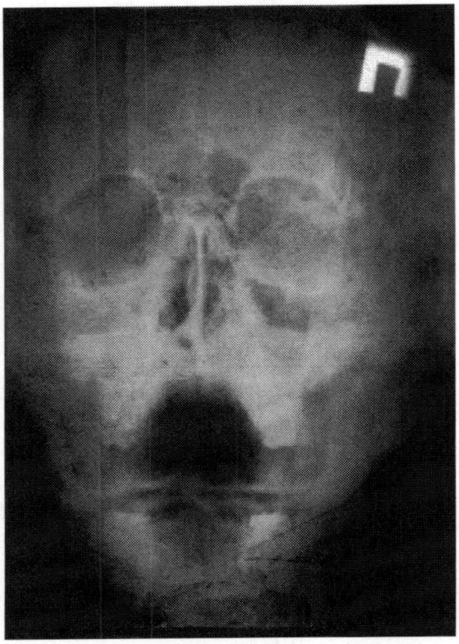

Abb. 3: Torsten Seidel, Portrait of this mortal coil #7, 2003

Die Antwort auf die Frage, was denn überhaupt ein künstlerisches Bild sei, muss aber notwendig schuldig bleiben, wer seinen Blick nicht von der Bildfläche zu lösen vermag. Dies jedenfalls legt Boris Groys in seiner *Topologie der Kunst* nahe, wenn er ausführt: »es gibt keine bestimmten ›Kunstbilder‹, vielmehr können alle Bilder im Kunstkontext verwendet werden.«[37] Trotzdem – oder: gerade deshalb – macht es, zumal vor dem Hintergrund des Begriffs der ›nicht-künstlerischen Bilder‹, Sinn, von ›künstlerischen Bildern‹ zu sprechen, und zwar unter genau der Voraussetzung, die Groys an gleicher Stelle geltend macht: »Strenggenommen können wir nur über Kunstorte – nicht über Kunstwerke – sprechen.«[38] Als Katalysator eines pragmatisch, nicht idealistisch gefassten künstlerischen Bildbegriffes gerät Groys dabei das Readymade-Verfahren, dessen Funktion darin besteht, »daß bestimmte seriell und industriell produzierte Objekte inklusive Fotos, Videos oder Filme als Kunstwerke in den Kunstkontext, ins Museum gestellt werden.«[39] Von daher gilt, dass Kunst im ganz sprichwörtlichen Sinne im Auge des Betrachters liegt – allerdings unter der bloßer Willkür Einhalt gebietenden Einschränkung, dass dieses Auge dem Betrachter nicht ausschließlich eigen und frei verfügbar, sondern als Blick immer auch kulturell vorgeprägt und zielführend ist. Etwa im musealen Kunstkontext, welcher eben ganz unzweideutig bestimmte ›Lesarten‹ von Bildern begünstigt. Von daher die wesentliche Bedeutung der Installation für die *Topologie der Kunst*, welche nicht nur die Frage, was ›künstlerische Bilder‹ wann und wo und aus welchem Grund sind, betrifft, sondern indirekt eben auch die Frage, was unter ›nicht-künstlerischen Bildern‹ verstanden werden kann.

Die künstlerisch motivierte Auseinandersetzung mit wissenschaftlichem oder medizinischem Bildmaterial erlaubt einen anderen Blick auf diese Bilder und befördert mithin ein anderes Wissen durch und um sie. So unterliegen etwa Röntgenbilder einem grundlegenden Bedeutungswandel, wenn sie von der klinischen Diagnostik in den *White Cube* wandern, um dort in überlebensgroßer Tafelbildmanier ausgestellt zu werden.[40] (Abb. 3, 4) Dabei muss dieser Bedeutungswandel auf den ersten Blick nicht einmal notwendig augenfällig werden, da er sich vor Ort nicht auf der Bildfläche vollzieht. Womit gleichzeitig schon eine mögliche Antwort auf folgende Frage Geimers formuliert ist: »Es fragt sich indessen, welches Artefakt zurückbleibt, wenn man von wissenschaftlichen Bildern die Wissenschaft abzieht.«[41]

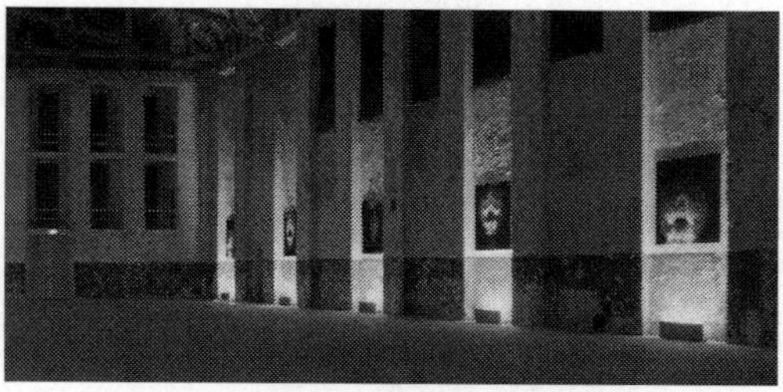

Abb. 4: Torsten Seidel, Portrait of this mortal coil, 2003, Installation, Dresden Hellerau

Die von Boehm aufgeworfene »sekundäre Ästhetisierung«[42] jedoch ist nicht allein auf künstlerische Praktiken zu beschränken, wie sie sich in obigem Fall anlässlich der Installation von Röntgenbildern im *White Cube* manifestieren. Auch kunstwissenschaftliche Praktiken, solche wissenschaftlichen Bilder als ›nicht-künstlerische Bilder‹ in den Blick zu nehmen, befördern ›Lesarten‹, welche sich wesentlich von dem eigentlich wissenschaftsspezifischen Umgang mit derartigen Bildern unterscheiden. Und zwar nicht bloß bildkulturell – also hinsichtlich des Wanderns von Bildern durch verschiedene Kulturen –, sondern auch historisch – also hinsichtlich einer sich in und mit der Zeit entwickelnden Bedeutungsverschiebung. Dies alles geht spätestens dann über den »Kunsthistoriker als Nachlassverwalter der Bildtraditionen«[43] hinaus, wenn sich Bilder durch druckgrafische Reproduktion oder digitale Verfügbarkeit in der Regel an verschiedenen Orten gleichzeitig antreffen lassen, anders als etwa die Ikone, die als Original entweder in der Kirche oder im Museum hängt.

Bei folgender Einschätzung Boehms hingegen handelt es sich um ein ganz einschlägig kunstwissenschaftliches Missverständnis: »Wissenschaftliche Bilder sind ›schwache Bilder‹, soweit sie ihren Zweck notwendigerweise außer sich selbst haben.«[44] Denn über die Autorität der Bilder in etwaigen medizinischen oder wissenschaftlichen Bildkulturen entscheidet sicherlich nicht die Kunstwissenschaft. Diese kann zwar unbestritten kompetent und womöglich sogar privilegiert über als Kunst verbuchte ›künstlerische Bilder‹ sprechen, ist aber nicht dazu aufgerufen, den Funktionshorizont wissenschaftlicher Bildgebung in den jeweiligen Wissenschaftskulturen ästhetisch zu reformulieren und damit qualitativ zu besetzen. Die Autorität des Bildes – davon abhängig seine etwaige Stärke oder Schwäche – liegt nicht einfach vor, sondern sie wird bildkulturell und medientechnisch ausgehandelt. Auch eine ›sekundäre Ästhetisierung‹ kommt nicht näher an eine etwaige wahre, echte, eigentliche Bildlichkeit heran. Ästhetik schließlich erweist sich als eine durchaus konventionelle ›Lesart‹ unter vielen, keineswegs aber als die authentische über allen. Entsprechend haben ästhetisch motivierte ›Lesarten‹ von Bildern ihre kulturökonomisch gewinnbringenden Orte in Museen, Ausstellungen und wie auch immer künstlerisch markierten Publikationen.

Wenn ein Bild – oder *das* Bild – als solches nicht vorliegt, gibt es freilich auch keinen Grund, bestimmten Kulturen, welche Artefakte als Bilder bedeutsam gestalten und sinnhaft verhandeln, abzusprechen, dass sie es mit Bildern zu tun haben, obwohl diese nicht restlos in künstlerischen oder kunstwissenschaftlichen Vorstellungen dessen, was ein Bild zu sein habe, aufgehen. Vergessen wir nämlich nicht: Wenn ein Radiologe ein Röntgenbild so betrachtet wie ein Kunstwissenschaftler, dann steht der Radiologe mit einem Bein im Gefängnis, der Patient mit einem Bein im Grab.

Methodenstreit: Formanalyse als Bildflächenfetischismus

Das zweite große Missverständnis, welchem die im Namen etwaiger Bildwissenschaften betriebene Kunstwissenschaft aufzuliegen Gefahr läuft, ist formanalytischer Art. So heißt es etwa im programmatischen Editorial zum ersten Band der *Bildwelten des Wissens*:

> »Die ›Bildwelten des Wissens‹ zum Gegenstand zu machen, ist ein ungeheuer komplexer und nicht eben geheuerer Anspruch. Er betrifft die Bildwelten der Geisteswissenschaften ebenso wie die der Massenmedien und der Populärkultur, der Naturwissenschaften und der Technikgeschichte.«[45]

Dieser Ausweitung des Untersuchungsgegenstandes, die aufs Ganze geht und sich für alles nur irgendwie Bildliche verantwortlich fühlt, entspricht eine ebenso gewaltige Engführung, welche eigentlich noch viel weniger geheuer erscheinen dürfte: »Wir erlauben uns jedoch eine einzige Strenge [...] Unser Begriff von Bildkritik setzt bei der Analyse der Form an, also dem, was die Spezifik von Bildern ausmacht.«[46] Schließlich gerät den Verfassern die Formanalyse zur *conditio sine qua non*:

> »Eine ›Bildwissenschaft‹ ohne Formanalyse wirkt, als würde jemand, der nie ein Pferd geritten hat, die Fähigkeiten eines Jockeys von einer fahrenden Limousine aus kommentieren.«[47]

Ganz abgesehen davon, dass dieser Vergleich hinkt – es beunruhigt, wenn Kunstwissenschaftler, die ›Bildwelten des Wissens‹ thematisieren wollen, derart unbedarft gegen eine der grundlegenden Einsichten der Wissens- und Wissenschaftsgeschichtsschreibung verstoßen. Diese ist an überaus prominenter Stelle von Georges Canguilhem formuliert worden und hat bis heute Gültigkeit: »Der Gegenstand der Wissenschaftsgeschichte hat mit dem Gegenstand der Wissenschaft nichts gemeinsam.«[48] Und weiter heißt es dort: »Der Gegenstand der Wissenschaftsgeschichte ist in der Tat die Geschichtlichkeit des wissenschaftlichen Diskurses.«[49] Wollte man den wohlfeilen Vergleich aus den *Bildwelten des Wissens* auf die Spitze treiben, müsste man wohl behaupten, nur Bildproduzenten selbst könnten über Bilder sprechen. Unter solch merkwürdigen Voraussetzungen jedoch ist Wissenschaft, in welcher Form und mit welcher Absicht auch immer, nicht mehr möglich – ganz unabhängig davon, ob es sich nun um Kunst-, Bild- oder Medienwissenschaften handelt.

Ohne ihren Stellenwert grundsätzlich in Frage stellen zu wollen, drängt sich der Verdacht auf, dass das einseitige Beharren einiger Kunstwissenschaftler auf der Formanalyse einem zweifachen Missverständnis aufliegt. Dies betrifft erstens den Umstand, dass selbstverständlich nicht nur die Kunstwissenschaft über formanalytische Methoden verfügt. Und zweitens ist zu bedenken, dass eine Formanalyse zwar sinnvoll und zielführend sein kann, es aber nicht sein muss. Bisweilen nämlich steht besagte Formanalyse den jeweiligen Bildforschern nachgerade im Weg. So geht etwa der Kunstwissenschaftler Martin Kemp in seinem Band *Bilderwissen*, welcher sich der *Anschaulichkeit naturwissenschaftlicher Phänomene* widmet, davon aus, »dass Wissenschaft und Kunst viele Vorgehensweisen gemeinsam haben«[50] und der Stil nachhaltiges Wissen »über die Wissenschaftler und Techniker, ihre Materialien, ihre Auftraggeber und Förderer sowie über die Verbreitung und Rezeption ihrer Ergebnisse«[51] befördere. Der Wissenschaftshistoriker Thomas S. Kuhn hingegen kommt zu folgendem Befund:

> »Wenn Kunst und Wissenschaft aufgrund einer sorgfältigen Analyse so merkwürdig ähnlich erscheinen, so könnte das weniger an ihrer tatsächlichen Ähnlichkeit liegen als an der Mangelhaftigkeit der Mittel unserer genauen Untersuchung.«[52]

Einer einfältigen Gleichschaltung von Kunst und Wissenschaft, formanalytisch begünstigt und auf der Bildfläche verortet, ist gerade deshalb Vorschub zu leisten, da es oftmals erst der Bildgebrauch ist, der einen Unterschied macht, allerdings ohne auf der Bildfläche ›anschaulich‹ zu werden. Von daher, dies wurde bereits angeführt, die Notwendigkeit, den Kulturbegriff nicht in einer ›umfassenden Kultur des Wissens‹ aufzuheben, sondern ihn gleichzeitig breiter zu fächern – etwa: Kulturtransfers – und tiefer zu staffeln – etwa: Bildpraktiken. Besagte Gleichschaltung auf der Bildfläche hingegen stellt ein forschungsstrategisches Einfallstor der Kunstwissenschaft dar und findet, auch dies wurde bereits angedeutet, ihren argumentativen Fluchtpunkt gerne in der frühneuzeitlichen Anatomie, dank derer der Kunstwissenschaftler scheinbar unvermittelt zum Wissenschaftshistoriker mutieren darf.

Bildwissenschaftlich interessant, zumal vor dem Hintergrund etwaiger ›Bildwelten des Wissens‹, ist mithin weniger der Ausweis der Verfahren, die zu einem Produkt, nämlich dem Bild, führen, als der Versuch, die Verfahren, mit denen besagtes Bild in der Folge aufgeführt wird, in den Blick zu nehmen. Dabei geht es in erster Linie nicht um Bildflächen, sondern um dasjenige, was um diese herum, also mit Bildern in Kulturen geschieht.[53] Damit eingeschlagen wird der Weg von einer ikonografisch geprägten Bildsemantik zu einer kulturell fundierten Bildpragmatik, welche nicht nur die Grenzen der Formanalyse kennzeichnet, sondern auch deren Gefahren verdeutlicht.

Erbstreit: die Tradition Warburg zwischen Mnemosyne und Lethe

Die ›Ausweitung des Bilddiskurses‹, von welcher eingangs die Rede gewesen ist und welche sich unter anderem in Begriffen wie ›nicht-künstlerische Bilder‹ und ›nonart images‹ niederschlägt, ist, dies wird nach und nach deutlich, durchaus auch als Ausweitung der disziplinären Kampfzone zu verstehen. Um in dieser bestehen zu können, ist es, zumal für solche Disziplinen, welche auf eine lange Geschichte zurückblicken können, ratsam, sich einer Tradition zu versichern, welche es ihnen erlaubt, sich entweder als schon dort, wo andere erst hinwollen, oder als über die Maße zukunftsfähig zu verkaufen. Für Kunstwissenschaftler, die es mit ›nicht-künstlerischen Bildern‹ und ›nonart images‹ zu tun kriegen, weil sie sich ihrer bildwissenschaftlichen Herausforderung stellen, gilt der Kulturwissenschaftler Aby Warburg mittlerweile als obligatorischer Passagepunkt.[54] Unbenommen des ohne Zweifel begründeten Interesses an Warburgs bedeutsamer Bildforschung hat dies bisweilen auch einen wissenschaftspolitischen Hintergrund.

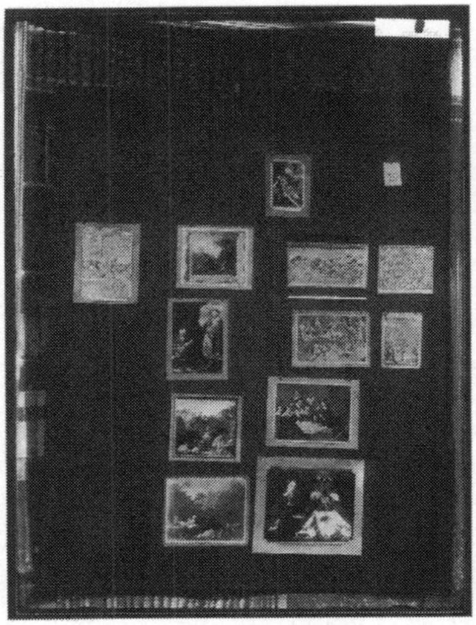

Abb. 5: Tafel 75 zu Aby Warburgs Bilderatlas Mnemosyne

Die heutige kunstwissenschaftliche Beschäftigung mit Warburg gibt, zumal dann, wenn sie zur Vereinnahmung gerät, durchaus dazu Anlass, in Anlehnung an Theodor W. Adornos ›Wunde Heine‹ auch von einer ›Wunde Warburg‹ zu sprechen. Vor diesem Hintergrund nämlich entfaltet folgende historiografische Einsicht ihre ganze Berechtigung: »Traditionen lassen vergessen, indem sie erinnern.«[55] Dies lässt sich besonders aufschlussreich am Beispiel des unvollendeten Bilderatlanten *Mnemosyne* aufzeigen (Abb. 5), welcher rückwirkend zu einem Gründungsakt der Kunstwissenschaft als Bildwissenschaft gerät, obwohl er das disziplinäre Selbstverständnis des Faches über Jahrzehnte hinweg überhaupt nicht berührt hat. So heißt es etwa bei Horst Bredekamp: »Der Bilderatlas formuliert die Essenz der Kunstgeschichte als Bildwissenschaft.«[56] Ganz abgesehen davon, dass es eine gewagte These ist, Warburgs *Mnemosyne* sei für heutige Bildwissenschaften wesentlich oder gar verpflichtend, wird, anders als Bredekamp im Anschluss behauptet, in den 1930er Jahren keinesfalls eine bereits irgendwie etablierte Tradition namens Warburg abgebrochen. Vielmehr findet Warburgs Forschung schon vorher innerhalb des disziplinären Rahmens der Kunstwissenschaft nur mehr Beachtung in der vor allem von Erwin Panofsky fortgeführten Ikonologie[57] – welche jedoch unter gänzlich anderen Vorzeichen als bei Warburg betrieben wird und auch kaum als Gründungsfigur etwaiger Bildwissenschaften herhalten kann. Die verschiedentlich in Anspruch genommene Traditionslinie Warburg ist mithin nicht durch einen historischen Mangel an Überlieferung geprägt, sondern durch eine historiografische Zugabe an fachlicher Einigkeit. Diese Tradition liegt nicht vor, und wenn sie jetzt bemüht wird, ist sie das Kind ihrer, also unserer Zeit.

Historiografisch schlüssiger, wenngleich in erster Linie auf eine bloße Ausweitung des Gegenstandsbereiches beschränkt, erscheint die Einschätzung von Karen Michels, die in ihrer Warburg-Biografie *Im Bannkreis der Ideen* erklärt, gerade die Kunstwissenschaft habe »etwa aus der in den Atlas einbezogenen Gebrauchsgraphik [...] die entscheidende Anregung für die Erweiterung ihres Stoffgebiets und ihre jüngste Entwicklung zur ›Bildwissenschaft‹ bezogen.«[58] In der heutigen Kunstwissenschaft aber zeichnet sich kaum ein Konsens darüber ab, ob und in welchem Ausmaß Warburgs Forschungen überhaupt als Teil des disziplinären Erbes angesehen werden können. Die Kunstwissenschaft, welche sich rückwirkend einer solchen Tradition versichern will, um schon immer Bildwissenschaft gewesen sein zu können, kann die Vielfalt der Standpunkte, welche die heutige Kunstwissenschaft erlaubt, in gar keinem Fall vertreten. Tatsächlich verleiht das Label ›Kunstwissenschaft‹ den in ihrem Namen stattfindenden, mannigfaltigen wissenschaftlichen Praktiken nur mehr eine imaginäre Kohärenz. Darauf, dass es also eigentlich nicht die eine Kunstwissenschaft gibt, hat Belting indes schon vor langer Zeit aufmerksam gemacht: »So läuft denn alles darauf hinaus, mehrere Kunstgeschichten nebeneinander zu betreiben, in denen jeder seine eigenen Fragen stellen mag.«[59]

5. *Nosce te ipsum*: über Bilder und mit im Bilde sein

Die gegenwärtige Vereinnahmung Warburgs durch einige Kunstwissenschaftler, die im Namen der Bildwissenschaften von ›nicht-künstlerischen Bildern‹ reden, mag zweierlei Stoßrichtungen aufweisen: nach innen, um innerhalb der Kunstwissenschaft an Einfluss zu gewinnen, indem mannigfaltige wissenschaftliche Praktiken auf eben diese, vermeintlich oder tatsächlich zukunftsfähige Tradition verpflichtet werden; nach außen, um im Rahmen einer breit gefächerten Diskussion über etwaige Bildwissenschaften immer schon am Ziel gewesen zu sein. Ferner, dies wurde aufgezeigt, ist es ihnen ein Anliegen, den eigenen Verantwortungsbereich bis ins Unendliche auszuweiten und gleichzeitig den eigenen Methodenbereich bis ins Unendliche zu verschärfen, um für künstlerische Bildwelten exklusiv und für alle anderen privilegiert zuständig zu sein. Andere Bildforscher dürfen an Bildwissenschaften, was auch immer das im Einzelnen sei, nur teilnehmen, wenn sie sich dem kunstwissenschaftlichen Diskurs anverwandeln. Da dieser am Tropf der Formanalyse hängt, können eigentlich nur Kunstwissenschaftler Bildwissenschaften betreiben oder solche, die bei ihnen in die Schule gehen.

Vor einem solchen Schulbesuch ist jedoch, zumindest in Hinblick auf wissenschaftliche oder medizinische Bildwelten, eher abzuraten. Denn dort lernt man zwar viel und unbestritten Kompetentes über Stilgeschichte und Ikonografie, über Formen und Ähnlichkeiten, über Einflüsse und Ursprünge. Man lernt indes schon deutlich weniger über ›Bild als kulturelle Handlung‹. Wenn kulturelle Handlungen in den Blick geraten, dann ausschließlich solche, die in das Bild münden, also etwa: wissenschaftliche Theorien, technisch-apparative Voraussetzungen, soziokulturelle Einigungsprozesse, Bildtraditionen usf. Dabei ist erstens die fälschliche Annahme grundlegend, alles das Bild irgendwie Betreffende schreibe sich auf der Bildfläche ein; und zweitens wird davon ausgegangen, es sei auf dieser Bildfläche auch immer wieder eins zu eins zu bergen. Ein derartiger Bildflächenfetischismus vergisst, dass kulturelle Handlungen nicht nur für Bilder und auf Bildern, sondern auch mit Bildern stattfinden. Schließlich lernt man leider kaum etwas über Wissens- oder gar Wissenschaftskulturen oder etwaige in der Wissenschaftsgeschichtsschreibung erprobte Modi, diese angemessen zu erfassen.

In *Vom Bild zum Kunstsystem* heißt es: »Auch Kunsthistorik ist nicht davor gefeit, immer schon mit im Bild zu sein.«[60] Dies wird deutlich in der disziplinär markierten Rede von ›nicht-künstlerischen Bildern‹, die genau dasjenige in Frage stellt, was eigentlich in Angriff genommen wird, nämlich eine bildwissenschaftlich angemessene Auseinandersetzung mit unterschiedlichen Bildwelten: ›nicht-künstlerische Bilder‹ jedenfalls sind Bilder, die von Kunstwissenschaftlern, die sich als Bildwissenschaftler verstehen, nach den Regeln der Kunstwissenschaft untersucht werden. Dies wird ebenfalls deutlich in der nicht minder disziplinär markierten Rede von ›starken‹ und ›schwachen Bildern‹, die ihrerseits vergessen lässt, dass auch Maßstäbe jenseits einstudierter ästhetischer Lesarten an Bildern geltend gemacht werden können und dass diese in verschiedenen Bildkulturen gerade deshalb bedeutsam sind.

Eigentlich ist der Umstand, dass auch Kunstwissenschaft mit im Bild ist, legitim, da unausweichlich. Legitim ist aber auch das Anliegen dieses Beitrags. Es besteht darin, die oben skizzierte kunstwissenschaftliche Forschungspraxis, selbst wenn sie im Namen etwaiger Bildwissenschaften stattfindet, nicht mit solchen zu verwechseln.

---

1 Bruno Latour: »How to Be Iconophilic in Art, Science, and Religion?« In: C. A. Jones, P. Galison (Hg.): *Picturing Science, Producing Art*. New York/London 1998, S. 418–440, hier S. 417.

2 James Elkins: »Art History and Images That Are Not Art« In: *The Art Bulletin*, Vol. LXXVII, Dezember 1995, S. 553–571.

3 Eine terminologische Differenzierung zwischen ›Kunstgeschichte‹ und ›Kunstwissenschaft‹, wie sie systematisch plausibel und historisch manifest ist, findet hier nicht statt, da sie in der disziplinären Praxis der jeweilig so benannten Institute heutzutage keine konkrete Entsprechung mehr hat. Im Folgenden wird also – trotz einer zugegebenen historiografischen Unschärfe – ausschließlich von ›Kunstwissenschaft‹ die Rede sein.

4 Elkins 1995 (wie Anm. 2), S. 554.

5 Horst Bredekamp: »Bildwissenschaft« In: Ulrich Pfister (Hg.): *Metzler Lexikon Kunstwissenschaft. Ideen, Methoden, Begriffe*. Stuttgart 2003, S. 56–58, hier S. 56.

6 Gottfried Boehm: »Zwischen Auge und Hand. Bilder als Instrumente der Erkenntnis« In: Jörg Huber, Martin Heller (Hg.): *Konstruktionen Sichtbarkeiten*. Wien/New York 1999, S. 215–227, hier S. 216 f.

7 Dabei ergeben sich unter anderem folgende Kriterien: digital/analog, technisch-apparativ/manuell, transportabel/installativ, projiziert/appliziert, bewegt/unbewegt. Diese können ihrerseits etwa an CTs, Filmen, Fotografien, Radierungen, Kupferstichen, Gemälden oder Mosaiken geltend gemacht werden.

8 Dabei sind zum Beispiel folgende Kriterien erkenntnisleitend: intern/extern, imaginär/medial, ›picture‹/ ›image‹ (W. J. T. Mitchell: »Der Mehrwert von Bildern« In: Stefan Andriopoulos, Gabriele Schabacher, Eckhard Schumacher (Hg.): *Die Adresse des Mediums*. Köln 2001, S. 158–184), ›Bild‹/›Körper‹/›Medium‹ (Hans Belting: *Bild-Anthropologie. Entwürfe für eine Bildwissenschaft*. München 1999), ›tableau‹/›image‹ (Gernot Böhme: *Theorie des Bildes*. München 1999), ›Bildobjekt‹/›Bildträger‹ (Lambert Wiesing: *Artifizielle Präsenz. Studien zur Philosophie des Bildes*. Frankfurt/M. 2005).

9 Immer noch maßgeblich ist hier die Einteilung der Zeichen in ›Ikon‹/›Index‹/›Symbol‹, wie sie von Charles Sanders Pierce vorgenommen wurde. Vgl. dazu zuletzt: Beat Wyss: *Vom Bild zum Kunstsystem*. Band 1. Köln 2006.

10 Einerseits begünstigt eine solche Einteilung die Rede von ›bildmedialen Zeitaltern‹ – etwa: Herta Wolf: *Paradigma Fotografie. Fotokritik am Ende des fotografischen Zeitalters*. Frankfurt/M. 2002 –, andererseits von mehr oder weniger in sich geschlossenen bildkulturellen Epochen wie Mittelalter, Frühe Neuzeit, Moderne usf. Sie mag auch für nahezu geschichtsphilosophische Anverwandlungen herhalten, so etwa in: Régis Debray: *Jenseits der Bilder. Eine Geschichte der Bildbetrachtung im Abendland*. Rodenbach 1999. Bisweilen tendiert sie – wenngleich unter Zuhilfenahme vor allem medientechnischer Gesichtspunkte – dazu, vermeintlich ›traditionelle‹ gegen vermeintlich ›revolutionäre‹ Bilder und Bildwelten gegeneinander auszuspielen. Vgl. dazu kritisch: Anette Hüsch: »Ein Relikt vergangener Zeiten? Anmerkungen zum Begriff des traditionellen Bildes« In: Birgit Mersmann, Martin Schulz (Hg.): *Kulturen des Bildes*. München 2006, S. 345–353; sowie: Markus Buschhaus: »Am einen &

am anderen Ende der Gutenberg-Galaxis. Von Büchern, Bildern & Revolutionen« In: Sven Grampp u.a. (Hg.): *Revolutionsmedien – Medienrevolutionen*. Konstanz 2008 (im Druck).

11 Dabei stehen die Kulturen, in welchen Bilder verortet werden und durch welche sie zur Aufführung geraten, im Vordergrund, zum Beispiel also religiöse, wissenschaftliche oder auch künstlerische Bildwelten. Vgl. dazu: Mersmann, Schulz 2006 (wie Anm. 10), S. 9–17.

12 Elkins 1995 (wie Anm. 2).

13 Dazu stellvertretend Boris Groys: »Kunst besteht eben nicht nur aus Bildern [...]« (Boris Groys: *Topologie der Kunst*. München 2003, S. 27).

14 Dazu stellvertretend Elkins: »Most images are not art.« (Elkins 1995 (wie Anm. 2), S. 553).

15 Dazu kritisch: Susan Sontag: *Über Fotografie*. Frankfurt/M. 1980; sowie: Rosalind Krauss: *Das Fotografische. Eine Theorie der Abstände*. München 1998. Vgl. ferner Peter Geimer: »[...] in der retrospektiven Sichtung des Bildmaterials wurde die künstlerische Absicht jetzt auch solchen Fotografien unterstellt, deren historische Funktionen ganz andere gewesen waren.« (Peter Geimer: »Einleitung« In: Ders. (Hg.): *Ordnungen der Sichtbarkeit. Fotografie in Wissenschaft, Kunst und Technologie*. Frankfurt/M. 2002, S. 7–25, hier S. 11).

16 Belting 2001 (wie Anm. 8), S. 17.

17 Vgl. dazu etwa: Kristin Marek, Raphaèle Preisinger, Marius Rimmele, Katrin Kärcher (Hg.): *Bild und Körper im Mittelalter*. München 2006.

18 Boehm 1999 (wie Anm. 6), S. 227.

19 Horst Bredekamp, Gabriele Werner (Hg.): *Bildwelten des Wissens. Kunsthistorisches Jahrbuch für Bildkritik*. Berlin 2003.

20 Martin Kemp: *Bilderwissen. Die Anschaulichkeit naturwissenschaftlicher Phänomene*. Köln 2003.

21 Olaf Breidbach: *Bilder des Wissens. Zur Kulturgeschichte der wissenschaftlichen Wahrnehmung*. München 2005.

22 Inge Hinterwaldner, Markus Buschhaus (Hg.): *The Picture's Image. Wissenschaftliche Visualisierung als Komposit*. München 2006.

23 Christa Maar: »Envisioning knowledge – Die Wissensgesellschaft von morgen« In: Dies., Hans-Ulrich Obrist, Ernst Pöppel (Hg.): *Weltwissen – Wissenswelt. Das globale Netz von Text und Bild*. Köln 2000, S. 11–19, hier S. 15.

24 Bettina Heintz, Jörg Huber: »Der verführerische Blick: Formen und Folgen wissenschaftlicher Visualisierungsstrategien« In: Dies. (Hg.): *Mit dem Auge denken. Strategien der Sichtbarmachung in wissenschaftlichen und virtuellen Welten*. Wien/New York 2001, S. 9–37, hier S. 9.

25 Horst Bredekamp, Angela Fischel, Birgit Schneider, Gabriele Werner: »Bildwelten des Wissens« In: Bredekamp, Werner 2003 (wie Anm. 19), S. 9–20, hier S. 19.

26 Manfred Faßler: *Bildlichkeit. Navigationen durch das Repertoire der Sichtbarkeit*. Köln/Weimar/Wien 2002, S. 65.

27 So betont Snow nachdrücklich: »the scientific culture really is a culture, not only in an intellectual but also in an anthropological sense.« (C. P. Snow: *The two cultures and a second look*. Cambridge 1965, S. 9) Ein solcher Kulturbegriff muss ›Kultur‹ nicht mehr als Differenzkriterium etwa zu ›Zivilisation‹, ›Technik‹ oder ›Naturwissenschaften‹ denken. Vielmehr kann er die grundsätzlich kulturelle Verfasstheit auch dessen, was traditionell als außerhalb der Sphäre des Kulturellen befindlich verstanden wurde, betonen.

28 Einmal ganz abgesehen von systemtheoretischen Standards, denen diese eine ›umfassende Kultur einer Arbeit am Wissen‹ vollständig zuwiderläuft, ist auch der Wissensbegriff, wie er etwa von Michel Foucault geprägt worden ist, damit unvereinbar. Zwar bewegt sich das Wis-

sen gemäß Foucault quer zu verschiedenen Kulturen, doch findet es dort jeweils eine Spezifizierung. Dies zeigt sich in den Wissenschaften etwa dadurch, dass besagtes Wissen die Schwelle der Wissenschaftlichkeit überschreitet, indem es disziplinär spezifiziert und somit autorisiert wird. Vgl. dazu: Michel Foucault: *Archäologie des Wissens*. Frankfurt/M. 2002; sowie: Ders.: »Titel und Arbeiten« In: Ders.: *Schriften I*. Frankfurt/M. 2001, S. 1069–1075.

29 Darauf weist – unabhängig von Snows Ausführungen – etwa Lorenz Engell hin: »Das Verständnis der Kultur erscheint nun in abnehmendem Maße als Differenz zwischen dem, was Kultur ist und dem, was nicht Kultur ist, sondern zunehmend durch Binnendifferenzierung, nach innen hin, zwischen den verschiedenen Erscheinungsformen von Kultur.« (Lorenz Engell: »Ausfahrt nach Babylon. Die Genese der Medienkultur aus Einheit und Vielfalt« In: Ders.: *Ausfahrt nach Babylon. Essais und Vorträge zur Kritik der Medienkultur*. Weimar 2000, S. 263–303, hier S. 273).

30 Peter Geimer: »Weniger Schönheit. Mehr Unordnung. Eine Zwischenbemerkung zu ›Wissenschaft und Kunst‹« In: *Neue Rundschau*, 2003, Heft 3, S. 26–38, hier S. 33.

31 Von in der Tat unzähligen Arbeiten seien hier lediglich drei angeführt: Lovis Premuda: *Storia dell'iconografia anatomica*. Mailand 1957 – Bernard Schultz: *Art and anatomy in Renaissance Italy*. Ann Arbor 1985 – Harald Moe: *The art of anatomical illustration in the Renaissance and Baroque periods*. Rhodos/Copenhagen 1995.

32 So wirft dieser 1931 die Frage auf, »ob die Entdeckung der Perspektive als eines außerkünstlerischen Prinzips nicht als ein störendes Moment in die Malerei gekommen ist, ob nicht mit der Perspektive eine jener Bedrohungen gekommen ist, wie hernach mit Anatomie und Richtigkeit.« (Theodor Hetzer: *Zur Geschichte des Bildes von der Antike bis Cézanne*. Stuttgart 1998, S. 59)

33 Panofsky stimmt in den Chor jener mit ein, die die Ausformung einer professionellen Anatomie mit derjenigen einer professionellen Kunst verwechseln, wenn er ausführt: »it has been said, not without justification, that in the Renaissance the greatest advances in natural science were made by engineers, instrument-makers and artists rather than professors.« (Erwin Panofsky: »Artist, scientist, genius: notes on the ›Renaissance-Dämmerung‹« In: Wallace K. Ferguson (Hg.): *The Renaissance: Six essays*. New York/Evanston 1962, S. 123–182, hier S. 136).

34 Vgl. dazu: Markus Buschhaus: *Über den Körper im Bilde sein. Eine Medienarchäologie anatomischen Wissens*. Bielefeld 2005, S. 220–234.

35 Faßler 2002 (wie Anm. 26), S. 55.

36 Mersmann, Schulz 2006 (wie Anm. 10), S. 13.

37 Groys 2003 (wie Anm. 13), S. 27.

38 Ebd., S. 23.

39 Ebd., S. 39.

40 Vgl.: Markus Buschhaus: »Re-Installationen. Portrait of this mortal coil & die Orte der Röntgenbilder« In: Torsten Seidel, Friederike Meyer (Hg.): *Röntgenportrait*. Berlin 2005, S. 79–89.

41 Geimer 2003 (wie Anm. 30), S. 31.

42 Boehm 1999 (wie Anm. 6), S. 227.

43 Wyss 2006 (wie Anm. 9), S. 262.

44 Boehm 1999 (wie Anm. 6), S. 227.

45 Bredekamp, Fischel, Schneider, Werner 2003 (wie Anm. 25), S. 7.

46 Ebd.

47 Ebd.

48 Georges Canguilhem: »Der Gegenstand der Wissenschaftsgeschichte« In: Ders.: *Wissenschaftsgeschichte und Epistemologie*. Gesammelte Aufsätze. Frankfurt/M. 2002, S. 22–37, hier S. 29.

49 Ebd., S. 30.

50 Kemp 2003 (wie Anm. 20), S. 15.

51 Ebd.

52 Thomas S. Kuhn: »Bemerkungen zum Verhältnis von Wissenschaft und Kunst« In: Ders.: *Die Entstehung des Neuen. Studien zur Struktur der Wissenschaftsgeschichte*. Frankfurt/M. 1978, S. 446–460, hier S. 447.

53 Vgl. diesbezüglich: Hinterwaldner, Buschhaus 2006 (wie Anm. 22), S. 9–19.

54 Vgl. etwa: Belting 2001 (wie Anm. 8), S. 15 f. – Thomas Hensel: »›Von der Kunstgeschichte zur Wissenschaft vom Bilde‹ (Aby Warburg) oder von der Geburt der Bildwissenschaft aus Sendetrommeln, Karoluszellen und Stromschwankungen.« In: Silke Walther (Hg.): *Carte Blanche. Mediale Formate in der Kunst der Moderne*. Berlin 2007, S. 131–167. – Martin Schulz: *Ordnungen der Sichtbarkeit. Eine Einführung in die Bildwissenschaft*. München 2005, S. 29–49. – Wyss 2006 (wie Anm. 9), S. 101–110.

55 Christoph Conrad, Martina Kessel: »Blickwechsel: Moderne, Kultur, Geschichte« In: Dies. (Hg.): *Kultur und Geschichte. Neue Einblicke in eine alte Beziehung*. Stuttgart 1998, S. 9–40, hier S. 24.

56 Bredekamp 2003 (wie Anm. 5), S. 57.

57 Vgl. insbesondere: Schulz 2005 (wie Anm. 54), S. 38 ff.

58 Karen Michels: *Aby Warburg. Im Bannkreis der Ideen*. München 2007, S. 115.

59 Hans Belting: *Das Ende der Kunstgeschichte. Eine Revision nach 10 Jahren*. München 1995, S. 164. Zu den vielfältigen, teils widersprüchlichen wissenschaftlichen Praktiken, die heute unter ›Kunstwissenschaft‹ laufen, vgl. insbesondere: Jutta Held, Norbert Schneider: *Grundzüge der Kunstwissenschaft. Gegenstandsbereiche – Institutionen – Problemfelder*. Köln/Weimar/Wien 2007.

60 Wyss 2006 (wie Anm. 9), S. 75.

Marius Rimmele

Bildwissenschaften und Mittelalter

›Bildwissenschaften‹ sind ein derart breites und vielfältig bestelltes Feld, dass der Blick auf die Zusammenhänge von Mittelalterforschung und allgemeinen Bildfragen manchen als ein sehr spezielles, ja marginales Unterfangen erscheinen könnte. Nun ist die historische Erforschung einer jeden Bildkultur im weiteren Sinne Bildwissenschaft, die eben den Einzelfall des Bildgebrauchs, der Bildsprache, des Bildkonzepts analysiert. In einer Dreiteilung, wie sie etwa Hans-Dieter Huber vorschlägt, lassen sich diese Fragen einer dritten Klasse, der »historischen Bildwissenschaft« zuordnen, die »unter Absehung des Allgemeinen und des Medienspezifischen« den Versuch unternimmt, »den historischen Wandel von Bildern in ihrem Verhältnis zu bestimmten, historischen Beobachtern und bestimmten historischen Milieus und Lebensstilen zu rekonstruieren«.[1]

1. Steinbruch Mittelalter

Nahe liegend ist zunächst auch, sich der besonderen Rahmenbedingungen einer Bildkultur zu erinnern, die zwischen den Polen des nur bedingt außer Kraft gesetzten biblischen Bilderverbots – man bedenke nur die lang anhaltende Ächtung dreidimensionaler Bildwerke und den legitimatorischen Aufwand bei deren Wiedereinführung[2] – und den auf das Bild ausgreifenden Realpräsenzen oszilliert, wie sie die Eucharistie und das Reliquienwesen darstellen.[3] Auch im Hinblick auf den Aspekt irrational anmutender »response«[4] steht das Mittelalter als Asservatenkammer für die Theoriebildung zur Verfügung: Es liegt nahe, in den Bildwundern und belegten wie unterstellten animistischen Bildpraktiken des Mittelalters aufschlussreiche Ausprägungen derjenigen Wirkmacht der Bilder zu vermuten, die ihnen zu allen Zeiten potentiell und im erhitzten Diskurs um die heutigen Bilder im Besonderen zugesprochen wird. Die interessantesten Ansätze gehen dabei trotz einer Unterscheidbarkeit der Bildkulturen von einer im Bild bzw. im Prozess der Repräsentation selbst verankerten Doppelung von Präsenz/Lebendigkeit und Absenz/Bezeichnung als Grunderfahrung aus, deren Einsicht durchaus auch den ›primitiven‹ Geistern zuzusprechen ist.[5] Im Sinne von Hartmut Böhmes Betonung einer (verdrängten) kulturellen Notwendigkeit des Fetischismus, und des gerne zitierten Bonmots von Bruno Latour, dass die Menschen nie modern gewesen seien, sind die hier angesprochenen mittelalterlichen Bildpraktiken weniger als jederzeit wieder drohende pathologische Entgleisungen zu analysieren.[6] Sie folgen wahrscheinlicher kaum minder als heutige Handlungsweisen einer anthropologischen und sozialen Notwendigkeit, bestimmten Bildern Wirkmacht zuzusprechen. Dies ist im Kern auch der Ansatz von W.J.T. Mitchells *What do pictures want?*, der von einer »Unheilbarkeit« des fetischistischen Komplexes ausgeht und nach den Möglichkeiten der Bildforschung sucht, eine Transformation in möglichst ungefährliche Ausprägungen zu bewerkstelligen.[7]

Besonders lohnend scheinen solche Rückgriffe auf das Mittelalter auch, weil es sich um die eigene Vergangenheit, den Wurzelgrund heutiger Bildbegriffe und -konzepte handelt. So betonte bereits Kurt Bauch 1960 in seinem bildwissenschaftlich kanonisierten Aufsatz zur *Imago*, »daß wir erst in der Schicht des Mittelalters auf die Entscheidungen treffen, die das Bild bestimmen, das heute fragwürdig erscheint. Damals ist alles Frühere verwandelt, alles Folgende begründet worden, bis heute.«[8] Es leuchtet unmittelbar ein, dass etwa Forschungen, die das historische wie systematische Verhältnis deiktischer Dimensionen in Schrift und Bild anpeilen, an den höchst interessanten Mischungsverhältnissen etwa im mittelalterlichen Manuskript nicht vorbei kommen.[9]

2. Mediävistik als Modell und Laboratorium

Nicht weniger, aber auch nicht mehr scheint sich hier demnach präsentieren zu lassen, als eine historische Bildkultur, die punktuell durchaus paradigmatischen Wert aufweist und sicher gewisse Auswirkungen bis heute zeitigt.

So wird es manchen überraschen, dass gerade die Mediävistik in der Kunstgeschichte offenbar für eine bildwissenschaftliche Öffnung ausschlaggebend war. Horst Bredekamp betont an programmatischer Stelle, dass die Mittelalterforschung, »die keine Einschränkung ihres Gegenstandsbereiches kannte [...] das Modell einer genuinen B[ildwissenschaft] war und bis heute geblieben ist«.[10] Sie hat im Verein mit Kunstgewerbe und Fotografie als Forschungsinteressen im 19. Jahrhundert unter dem Signum eines unspezifischen Kunstbegriffs zu einer Bildwissenschaft *avant la lettre* geführt, d.h. für Bredekamp vorrangig: zu einer wissenschaftlichen Beschäftigung mit visuellen Artefakten jedweder Stilhöhe und Materialität.[11] Nach einer Verschmälerung sowohl des Kunstbegriffs als auch der konsensfähigen Forschungsinteressen der Kunstgeschichte sieht Bredekamp auch die erneute Zuwendung zu den unkünstlerischen Bildern seit den 70er Jahren unter mediävistischen Vorzeichen.[12] Damit ist nicht gesagt, dass nicht bestimmte gesellschaftliche und wissenschaftliche Kurswechsel ebenfalls eine Erweiterung und Verschiebung der Perspektive von der Hochkunst auf die Bildwelten der Alltagskultur und der Wissenschaft hätten bewirken müssen. Entscheidend ist jedoch die Methodenfrage bzw. die prominente Problematik disziplinärer Zuständigkeiten. Die Mediävistik als proto-bildwissenschaftlicher Stachel im Fleisch der Kunstgeschichte war und ist Teil des Kanons und Curriculums. Daraus folgt – so lässt sich Bredekamps Diktum interpretieren –, dass man die heterodoxen Gegenstände ganz selbstverständlich auch z.B. einem formalen Zugang unterworfen hat. Im hauseigenen Laboratorium der Mittelalterforschung wurden und werden so besehen Kompetenzen geschult, die Routinen des Faches für Bildsphären *jenseits* der Kunst zu adaptieren, wofür die Kunstgeschichte für Bredekamp ja aufgrund ihrer historischen und formalen Kompetenzen privilegiert erscheint.

Andere haben über die Herausforderungen durch das mediävistische Material vorrangig ein Interesse für *neue Fragestellungen* entwickelt, die letztlich gravierender als eine Ausweitung der Gegenstandsbereiche aus dem kanonischen Feld kunsthistorischer Fragen herausführen bzw. sich anschicken, dieses zu verändern.

3. Mittelalterliche Bilder als Provokation kunsthistorischer Routinen

Das mittelalterliche Material verlangte offenbar, frühneuzeitliche und insbesondere dem Idealismus des 19. Jahrhunderts geschuldete Kategorien[13] hintanzustellen und provozierte stattdessen Fragen nach der intendierten Funktion, dem medialen Status und den vielfältigen Formen der Bildpraxis und Rezeption vor dem Hintergrund sozialhistorischer und anthropologischer Parameter. In Parenthese sei bemerkt, dass die fachinterne methodologische Diskussion immer noch von der offensichtlichen Andersartigkeit derjenigen Bilder profitiert, die sich aufgrund der komplexen Repräsentationsvorschriften des Christentums vermeintlich selbstverständlichen Normen verweigern. Wie Georges Didi-Huberman betont hat, betrifft dies z.B. die für die meisten Renaissancebilder durchaus zielführende Vorstellung, dass vorrangig handelnde Körper vor weniger bedeutsamen Hintergründen im Sinne einer ›Theaterhandlung‹ das Wesentliche eines Bildes vermittelten.[14] Im Gegensatz dazu weisen viele mittelalterliche Bilder allegorische Strukturelemente auf, die sich im Zusammenspiel von Vorder- und Hintergrund bzw. unter völliger Absehung von Gegenstandsgrenzen entfalten, ergänzt um suggestive Leerstellen bewusster Figurationsverweigerung.

Die – gemessen an kunstgeschichtlichen Interpretationsstandards – immer noch heterodoxen Strategien mittelalterlich-christlicher Bilder sind umsoweniger im *common sense* ›bildwissenschaftlicher‹ Theoriebildung angekommen. Zusammen mit den epistemischen Bildern der Wissenschaft stellen sie eine produktive Herausforderung für die oft unausgesprochen an hochkünstlerischen (Abb-)bildern orientierten Paradigmen etwa der philosophischen Definitionsansätze dar.[15]

Das Verhältnis von Bildsyntax und Bildsemantik ist jedoch nur ein spezieller Aspekt neben solchen, die prinzipiellere Geltung beanspruchen können. Die Leistung einzelner Künstler und das ›Wie‹ der Bilder, die den Blick auf die Kunst ab und seit der frühen Neuzeit durchaus mit Recht präokkupieren, treten – ohne für das Mittelalter ungültig zu sein – zwangsläufig zurück. Stattdessen stellt sich die Frage nach dem ›Was‹, dem ›Wo‹ und dem ›Wozu‹ des Bildes, nach Präsenzen, »äußeren Zugangsbedingungen«[16] einschließlich (para)liturgischer Kontexte und Bildbedürfnissen mit nicht zu ignorierendem Nachdruck. Nicht nur im Hinblick auf die Breite der Gegenstände tendiert mediävistische Bildforschung dazu, eine ›visuelle Kultur‹ ins Auge zu fassen.

Ausgehend von Hans Beltings Forschungen lässt sich einiges vom kulturwissenschaftlichen und medientheoretischen Mehrwert präzisieren, den die Mittelalterforschung erwirtschaftet hat. Mit seinem Ansatz einer ›Bild-Anthropologie‹ berücksichtigt man eine im Vergleich zu Bredekamp differierende bildwissenschaftliche Position in der deutschen Kunstgeschichte, die eher in methodologischer Hinsicht die Tendenz zeigt, aus dem Kanon herauszuführen.[17] Beat Wyss hat das Erscheinen von Hans Beltings Buch *Bild und Kult* (1990) in einen Zusammenhang mit einer »epochalen Sinnkrise« des Bildbewusstseins gestellt, die später unter dem Banner des ›pictorial turn‹ das bildwissenschaftliche Großprojekt stimulieren sollte.[18] Er erkennt eine Relevanz bzw. Symptomatik des Buches vor dem Hintergrund einer durch die Digitalisierung angestoßenen Neuverhandlung des Wahrheitsversprechens der Bilder. Weniger die Ästhetik der Bilder, als ihre mehr oder minder symbolische Stellvertretung des Heiligen sowie die sich an die Bilder heftenden Begehrens- und Verhaltensstrukturen und auch die Berücksichtigung der spezifischen Medialität standen mit diesem Werk neu im Fokus.

An Beltings Publikationen selbst lässt sich der Fortgang der angestoßenen Bewegungen ablesen: Zum Ersten hat er daraus ein Spektrum von bildanthropologischen Fragen gewonnen, das sich weit über eine historische Bildgattung oder -kultur hinaus erstreckt und nur im Zusammenspiel verschiedenster Disziplinen zu analysieren ist.

Wesentliche Fragen betreffen aber durchaus auch die Bilder im Zentrum der Kunstgeschichte, insofern sich in ihnen Verhandlungen über den Körper-Medien-Bezug, die Wahrnehmung, Ortsfragen des Bildes und grundlegende Repräsentationsdiskurse manifestieren. Dass die Bilder zuweilen explizit Theorie verhandeln, steht neben der Medienfrage in einem weiteren Folgebuch, das der frühniederländischen Malerei[19] gewidmet ist, im Zentrum.

Die hier behauptete Genese der Bild-Anthropologie aus den mediävistischen Forschungen wird nicht nur vom Autor eingeräumt,[20] sondern lässt sich an zahlreichen Beispielen, wie auch an Denkmodellen nachweisen – etwa einem Transfer von Bildern zwischen äußeren Medien und dem Körper als Bildträger –, die aus der mittelalterlichen Theoriebildung gewonnen sein könnten, sich mit dieser zumindest höchst kommensurabel zeigen.[21] Auch auf die hoch aktuellen mittelalterlichen Einsichten zum Verhältnis von materiellen Bildern, mentalen Repräsentationen und epistemologischen Fragen wird noch kurz zurückzukommen sein.

Das echte Bild (2005) hingegen verfolgt ätiologisch die in Spätantike und Mittelalter gesetzten und in modifizierter Form immer noch virulenten Erwartungen und Problemstellungen rund um das Bild bezüglich einer ›richtigen‹ Repräsentation. Etwas quer zur heute noch umstrittenen Frage in der Philosophie, ob man ein Bild besser als Zeichen oder als artifizielle Präsenz adressiert,[22] verfolgt Belting dabei auch die historischen Streitigkeiten um das Verhältnis zwischen dem potentiell präsentischen Bild und seinen semiologischen Disziplinierungsversuchen nach. Das mediävistische Wissen wird hier also in seiner kulturgeschichtlichen Dimension fruchtbar gemacht, um aktuelle Bilddiskurse zu erhellen. Halten wir bezüglich einer dritten Berührung von Mediävistik und Bildwissenschaft fest, dass zahlreiche Fragen, welche die Trennlinie zwischen Kultbildsphäre und Kunstsystem hervorgetrieben hat, sich als höchst relevant erweisen, um die anthropologische Rolle des Bildes[23] überhaupt in den Blick zu nehmen und zu verstehen. Dazu gehört auch eine über Kommunikationsaspekte hinaus zu befragende Medialität des Bildes als materielle Verkörperung und Verortung von etwas Imaginärem in seinem vielfältigen Bezug auf den Körper des Menschen. Rezente, von Beltings Ansatz ausgehende Forschungen belegen, dass sich selbst moderne Bildpraxen, wie die private Fotografie und deren Erinnerungskulte, in überraschende Traditionslinien des Medien-Körper-Bezugs einrücken lassen.[24] Natürlich sind solche Fragestellungen nur *ein* Feld innerhalb der Bildwissenschaften, wie auch das Kultbild alleine nicht in der Lage ist, *das* mittelalterliche Bildkonzept in der Kunstgeschichte zu repräsentieren.[25] Gerade die Forschung zur Bilderzählung, die naturgemäß auf eine ganz andere Klasse mittelalterlicher Bilder abzielt, hat mit der *Wiener Genesis* ihren Ausgang in einer Handschrift des 6. Jahrhunderts genommen und findet ihre komplexesten Gegenstände in der experimentierfreudigen Zeit zwischen der Ablösung des »distinguierenden Stils« nach Wickhoff und dessen dogmatischer Neuetablierung in der Renaissance.[26]

Auch kann man kritisch einwenden, dass bildanthropologische Ansätze dazu tendieren, auf der Suche nach Analogien begriffliche Differenzen einzuebnen, anstatt sich in Begriffsschärfung zu üben.[27] Doch auch wenn man den Status des materiellen Bildes in einem Geflecht von Symbolisierungen, Wahrnehmung und kognitiven Aspekten ins Auge fassen möchte, also epistemologische Fragen verfolgt, sieht man sich mit einer Weite des Bildbegriffs konfrontiert, der sich nicht im diskurshygienischen Handstreich erledigen lässt, ohne zentrale Zusammenhänge von vornherein auszuschließen.

4. Epistemologische Fragen an die Bilder und mittelalterliche Theorien

Wie bereits angedeutet, lassen sich gerade im Mittelalter die Ursprünge für heutige Begriffsunschärfen finden.[28] Für bildwissenschaftliche Fragen dürften dabei die möglichen Einsichten von vorrangigem Interesse sein, die hinter solchen Äquivokationen stehen. Der Religionshistoriker Thomas Lentes hat das (mittelalterliche) Christentum als eine »Religion des Bildes« bezeichnet.[29] Eine solche muss sich mit dem Bild notwendig theoretisch auseinandersetzen, wenn auch nicht zwingend auf den Feldern, die man als erstes vermuten würde. Explizite Bildtheorie, die sich aufs materielle Artefakt richtet, ist verhältnismäßig rar, zumindest aber wenig aufschlussreich. Auch wenn gewaltige kollektive Denkanstrengungen auf benachbarten Feldern unter den heute problematisch erscheinenden Setzungen der Theologie unternommen wurden – sie können doch stimulierend sein, als bildwissenschaftliches Forschungsfeld in der Mediävistik wie als Inspirationsquelle für aktuelle Bildtheorien. Seit Thomas S. Kuhn weiß man, dass im Verlauf von Paradigmenwechseln nicht alles nur besser erklärbar wird, sondern manche Fragen auch einfach aus dem Blickfeld verschwinden. So gesehen braucht man sich im Blick zurück auf mittelalterliche Theorien nicht unbedingt Antworten zu erhoffen – so manche alte Frage kann bereits neue Impulse geben. Aus dem verwirrenden Bündel der eng miteinander verwobenen mittelalterlichen Bildkonzeptionen kann ich hier nur zwei Knotenpunkte benennen, die beide eine epistemologische Dimension aufweisen: die Frage der Abbildhaftigkeit bzw. der Vorbild-Verhältnisse und die Problematik ›innerer Bilder‹.

Nicht nur die problematische Grenzziehung zu den eucharistischen Gestalten und die die eigene Identität stets bedrohende Idolatrie haben große Anstrengungen in der Theoriebildung bzw. Adaption präexistenter (insbesondere platonischer) Bildphilosophien abverlangt.[30] Vielmehr zeigt sich auch in der sprachlichen Verschleifung von materiellen Artefakten, anthropologischen Wesensbestimmungen sowie moralisch-ethischen Nachahmungsverhältnissen, dass der Bildbegriff im Mittelalter von essentieller Bedeutung war: Der Mensch als prekäres Ebenbild Gottes (Gen 1,26–27) und Christus als wahres Ebenbild (z. B. Kol 1,15) sowie das alles überspannende »Drama der Ähnlichkeit« (Didi-Huberman), also das heilsnotwendige Angleichen an das Vor-Bild Christi bis zum Gericht, machen die mittelalterliche Existenz zu einer Bilderfrage.[31] Das Bewusstsein mittelalterlicher Denker, selbst in einem Abbildverhältnis zum Göttlichen (als Objekt der Erkenntnis) zu stehen und dabei neben dieser als (abgestuften) Teilhabe begriffenen eigenen Verfasstheit nur noch auf eine ebenso bildhafte Schöpfung zurückgreifen zu können, deutet der Philosoph Johann Kreuzer als bemerkenswerte Einsicht in eine unhintergehbare Bildverhaftetheit des Menschen.[32] Auf einer abstrakt-epistemologischen Ebene fühlt man sich an W.J.T. Mitchell erinnert, der in seiner neusten Publikation aus der Einsicht in die nicht zu umgehende Verflochtenheit des Menschen in seine Bildwelten methodologische Konsequenzen ziehen will. Dazu gehört es, den ikonoklastischen Gestus ›entlarvender‹ Bildkritik (etwa im Feld der *visual culture*) zu überwinden:

> »This would be a mode of criticism that did not dream of getting beyond images, beyond representation, of smashing the false images that bedevil us, or even of producing a definitive separation between true and false images.«[33]

Doch mit der Ebenbildlichkeitsfrage sind zweifellos noch weitere, konkretere ›Bilder‹ verknüpft und spätestens in solchen Zusammenhängen sehen nicht mehr nur die Philosophen Parallelen zu aktuellen Forschungsdesideraten: So hat man Heilige, Lehrer und Standespersonen oder historische Exempel als ›Bilder‹ verstanden und damit als Spiegel, mit denen man sich umgestaltend auseinanderzusetzen hat, an denen das Selbst sich konstituiert.[34] Auch blieben der Abbildstatus des Menschen und die sichtbare Offenbarung Gottes als Dreh- und Angelpunkte mittelalterlicher Bildkonzeptionen in ihrer Bedeutung nicht auf das Kreatürliche oder auf seine soziale Dimension beschränkt: Jede Betrachtung eines Bildes, so die religiösen Anleitungen, soll nicht nur von der Einsicht in die Vermitteltheit der Repräsentation, sondern zugleich auch von einer Reflexion über die Vorbildhaftigkeit des Dargestellten und den eigenen Bildstatus im biographischen Fortschritt, z. B. von »Entbildung, Einbildung und Überbildung«[35] begleitet werden. Denn jedes materielle Bild wird vor diesem Hintergrund nicht nur zur Allegorie der kreatürlichen und kerygmatischen Bildbeziehungen, sondern wird immer auch als eine appellative Konkretion in einem wahren Koordinatensystem von Fluchtungen wahrgenommen. Als spätes, aber für frühere Konzeptionen durchaus symptomatisches Beispiel sei aus der *Tewtschen Theologey* des Bischofs Berthold Pürstinger (1465–1543) zitiert, der den angemessenen Blick auf eine Darstellung der Verkündigung einübt: »Aus anschawen des pildes mag einer bewegt werden danckzesagen, daz got zuo seiner gleichnuss ain solhe heilige pildnusz, als maria an jrselbs ist, beschaffen hat, vnd daneben mariam anrueeffen, daz sy als vormundinn von got erlang rainigung vnserr vermailigten pildnusz.«[36] Insbesondere die Forschung zur *Vera Ikon* als überdeterminiertem Knotenpunkt der verschiedenen, aber aufeinander bezogenen Bilddiskurse belegt die Virulenz solcher Verweisungen auch am Beispiel des Christusporträts, gesteuert durch ablassträchtige und damit massenhaft rezipierte Gebetstexte.[37]

In dieselbe Logik einbeschlossen war die normative Kraft exemplarischer Geschehnisse, etwa im Zuge typologischer und tropologischer Auslegungen, die nicht nur analytische, sondern durchaus auch handlungssteuernde Wirksamkeit entfalten konnten.[38] Auch hier konkretisiert sich das Denkmuster im Bild. Bereits Erich Auerbach hat die Frage formuliert, inwieweit »das Kunstwerk als figura einer noch unerreichbaren Erfüllungswirklichkeit aufgefaßt wird.«[39]

Vom dialogischen Andachtsbild[40] oder der symbolischen Inszenierung eines Herrschers über Exempla aus Natur und Geschichte bis zur anthropologischen (und damit zugleich erkenntnistheoretischen) Wesensbestimmung des Menschen – alles funktioniert im Bewusstsein einer Nachbildung als ontisch abgestufter Teilhabe, die zugleich aktuelle Apellfunktion hat und stets auf ein zukünftig zu realisierendes Ideal bezogen bleibt. Hinter den Analogien scheint eine jede Metaphorik übersteigende Einsicht in strukturelle Analogien und Bedingtheiten zu stehen. Bilder – seien es gemalte oder im Sinne von Nachahmungs- und Vorbildverhältnissen – werden mit hohem Bewusstheitsgrad als Schnittstellen wahrgenommen. Sie vermitteln zwischen kollektiv geteilten (und göttlich sanktionierten) Normen und dem Individuum, das sich in der Welt zu orientieren und als Bild im Prozess der Bearbeitung selbst umzugestalten hat. So besehen fordert Bischof Pürstinger mit dem Umschlagen von der Wahrnehmung zur Reflexion verschiedener Bildverhältnisse nicht nur eine reflexartige Entmächtigung des Weltlichen ein. Die Aufforderung zeugt genauso von zeitlos relevanten Einsichten in die notwendige Bildverhaftetheit der Erfahrung und das Eingebundensein in bildlich strukturierte Rahmenbedingungen der Erkenntnis. So verspricht die Koppelung von materiellen, kreatürlichen, normativen und epistemischen Bildverhältnissen hohe Aktualität für all diejenigen bildwissenschaftlichen Positionen, die Einblicke in die epistemologische und kognitionspsychologische Dynamik von Bildbezügen anstreben.[41] Hier widmet man sich der Frage, wie die wahrnehmbaren Bilder an der kollektiven und individuellen ›Welt-Bildung‹ beteiligt sind, also immer schon in ein Geflecht von phänomenologischen und hermeneutischen Prozessen, überlebensnotwendigen Vorurteilen, kognitiv essentiellen Stereotypisierungen, Symbolisierungen und Nachahmungsdynamiken eingebunden bleiben.[42] Auch das ständige Denken in Analogien und häufig irritierend ontologisierten Metaphern sollte uns nicht nur zum Schmunzeln bringen. Es mag nach Foucault die *episteme* einer vergangenen Epoche sein, aber das heißt nicht, dass dahinter nicht wichtige Einsichten in die Art und Weise kognitiver Welterschließung stehen.[43]

Der Kulturwissenschaftler Thomas Macho hat jüngst erst auf die bislang theoretisch vernachlässigte Dimension des *in die Zukunft gerichteten Bildes* hingewiesen. Es steuert Handlungen als normatives Ideal, bei Platon bereits im Denkmuster eines Züchtungsideals entworfen.[44] Die mittelalterliche Theorie hat in ihren Bildkonzeptionen diesem Aspekt, der nach Macho in heutigen virtuellen und bildpragmatischen Zusammenhängen wieder von höchster Relevanz ist, einen enormen Stellenwert beigemessen.

Es ist zu vermuten, dass sowohl eine Reflexionsgeschichte »ikonischer Episteme« wie sie etwa Gottfried Boehm verfolgt,[45] als auch eine ihrer eigenen Beschränktheit bewusste Bildkritik im Sinne Mitchells von den Ergebnissen mittelalterlicher Reflexion über ›Bild und Wahrheit‹ durchaus profitieren dürften. Dabei sind es keineswegs nur die theologischen Auseinandersetzungen mit dem unter Metaphernverdacht stehenden Bildbegriff der Ebenbildlichkeitsfrage, sondern natürlich auch explizit epistemologische Reflexionen unter Einschluss materieller oder mentaler Bilder in einer symboltheoretischen und mnemotechnischen Traditionslinie, welche sich bildwissenschaftlicher Erschließung anbieten.[46] So betrachtet etwa Lentes in einem skizzierten Forschungsprogramm – neben der für einen Historiker überraschenden Betonung bildimmanenter Reflexionsleistungen – den Zugang über die Wahrnehmungstheorien als Desideratum und potentiellen Königsweg in einer an schriftlichen Quellen zum materiellen Bild eher armen Kultur.[47] Durchaus beachtlich ist nämlich der theoretische Aufwand, der im Mittelalter der Wahrnehmung sowie dem Wesen innerer Bilder (Imaginationen, künstliche und natürliche Gedächtnisbilder, *phantasmata* als Grundlage des Denkens) und deren Zusammenhängen untereinander gewidmet wurde.[48] Sowohl die unterstellte Materialität des Sehvorgangs[49] als auch die enormen Auswirkungen, die man der Imagination bis in die frühe Neuzeit zubilligte,[50] lassen die heute oft vorgenommene Trennung zwischen mentalen und äußeren Bildern als höchst problematische Distinktion erscheinen, was sich mit aktuellen Erkenntnissen der Neurowissenschaften ebenso deckt wie mit phänomenologischen Bildtheorien.[51] Die meisten der genannten Aspekte bieten sich einer eher kulturgeschichtlichen Forschung an, erlangen aber durchaus auch Relevanz für kunsthistorische Studien. So lässt sich z.B. nach den subtilen Strategien fragen, mit denen Andachtsbilder – also Vorlagen für eine innere Bildproduktion – auf ihren endgültigen Speicher im Inneren des Gläubigen bezogen werden. Insofern hier Gestaltungsstrategien und Semantisierung von Trägermedien anschließen, sind damit sogar im engsten Sinne kunsthistorische Interessen berührt.[52]

5. Was wäre der kunstwissenschaftliche Beitrag zu einer mediävistischen Bildwissenschaft?

Auch wenn die Kunstgeschichte schon immer recht flexibel fachfremde Ansätze und Theorien aufgegriffen hat – Bredekamp hat gute Gründe, gewisse formale Sensibilitäten ins Zentrum kunsthistorischer Kompetenz zu stellen. Genauso bleibt die Frage nach der Kunst prekär. Wie betreibt man als Kunsthistoriker mit mittelalterlichem Material ›Bildwissenschaft‹, ohne zu dilettieren oder sich zwingend an den äußeren Rändern seines Faches zu positionieren? Was können Kunsthistoriker beitragen, das andere kulturhistorisch ausgerichtete Forscher nicht auch oder gar besser könnten, jetzt, wo die Bildfrage allein keine Disziplin mehr konturieren kann?

Eine mögliche Antwort[53] ist aus der Debatte um die heuristische Rolle des Kunstbildes zu gewinnen bzw. aus dem Abarbeiten einer Disziplin namens ›Kunst-geschichte‹ am »unerledigten Problem« der Grundspannung zwischen künstlerisch-ästhetischer und historisch rekontextualisierender Betrachtung von Bildern.[54] Methodologisch lässt sich hier eine weitere prominente Strömung kunsthistorischer Bildwissenschaft anführen, die Steffen Bogen in einer Übersichtsdarstellung »bildwissenschaftliche Kunsthistoriker« getauft hat. Sozusagen aus dem Herzen der Kunstgeschichte wird hier die »offene Frage nach der Kunst über die ebenso offene Frage nach dem Bild« neu verhandelt.[55] So hat etwa Gottfried Boehm häufiger den besonderen Wert der Kunst des 20. Jahrhunderts betont, wenn es um die Reflexion dessen geht, was ein Bild ausmacht.[56] Viele Kunstbilder gelten in diesem Sinne als ›starke Bilder‹, die einen weitaus höheren epistemischen Wert aufweisen als andere. Moderne Kunst ist anerkanntermaßen selbstbezüglich und damit theoriehaltig. Kunstinterpretation wird folgerichtig zur praktizierten Bildtheorie, auch in der Tradition von Imdahls ›Ikonik‹ als einer in formaler Hinsicht höchst sensiblen Befragung der Bilder nach ihrer »Identität und Nichtsubstituierbarkeit«.[57] Nun hat Victor I. Stoichitas bahnbrechende Studie zur Metamalerei die historische ›Ausdehnung‹ des Konzepts vom theoriehaltigen Bild bis zum Beginn des frühneuzeitlichen Kunstsystems zurück evident gemacht.[58] Klaus Krüger und Gerhard Wolf rekonstruieren solche selbstbezüglichen Diskurse sogar von den bildtheologischen Problemstellungen des Mittelalters her.[59] Für Krüger braucht es aber das ästhetische System des »transparenten« Bildes, um bildimmanente und nicht bloß kontextuelle theoretische Verhandlungen zu ermöglichen.[60] Entsprechend betont auch Valeska von Rosen, die in ihrem Lexikonartikel zum Lemma »Selbstbezüglichkeit« die neu ins Bewusstsein getretene prinzipielle Möglichkeit eines selbstreflexiven Bildes nachzeichnet, das Bestehen eines Kunstsystems als *conditio sine qua non* und damit die frühe Neuzeit als Schwelle.

Wenn man aber den Weg von Krüger und Wolf konsequent fortschreitet und nicht nur ästhetische und künstlerische Parameter als konstitutiv für eine immanente Bildtheorie heranzieht, dann lässt sich die Grenze auch endgültig zum Mittelalter hin überschreiten. Nehmen wir als Beispiel die oben erwähnten Aspekte der Wahrnehmungstheorie oder die theoretisch zentralen Dispute über die Materialität der Bilder. Auch hier gibt es ›starke‹ Bilder und – meist im Umweg über eine Gegenstandsreferenz – ein theoretisches Abarbeiten an Problemen der Repräsentation des Numinosen, der Materialität, des Aufeinander-Bezogenseins der verschiedenen skizzierten ›Bildlichkeiten‹. Wolf konnte etwa eine ganze Traditionslinie aufzeigen, Bildtheoretisches in den Darstellungen der *Vera Icon* zu verhandeln. Andere Bilder erscheinen subtil gerahmt durch Hinweise auf ihre adäquate Rezeption oder auf ihre letztgültige Verinnerlichung nach einem Transfer in die somatischen Speichermedien des Betrachters.[61] Silke Tammen hat jüngst am Beispiel von Bildern der Seitenwunde demonstriert, wie die Hersteller vermeintlich auf irrationale ›response‹ abzielender Visions- oder Reliquiensubstitute mediale Reflexionen erzwingen, indem sie das begehrte Objekt subtil entziehen.[62] Die Gläubigen bekommen, was sie begehren, nur in explizit vermittelter Form. Hier ließen sich auch sozialhistorische Fragen anschließen, insofern solche ›subversiven‹ Entzugsstrategien sich paradoxerweise gegen eine Selbstermächtigung der Gläubigen richten und dem kirchlichen Anspruch auf Mittlerschaft in die Hände spielen.

Es gibt einen gewichtigen Unterschied zwischen den oben skizzierten mittelalterlichen Theorien des Bildes, die sich punktuell den Bildern annähern sowie bestimmte Bilder erklären helfen, und einer Theoriegenese im Bild, die auch nur an den Bildern rekonstruiert werden kann. Die Praxis der Bildprofis wirft auch im Mittelalter Fragen auf, die eine kodifizierte Theorie überhaupt nicht zu stellen interessiert ist. Überall, wo sich derart Bildwissen visuell manifestiert, sind die Kunsthistoriker gefragt, mit ihren ikonographischen und formalen Kompetenzen, mit dem eigenen disziplinären Bildwissen, das benötigt wird, um sinnhaltige Abweichungen von der Norm oder überhaupt die Signifikanz von Variationen zu erkennen. Hier gibt es eine Fülle an Aufgaben für den Kunsthistoriker/-wissenschaftler im Feld einer aufs Mittelalter gerichteten Bildwissenschaft. So lassen sich genuin fachspezifische Kompetenzen ohne Substanzverluste einbringen in ein interdisziplinäres Projekt, ohne dass umgekehrt die sehr viel breiter interessierte kunsthistorische Mediävistik zur reinen Bildwissenschaft zu werden drohte.

---

1 Hans Dieter Huber: »Systemische Bildwissenschaft« In: Klaus Sachs-Hombach (Hg.): *Bildwissenschaft zwischen Reflexion und Anwendung*. Köln 2005, S. 155–162, hier: S. 156.

2 Vgl. Kurt Bauch: »Imago« In: Gottfried Boehm (Hg.): *Was ist ein Bild?* München 1994, S. 275–299. – Hans Belting: *Bild und Kult*. München 1990. – Zuletzt: Beate Fricke: *ecce fides. Die Statue von Conques. Götzendienst und Bildkultur im Westen*. München 2007.

3 So sieht etwa Carlo Ginzburg einen Wandel im Konzept der Repräsentation parallel zur Durchsetzung der Realpräsenz in der Eucharistie. Carlo Ginzburg: »Repräsentation – das Wort, die Vorstellung, der Gegenstand« In: *Freibeuter*, Jg. 53, 1992, S. 3–23. – Siehe auch Thomas Lentes: »Auf der Suche nach dem Ort des Gedächtnisses. Thesen zur Umwertung der symbolischen Formen in Abendmahlslehre, Bildtheorie und Bildandacht des 14.–16. Jahrhunderts.« In: Klaus Krüger, Alessandro Nova (Hg.): *Imagination und Wirklichkeit. Zum Verhältnis von mentalen und realen Bildern in der Kunst der frühen Neuzeit*. Mainz 2000, S. 21–46.

4 Bes. David Freedberg: *The Power of Images. Studies in the History and Theory of Response.* Chicago 1989. – Zuletzt ein Überblick durch Keith Moxey: »Response« In: *Kritische Berichte*, Jg. 35, 2007, Heft 3, S. 28–30.

5 Siehe etwa Hans Belting: *Bild-Anthropologie. Entwürfe für eine Bildwissenschaft.* München 2001. – W.J.T. Mitchell: *What Do Pictures Want? The Lives and Loves of Images.* Chicago 2005, bes. S. 5–11.

6 Hartmut Böhme: *Fetischismus und Kultur. Eine andere Theorie der Moderne.* Reinbek 2006. – Bruno Latour: *Wir sind nie modern gewesen. Versuch einer symmetrischen Anthropologie.* Berlin 1995.

7 »My own position is that the subjectivized, animated object in some form or other is an incurable symptom, and that Marx and Freud are better treated as guides to the understanding of this symptom and perhaps to some transformation of it into less pathological, damaging forms. In short, we are stuck with our magical, premodern attitudes toward objects, especially pictures, and our task is not to overcome these attitudes but to understand them, to work through their symptomatology.« Mitchell 2005 (wie Anm. 5), S. 30.

8 Bauch 1994 (wie Anm. 2), S. 275. – Ähnlich zum Nachhall der ›visual culture‹ des Mittelalters auch Kathryn Starkey: »Visual Culture and the German Middle Ages« In: Dies., Horst Wenzel (Hg.): *Visual Culture and the German Middle Ages.* New York u. a. 2005, S. 1–13, bes. S. 2.

9 Vgl. zahlreiche Beiträge in Starkey, Wenzel 2005 (wie Anm. 8). – Auch dem ›Dritten‹ dazwischen, dem Diagramm, wurde gerade in einem mediävistischen Sammelband eine grundlegende bildwissenschaftliche Würdigung zuteil: Steffen Bogen, Felix Thürlemann: »Jenseits der Opposition von Text und Bild. Überlegungen zu einer Theorie des Diagramms und des Diagrammatischen« In: Alexander Patschovsky (Hg.): *Die Bildwelt der Diagramme Joachims von Fiore. Zur Medialität religiös-politischer Programme im Mittelalter.* Ostfildern 2003, S. 1–22.

10 Horst Bredekamp: »Bildwissenschaft« In: Ulrich Pfisterer (Hg.): *Metzler Lexikon Kunstwissenschaft. Ideen, Methoden, Begriffe.* Stuttgart/Weimar 2003, S. 56–58, hier: S. 56.

11 »Die Präsentierung von Heiligen auf Gebäck, unscheinbaren Holzschnitten, gestanzten Tonfiguren sowie Holz- und kostbaren Metallskulpturen z.B. hat die Grenze von High und Low nie akzeptiert.« Hans Dieter Huber, Gottfried Kerscher: »Kunstgeschichte im ›Iconic Turn‹. Ein Interview mit Horst Bredekamp« In: *Kritische Berichte*, Sonderheft Netzkunst, Jg. 26, 1998, Heft 1, S. 85–93, hier: S. 85. – Er nennt insbesondere die Forschungsinteressen der Wiener und der Hamburger Schule als Beispiele für eine akademische Kunstgeschichte mit der Breite heutiger ›Bildwissenschaften‹, vgl. ebd. S. 91.

12 Vgl. Bredekamp 2003 (wie Anm. 10), S. 57.

13 Vgl. dazu insbesondere Georges Didi-Huberman: *Vor einem Bild.* München/Wien 2000.

14 Ebd. und Georges Didi Huberman: *Fra Angelico. Unähnlichkeit und Figuration.* München 1995, S. 19–22.

15 Vgl. meine Rezension von: Klaus Sachs-Hombach (Hg.): Bildwissenschaft zwischen Reflexion und Anwendung. Köln 2005. In: *sehepunkte* 6, 2006, Nr. 10 [15.10.2006], URL: http://www.sehepunkte.de/2006/10/9451.html (28.02.2008). – In Kenntnis des historischen Materials täte sich ein Philosoph schwerer zu statuieren, dass im Gegensatz zum Wandel im Sprachgebrauch »kein Verwendungszusammenhang […] aus einem Bild, das morphologisch der Gestalt eines Elefanten entspricht, das Bild einer Mücke machen« könne, so Ferdinand Fellmann: »Anthropologische Grundlagen der Bildsemantik«, ebd., S. 45–55. – Hier erinnert man sich z.B. eines Pseudo-Dionysius Areopagita, der empfahl, Gott am besten durch das

Bild eines Wurms darzustellen, um irreführenden Gewissheiten vorzubeugen, vgl. Didi-Huberman 1995 (wie Anm. 14), S. 57.

16 Vgl. Wolfgang Kemp: »Kunstwerk und Betrachter: Der rezeptionsästhetische Ansatz« In: Hans Belting u.a. (Hg.): *Kunstgeschichte. Eine Einführung*. 5. überarb. Auflage, Berlin 1996, S. 241–258.

17 Vgl. den Überblick von Steffen Bogen: »Kunstgeschichte/Kunstwissenschaft« In: Sachs-Hombach 2005 (wie Anm. 1), S. 52–67.

18 Beat Wyss: *Vom Bild zum Kunstsystem*, Bd. 1, Köln 2006, S. 17.

19 Hans Belting, Christiane Kruse: *Die Erfindung des Gemäldes. Das erste Jahrhundert der niederländischen Malerei*. München 1994.

20 Vgl. etwa Hans Belting: *Das echte Bild. Bildfragen als Glaubensfragen*. München 2005, S. 217.

21 Vgl. Thomas Lentes: »Inneres Auge, äußerer Blick und heilige Schau. Ein Diskussionsbeitrag zur visuellen Praxis in Frömmigkeit und Moraldidaxe des späten Mittelalters« In: Klaus Schreiner (Hg.): *Frömmigkeit im Mittelalter. Politisch-soziale Kontexte, visuelle Praxis, körperliche Ausdrucksformen*. München 2002, S. 179–219. – Silke Tammen: »Wahrnehmung. Sehen und Bildwahrnehmung im Mittelalter« In: Pfisterer 2003 (wie Anm. 10), S. 380–385. – Marius Rimmele: »Heilsleitern. Medien des Bildes und Medien zu Gott im Triptychon des Antonius van Tsgrooten (1507)« In: Birgit Mersmann, Martin Schulz (Hg.): *Kulturen des Bildes*. München 2006, S. 203–222.

22 Siehe zahlreiche Beiträge in Sachs-Hombach 2005 (wie Anm. 1).

23 Damit ist mitnichten eine Unwandelbarkeit bestimmter »ewiggleicher« Bildfaktoren wie der Bezug zum Tod u. Ä. gemeint, sondern ein Fokus auf die menschlichen Bedürfnisse und symbolischen Praktiken, die durchaus große Veränderungen durchlaufen.

24 Siehe Ilka Brändle: »Das Foto als Bildobjekt. Aspekte einer Medienanthropologie« In: Hans Belting (Hg.): *Bilderfragen. Die Bildwissenschaften im Aufbruch*. München 2007, S. 83–100.

25 Vgl. das Interview von Klaus Sachs-Hombach mit Felix Thürlemann in: *Wege zur Bildwissenschaft. Interviews*. Köln 2004, S. 200–215.

26 Vgl. Karl Clausberg: *Die Wiener Genesis. Eine kunstwissenschaftliche Bilderbuchgeschichte*. Frankfurt/Main 1984. – Wolfgang Kemp: »Bilderzählung« In: Pfisterer 2003 (wie Anm. 10), S. 46–48.

27 Vgl. etwa Lambert Wiesing: *Artifizielle Präsenz. Studien zur Philosophie des Bildes*. Frankfurt/Main 2005, S. 23–25.

28 Dies gilt natürlich in besonderem Maße für die mittelhochdeutsche Universalvokabel ›bilde‹, vgl. Horst Wenzel: »Zur Narrativik von Bildern und zur Bildhaftigkeit der Dichtung. Plädoyer für eine Text-Bildwissenschaft« In: Belting 2007 (wie Anm. 24), S. 317–332, hier: S. 320–322.

29 Thomas Lentes: »Von der Wirklichkeit und Wahrheit des Bildes im Mittelalter. Transdisziplinäre Bildforschung in der VW-Nachwuchsgruppe ›Kulturgeschichte und Theologie des Bildes im Christentum‹« In: *Kritische Berichte*, Jg. 29, 2001, S. 34–46, hier: S. 40. – Ders.: »Wir sind alle Bildgebärer. Wider die Rede vom Christentum als einer Schriftreligion« In: *Orientierung*, Jg. 67, 2003.

30 Vgl. Lentes 2000 (wie Anm. 3)

31 Vgl. *Lexikon für Theologie und Kirche*, Bd. 4, Freiburg/Br. u.a. 1995, Lemma: »Gottebenbildlichkeit«, S. 871–878. – *Theologische Realenzyklopädie*, Bd. 6, Berlin/NewYork 1980, Lemma: »Bild Gottes II–IV«, S. 499–515. – Didi-Huberman 2000 (wie Anm. 13), S. 217.

32 Johann Kreuzer: »Bewusstsein des Bildes. Zur Aktualität mittelalterlichen Denkens. Mit einer Nachbemerkung zu Wittgenstein« In: Siegfried Blasche, Mathias Gutmann, Michael Weingarten (Hg.): *Repraesentatio Mundi. Bilder als Ausdruck und Aufschluss menschlicher Weltverhältnisse. Historisch-systematische Perspektiven*. Bielefeld 2004, S. 15–42.

33 Mitchell 2005 (wie Anm. 5), S. 8f.

34 Siehe etwa Wenzel 2007 (wie Anm. 28). – Frank O. Büttner: *Imitatio Pietatis. Motive der christlichen Ikonographie als Modelle zur Verähnlichung*. Berlin 1983.

35 Vgl. dazu Wolfgang Wackernagel: »Subimaginale Versenkung. Meister Eckharts Ethik der Bild-ergründenden Entbildung« In: Boehm 1994 (wie Anm. 2), S. 184–207.

36 Zitiert nach Klaus Schreiner: *Maria. Jungfrau, Mutter, Herrscherin*. München/Wien 1994, S. 254.

37 Siehe v. a. Gerhard Wolf: *Schleier und Spiegel. Traditionen des Christusbildes und die Bildkonzepte der Renaissance*. München 2002.

38 Vgl. Friedrich Ohly: »Typologie als Denkform der Geschichtsbetrachtung« In: Volker Bohn (Hg.): *Typologie*. Frankfurt/Main 1988, S. 22–63.

39 Erich Auerbach: »Figura«. In: Ders.: *Gesammelte Aufsätze zur romanischen Philologie*. Hg. von Gustav Konrad. Bern/München 1967, S. 55–92, hier: S. 83.

40 Vgl. v. a. Hans Belting: *Das Bild und sein Publikum im Mittelalter. Form und Funktion früher Bildtafeln der Passion*. Berlin 1981.

41 Vgl. als Einführung Hans Ulrich Reck: »Kunstgeschichte und Epistemologie der Bilder. Eine sondierende Skizze« In: Klaus Sachs-Hombach (Hg.): *Bild und Medium. Kunstgeschichtliche und philosophische Grundlagen der interdisziplinären Bildwissenschaft*. Köln 2006, S. 27–69.

42 Vgl. aktuell Mitchell 2005 (wie Anm. 5), S. XVII.

43 Vgl. etwa George Lakoff, Mark Johnson: *Metaphors We Live By*. Chicago 1980. – Stefan Majetschak: »Sichtbare Metaphern. Bemerkungen zur Bildlichkeit von Metaphern und zur Metaphorizität in Bildern« In: Richard Hoppe-Sailer u. a. (Hg.): *Logik der Bilder. Präsenz – Repräsentation – Erkenntnis*. Berlin 2005, S. 239–253.

44 Thomas Macho: »Körper der Zukunft. Vom Vor- und Nachleben der Bilder« In: Belting 2007 (wie Anm. 24), S. 181–194.

45 Gottfried Boehm: »Das Paradigma ›Bild‹. Die Tragweite der ikonischen Episteme« In: Belting 2007 (wie Anm. 24), S. 77–82.

46 Katrin Kärcher: »Wer etwas in seinem Geist begreift, male ein Bild. Zur epistemischen Funktion des Bildlichen im Mittelalter« In: Mersmann, Schulz 2006 (wie Anm. 21), S. 167–182. – Christel Meier: »Malerei des Unsichtbaren. Über den Zusammenhang von Erkenntnistheorie und Bildstruktur im Mittelalter« In: Wolfgang Harms (Hg.): *Text und Bild. DFG-Symposion 1988*. Stuttgart 1990, S. 35–65.

47 Lentes 2001 (wie Anm. 29), bes. S. 39

48 Vgl. Tammen 2003 (wie Anm. 21), S. 380–385. – Michael Camille: »Before the Gaze. The Internal Senses and Late Medieval Practices of Seeing« In: Robert S. Nelson (Hg.): *Visuality before and beyond the Renaissance. Seeing as Others Saw*. Cambridge 2000, S. 197–223.

49 Vgl. Tammen 2003 (wie Anm. 21). – Suzannah Biernoff: *Sight and Embodiment in the Middle Ages*. Basingstoke 2002.

50 Vgl. Lentes 2002 (wie Anm. 21). – Jean-Claude Schmitt: »L'imagination efficace« In: *Le corps des images. Essais sur la culture visuelle au Moyen Âge*. Paris 2002, S. 345–362.

51 Vgl. Wyss 2006 (wie Anm. 18), S. 87–116, bes. 88f.

52 Vgl. Rimmele 2006 (wie Anm. 21). – Ders.: »Selbstreflexivität des Bildes als Ansatzpunkt historischer Bildforschung: Ein Diskussionsbeitrag zur Rolle des Trägermediums« In: Ingeborg Reichle, Steffen Siegel, Achim Spelten (Hg.): *Verwandte Bilder. Die Fragen der Bildwissenschaft*. Berlin 2007, S. 15–32.

53 Formale Kompetenzen sind etwa auch bei der Rekonstruktion von Kontextmarkierungen bzw. allgemein rezeptionsästhetischen Strategien in Bildern gefragt, die letztlich ebenfalls genuine Zugänge zu historischem Bildwissen eröffnen, vgl. Wolfgang Kemp: »Kunstwissenschaft und Rezeptionsästhetik« In: Ders. (Hg.): *Der Betrachter ist im Bild: Kunstwissenschaft und Rezeptionsästhetik*. Berlin 1992, S. 7–28, bes. S. 23.

54 Vgl. Gottfried Boehm: »Die Wiederkehr der Bilder« In: Boehm 1994 (wie Anm. 2), S. 11–38, hier: S. 36. – Siehe auch Klaus Krüger: »Geschichtlichkeit und Autonomie. Die Ästhetik des Bildes als Gegenstand historischer Erfahrung« In: Otto Gerhard Oexle (Hg.): *Der Blick auf die Bilder. Kunstgeschichte und Geschichte im Gespräch*. Mit Beiträgen von Klaus Krüger und Jean-Claude Schmitt (Göttinger Gespräche zur Geschichtswissenschaft, 4). Göttingen 1997, S. 55–85.

55 Bogen 2005 (wie Anm. 17), S. 54.

56 Siehe etwa Boehm 1994 (wie Anm. 54).

57 Max Imdahl: *Giotto. Arenafresken. Ikonographie, Ikonologie, Ikonik*. München 1988, S. 13.

58 Victor I. Stoichita: *Das selbstbewußte Bild. Vom Ursprung der Metamalerei*. München 1998. – Zur Bedeutung dieser Arbeit und zur Ausweitung des Metapikturalen siehe die Rezension von Christiane Kruse in: *Zeitschrift für Kunstgeschichte*, Jg. 62, 1999, S. 585–594.

59 Klaus Krüger: *Das Bild als Schleier des Unsichtbaren*. München 2001 – Wolf 2002 (wie Anm. 37).

60 Krüger 2001 (wie Anm. 59), S. 26f.

61 Vgl. Anm. 52.

62 Silke Tammen: »Blick und Wunde – Blick und Form: Zur Deutungsproblematik der Seitenwunde Christi in der spätmittelalterlichen Buchmalerei« In: Kristin Marek u.a. (Hg.): *Bild und Körper im Mittelalter*. München 2006, S. 85–114.

Götz Grossklaus

Bild als Zeichen. Der kultursemiotische Ansatz im Vergleich

I.

1. Der Entwurf von Zeichen für etwas: für etwas Nicht-Anwesendes, Erinnertes oder Vorgestelltes – für etwas Nicht-Anwesendes: gerade Fehlendes, räumlich Entferntes – gehört zu den Leistungen des menschlichen Bewusstseins. Piaget[1] unterscheidet in der Entwicklungsgeschichte des Kindes Phasen in der Ausbildung des Wahrnehmungs- und Denkvermögens, die sich darauf beziehen, dass das Kind schrittweise den Umgang mit »inneren Bildern« erlernt. Piaget spricht von zwei Kategorien »innerer Bilder«: »den reproduktiven Bildern, die [...] bereits bekannte und früher wahrgenommene Anblicke in Erinnerung rufen« und: »den antizipierenden Bildern, die [...] Bewegungen und Veränderungen [...] verbildlichen [...] ohne bei ihrer Verwirklichung dabei gewesen zu sein.«[2]

Mentale Erinnerungs-Bilder und Vorstellungs-Bilder ermöglichen frühzeitig den Umgang mit Objekten und Vorgängen, die im Gegenwartsfeld nicht wahrnehmbar sind. Die mentalen Bilder üben die Kinder schon früh ein in den Gebrauch von Stellvertretern für abwesende Dinge oder auch Personen; interne Repräsentationen werden das Material aller Imaginationen. Piaget spricht vom Auftreten einer semiotischen Funktion, von entsprechenden Verhaltensweisen schon im Laufe des zweiten Lebensjahres, »die ... den vorstellungsmäßigen Hinweis auf einen nicht vorhandenen Gegenstand oder ein nicht stattfindendes Ereignis beinhalten und [...] folglich den Aufbau [...] von differenzierenden Zeichen voraussetzen.«[3]

2. Wechseln wir von der ›Ontogenese‹ zur ›Phylogenese‹, und zwar zur Kulturgeschichte, so ist zu beobachten, dass es immer darum ging, den mentalen Prozessen des Erinnerns, Wahrnehmens und Vorstellens eine bleibende mediale Form in Gestalt von visuellen Symbolen und Zeichen zu verleihen. Zwischen den Innenzuständen unseres Bewusstseins und den Außenzuständen der kulturellen Welt vermitteln immer schon Zeichen und Symbole. Das historisch jeweils dominante Leitmedium – sei es das Bild, die gesprochene oder geschriebene Sprache – »organisiert den Rapport der Subjekte mit dem intersubjektiven Raum«[4].

Zwischen Natur und Mensch, zwischen Objekt und Subjekt, zwischen Außen und Innen, Welt und Ich, tritt die neue Welt der Zeichen. »Dem Zeichen kommt« – so heißt es bei Cassirer – »im Gegensatz zu dem realen Wechsel der Einzelinhalte des Bewusstseins eine bestimmte ideelle Bedeutung zu, die als solche beharrt.«[5] Diese Transkription von interner Bewusstseinsform in externe Zeichenform kann als generelle Externalisierung von Erinnerung, Vorstellung und schließlich auch von gegenwärtiger Wahrnehmung im Medium von Bild und Schrift gesehen werden. Die ganze Entwicklung der Bild- und Sprachzeichen sieht Cassirer als den historisch fortschreitenden Prozess »der Trennung des Ideellen vom Reellen«[6], als Scheidung der Welt des unmittelbaren Seins und der Welt der mittelbaren Bedeutungen, wie sie im Gegensatz von Zeichen und Sache befestigt wird. Es ist jedoch gerade diese Trennung, die uns Freiheit und Distanz vom Druck des ›Realen‹, von den Zwängen der ›Wirklichkeits-Haftung‹ gewährt.

> »Denn das Zeichen ist keine bloß zufällige Hülle des Gedankens [des Sinns], sondern sein notwendiges und wesentliches Organ. Es dient nicht nur dem Zweck der Mitteilung eines fertig gegebenen [Gedanken] Inhalts, sondern ist ein Instrument, kraft dessen dieser Inhalt selbst sich herausbildet.«[7]

So weit Cassirer, der sich – wie aus dem Zitat ersichtlich – hier den Auffassungen des erkenntnistheoretischen Konstruktivismus annähert. Wenn Cassirer von der Trennung des Ideellen vom Reellen spricht, so kehrt dieser Gedanke in der konstruktivistischen Annahme wieder, dass es »keinen direkten Zusammenhang zwischen den Vorgängen in der Welt und den Inhalten unserer Wahrnehmung gibt«[8]. Immer schon orientieren wir uns – evolutionsgeschichtlich in unterschiedlichen Graden der Selbstbewusstheit und der Verfügung über mehr oder weniger elaborierte Zeichensysteme – im Rahmen von »Konstruktions- und Interpretationsversuchen, die auf der Grundlage von Erregungszuständen der Sinnessysteme ablaufen«[9].

Zu unterscheiden sind in unserem Zusammenhang medientheoretisch primär selektive Konstrukte unserer Wahrnehmung, unseres Gedächtnisses, unserer Imagination etc. als Akte unseres Bewusstseins von sekundären Konstrukten der Zeichen und Symbole, wie sie im Laufe der Evolutionsgeschichte von unterschiedlichen Medien zur Verfügung gestellt werden. Anzunehmen sind Mehrfach-Transkriptionen und Übersetzungen von Daten und Signalen, die von ›draußen‹, aus der ›bewusstseins-unabhängigen Welt‹ aufgenommen werden. Die intern – z.B. als innere Bilder – gewonnenen Ansichten, ›bedeutungsvolle Gestalten und Geschehnisse‹, erfahren in der Veräußerung zu materialen Zeichen-Gebilden einen weiteren Bedeutungs-Gewinn. Der Prozess, der sich – im Sinne Cassirers – vertiefenden Trennung von Zeichenwelt und Realwelt vollzieht sich in konstruktivistischer Sicht gegenüber unserer primären internen Bewusstseinswelt als Prozess zunehmender Elaboration und Autarkie der sekundär-externen Zeichen- und Symbolwelten.

3. Anzunehmen sind die folgenden historischen Etappen symbolischer Verselbständigung und Etablierung von Bedeutung setzenden Zeichensystemen:

a) Dem Mythos und dem magischen Bewusstsein sind diese Trennungen und Ablösungen noch fremd. Das magische Kult-Bild stellt die Sache nicht dar, verweist nicht auf sie, sondern behauptet, die Sache zu sein und wie sie zu wirken.[10] »Wortzauber, Bildzauber und Schriftzauber bilden den Grundbestand der magischen Betätigung.«[11] Das magische Bild oder Schriftzeichen »dient der magischen Besitznahme oder der magischen Abwehr«[12] und gewinnt seine Kraft aus der Identität.

b) Erst das religiöse Bewusstsein verwirft das magische Bild mit seiner Ineins-Setzung von Bild und Sache, von Bild und göttlichem Sein als Götzenbild. »Was der gemeinen, profanen Weltansicht als die unmittelbar gegebene Wirklichkeit der Dinge e r s c h e i n t – das wandelt die religiöse Auffassung in eine Welt der Zeichen um.« »Alles Physische und Materielle, jegliches Dasein und jegliches Geschehen wird jetzt zum Gleichnis: zum leiblich-bildhaften Ausdruck eines Geistigen.«[13]

c) Im neuzeitlich-ästhetischen Bewusstsein kann das Bild nicht mehr »Teil der Dingwelt«[14] sein wie im Mythos, aber auch nicht mehr Zeichen des Heilsplanes und des Überirdischen[15] wie im religiösen Bewusstsein, sondern es wird zunächst als Kunstbild[16] gegenüber dem traditionellen Kultbild »eine rein immanente Bedeutsamkeit«[17] gewinnen etc.

d) Das moderne, säkular-profane und technische Bild und die jeweiligen medialen Apparate seiner Veröffentlichung entfalten ihre Wirksamkeit im Kontext einer Bildgeschichte der Emanzipation vom magischen und religiösen Ritual[18] und der Trennung von Zeichen und Sache. Gerade die technischen Bild-Systeme haben diese Trennungen sichtbar vorangetrieben und sich als autonome Institutionen etabliert. Die »vermittelnde Sphäre des [...] Bezeichnens und Bedeutens«[19] erfährt somit gerade in den neuen Zeichenwelten der elektronischen Bilder eine ungeheure Ausdehnung, wodurch sich nur bestätigt, dass die wachsende Entfernung vom »Paradies der reinen Unmittelbarkeit«[20] im Kulturprozess notwendig angelegt ist. Die Klage um den Verlust der Unmittelbarkeit und Ursprünglichkeit des Lebens hat den Zivilisationsprozess als zunehmende Verselbständigung der vermittelnden Instanzen – der Zeichen und Symbole – begleitet und immer wieder Rückkehr-Wünsche wachgerufen nach dem unvermittelten, zeichenlosen »Seinsgrund« und seiner »intuitiven Schau«.

Wenn aber in konstruktivistischer Sicht, »jede Aussage über die Existenz einer bewusstseinsunabhängigen Welt eine Aussage in der Bewusstseinswelt ist«[21], dann bleiben wir mit dem Rückkehr-Wunsch ins Reich der Unmittelbarkeit in einem Zirkel befangen. Auf der anderen Seite ist gerade für das komplex vermittelte Live-Bild der elektronischen Medien zu beobachten, dass es uns seine Vermitteltheit vergessen lassen möchte und uns in der Illusion einer (zweiten) Unmittelbarkeit bestärkt.

Für die neuen Bildwissenschaften trennen sich hier schon die Wege: Die anthropologisch ausgerichtete Theorie (H. Belting) ebenso wie die eher phänomenologisch argumentierende Theorie (G. Boehm, L. Wiesing) verstehen das Bild als »Ereignis des Zeigens«, als »sich selbst offenbarende Erscheinung«,[22] als »symbolischen oder virtuellen Körper« in direktem Bezug zu unserer körpereigenen Bilderzeugung: der Erinnerung und der Vorstellung.[23] Gemeinsam sind diesen Ansätzen, jene Trennungen »der Welt der Zeichen von der Welt der Körper«[24], der Sprache von der Sache, der Welt der Zeichen von der Welt des Sichtbaren[25] wieder aufheben zu wollen in Akten der »Animation« oder der Teilhabe am ›Ereignis des Zeigens‹. Eine kultursemiotische Lesart des Bildes geht von einem unhintergehbaren Prozess der Entfernung von aller Unmittelbarkeit aus, vom Prätext einer langen Geschichte vermittelnder Zeichen und Symbole; dem Bild als kulturellem Artefakt gesteht sie seinen zeichentheoretischen Sonderstatus zu, postuliert aber den ›Ort der Bilder‹ im Kontext einer Welt der Zeichen, ohne den Austausch außer Acht zu lassen, in dem das materiale, externe Bild und das immaterielle, interne Bild unserer Erinnerung und Vorstellung, unserer Träume und Imaginationen immer stehen.

II.

Ein kultursemiotischer Ansatz zur Beschreibung von Merkmalen vornehmlich technischer Bilder seit der Fotografie geht von einer Reihe kulturanthropologischer Voraussetzungen aus: In kognitiven Akten der Wahrnehmung, der Erinnerung und der Vorstellung werden uns bestimmte innere und äußere Geschehnisse oder Abläufe bewusst.[26] Wahrnehmend, erinnernd und vorstellend werden ursprünglich am Körper gemachte elementare Erfahrungen einer Verortung und einer Verzeitlichung ins Bewusstsein gehoben. Am Körper werden erste Elemente einer räumlichen Orientierung ablesbar; das Bild des menschlichen Leibes vermittelt die Anschauung von räumlichen Indices wie oben/unten, vorn/hinten, rechts/links und vor allem von innen/außen. Der menschliche Körper als erstes Medium vermittelt auch erste Elemente einer zeitlichen Orientierung: in der Erinnerung an Zustände, die vergangen sind, in der Wahrnehmung an Zustände, die augenblicklich erlebbar sind, und in der Vorstellung von Zuständen, die als kommend erwartet werden. In Wahrnehmung, Erinnerung und Vorstellung entwirft unser Bewusstsein jenen Strom innerer Bilder, die immer mit diesen elementaren Annahmen eines Vorher und Nachher, eines Innen und Außen etc. verknüpft sein werden. Schließlich: die eigentlich kultursemiotische Annahme, dass es im Prozess der Kultur darum geht, die flüchtigen inneren Bilder in die bleibende Form äußerer Bild-Zeichen zu übersetzen und zu externalisieren – so wie sie ihrerseits wieder ›zurückfließen‹ können, um sich mit dem Strom der inneren Bilder zu vermischen.

Auszugehen ist von dieser Wechselbeziehung mentaler und kultureller Bilder und von den drei Aspekten, mit denen die externen Bilder mit den inneren Bildern verknüpft bleiben: als wahrnehmungsnahe Zeichen,[27] als erinnerungsnahe Zeichen und als vorstellungsnahe Zeichen. Das Bild-Zeichen transkribiert in diesem Sinn das vorgängig am Körper gewonnene raumzeitliche Orientierungs-Schema in das Reich der kulturellen Symbole. Mit dem Rekurs auf den Körper und den internen Bilderstrom unseres Bewusstseins trifft sich der kultursemiotische Ansatz in einigen Punkten mit der anthropologischen Bildtheorie (Belting), unterscheidet sich aber in der konsequenten Thematisierung des Bildes als Zeichen, in der Geschichte seines Wandels und im Kontext des jeweils historischen Medien- und Symbol-Systems.

Übereinstimmend beziehen der anthropologische und der kultursemiotische Ansatz die kognitiven Akte des Erinnerns und Vorstellens (des Imaginierens) und der Wahrnehmung als konstitutiv für das mentale Bild ein und rechnen mit produktiven Transfers zwischen inneren und äußeren Bild-Konstrukten. Kultursemiotisch aber können diese Transfers nicht unmittelbar zwischen ›Körpern‹ ablaufen: zwischen »dem Körper als lebendes Medium«, als »Ort des Gedächtnisses«, als »Ort der Bilder« und dem »Körper der Bilder« und »dem Betrachter als ein(em) Körper«[28]. Kultursemiotisch gilt es dagegen, die Energie-Transfers zwischen Innen und Außen, zwischen Bild und Betrachter als ›Übersetzungen‹ zu beschreiben: als Transkriptionen über vermittelnde Zeichen und Symbole. Jederzeit ist das externe Bild auf die Vermittlung durch kollektiv eingespielte Zeichen angewiesen. Erst so nimmt es teil an der kulturellen Zirkulation der Symbole. Zweifellos behauptet das Bild als Zeichen einen Status sui generis und unterscheidet sich im Signifikationsmodus grundsätzlich vom sprachlichen Zeichen und seiner Grammatik – soweit es nicht narrativ in Dienst genommen wird.

III.

Die Frage ist, wie Bild-Zeichen unter diesen Voraussetzungen so etwas wie Sinn oder Bedeutung entwerfen oder erzeugen. Die anthropologische und phänomenologische Bild-Theorie berufen sich bei der Beantwortung dieser Frage – ohne Rekurs auf Zeichen und Symbole – ganz auf die Eigenart des Bild-Körpers, auf eine »Logik der Bilder«[29] und die entsprechende Besonderheit einer »Bildwahrnehmung als Akt der Animation«[30]. Die Abkehr vom Zeichen wird mit der Annahme begründet, dass Zeichen sich generell »an eine kognitive statt an eine sinnliche, körperbezogene Wahrnehmung wenden«[31] und überdies ganz dem Primat der Sprache als Leitsystem unterworfen bleiben. Für einen verengten, am Saussure'schen zweistelligen Modell orientierten Zeichenbegriff mag das von Fall zu Fall zutreffend sein. Aber schon das Peirce'sche Zeichenmodell als dreistellige Relation hat den Bezugsrahmen erheblich erweitert. Außerdem lässt diese Zeichen-Kritk außer Acht, dass für Zeichen grundsätzlich zwei Signifikationsmodi zur Verfügung stehen: neben der Denotion (designativ, kognitiv) immer auch die Konnotation (assoziativ, symbolisch) – von den unterschiedlichen Zeichenfunktionen im Gebrauch (z. B. referentiell, emotiv, appellativ etc.) ganz zu schweigen. Von einer Signifikationsbeschränkung auf das Nur-Kognitive kann somit keine Rede sein.

Auch das ikonische Zeichen lässt sich unschwer als dreistelliges Relationsverhältnis beschreiben, in dem der Zeichenträger (als wahrnehmbarer Repräsentant), das Zeichenobjekt (als repräsentierte Einheit) und der Zeicheninterpretant (als Interpretationshorizont, unter dem sich die Repräsentation vollzieht) in Beziehung stehen.[32] Für den kultursemiotischen Ansatz und die Frage danach, wie es zu einer spezifisch ikonischen Form der Sinn-Erzeugung kommt, verspricht gerade das triadische Modell einen Weg zu weisen. Besonders die Vorstellung eines vom Zeicheninterpretanten ›ausgelösten‹ semiotischen Prozesses – als Wirkung des Zeichens im Bewusstsein eines Interpreten – könnte fruchtbar gemacht werden zur Erfassung der spezifisch-ikonisch nicht-linearen, simultanen Sinn-Konstitution des Bildes. Wenn das zweistellige, wortorientierte Zeichenmodell Saussures nahe legt, dass ein starrer Code jedem Signifikanten systematisch ein festes Signifikat zuordnet, so erscheint das triadische Modell besser geeignet, den offenen relationalen Sinn-Entwurf des Bildes zu erfassen und zu beschreiben.

IV.

Die Entscheidung für eine bestimmte Bildsorte oder -klasse ist immer auch eine Entscheidung im Rahmen eines historisch vorgegebenen medialen Systems: Z.B. unterliegt ein Kultbild im Veröffentlichungs-Medium des Tafelbildes, ein Kunstbild im Veröffentlichungs-Medium der technischen Fotografie oder ein Werbebild im Veröffentlichungs-Medium des Fernsehens etc. jeweils ganz bestimmten Regeln der medialen Ausdrucksform (z.B. manuell/technisch, bewegt/unbewegt etc.). Als medialer Rahmen ist das jeweils gesellschaftlich etablierte Mediensystem zu verstehen, innerhalb dessen das Bild immer in einem intermedialen Wechselverhältnis zum traditionellen Leitmedium von Sprache, Schrift, Buch und Text steht. So kann von Sprach-Bildern (Allegorien, Embleme, Metaphern etc.) ebenso gesprochen werden wie von Bild-Sprachen (Comics etc.).

Kehren wir zurück zur Frage der Konstitution von Sinn im einzelnen Bild-Zeichen. Im Reich der Zeichen »nehmen wir nicht etwas wahr, sondern wir nehmen etwas als etwas in einem bestimmten Interpretationshorizont wahr«[33]. Gottfried Boehm spricht in diesem Zusammenhang von »ikonischer Differenz«[34], nur schreibt er diesen Sachverhalt oder diese Leistung nicht dem Zeichen oder dem Symbol zu. Kultursemiotisch betrachtet aber ist dieser epistemische Sprung, die Setzung »von etwas als etwas«, gerade als die spezifische Leistung des Zeichens anzusehen. Zeichen und Symbole zeigen und bezeichnen ikonisch etwas als etwas Anderes: als Abwesendes, etwas Verlorenes, Vergangenes oder augenblicklich Vergehendes oder noch nicht Erschienenes.

Wie vollzieht sich dieses Zeigen und Verweisen im künstlichen Raum des Bildes? Es gehört zu der Besonderheit des Bildzeichens, dass der materielle Zeichenträger als Repräsentatem aufs engste mit dem Zeichenobjekt, das er ja repräsentiert, verknüpft ist. »Bilder sind in Materialitäten tief eingesenkt«, heißt es bei Gottfried Boehm.[35] Für das sprachliche Zeichen spielt auf andere Weise die spezielle materiale Zeichenbasis (als Schrift und Ausdrucksform) für die Übermittlung der Zeichenbedeutung keine Rolle. Die Schriftzeichen können frei in der Form und Anordnung variieren. Für das ikonische Zeichen kann es eine Abweichung von der gefundenen materiellen Anordnung der einzelnen Bild-Zeichenelemente nicht geben, ohne dass eine folgenreiche Verschiebung im gesamten Relationsgefüge von Repräsentant, Objekt und Interpretant einträte – und damit eine Veränderung des Bildsinns.

Die phänomenologische und anthropologische Bildtheorie begründet mit dieser medialen Differenz von Bild und Sprache, Schrift und Text ihre Grundprämisse: Bilder können keine Zeichen sein. Der kultursemiotische Ansatz geht nicht von irgendwie substantiell fest gefügten Einheiten aus,[36] von autonom den Objekten innewohnenden Bedeutungen, sondern von dem Gedanken, dass sich Sinn oder Bedeutung immer erst in relationalen Bezügen herstellen kann. So können Zeichen immer nur als Relationsverhältnisse begriffen werden, in denen Träger (Repräsentant), Objekt (Repräsentiertes) und Interpretant auf engste miteinander verbunden sind. Auch für das ikonische Zeichen gilt: »Objekt A wird in der Repräsentation B so repräsentiert, dass es die Interpretation C bestimmt.«[37] Die Zeichenelemente als Relate sind somit aus dem jeweiligen Relationsverbund nicht zu lösen.

Kultursemiotisch lässt sich für das Bildzeichen sein Zeichenträger oder Repräsentamen, der jeweilige materiale Bild-Raum, einmal als syntaktisches Feld beschreiben, als Matrix, in der den einzelnen Objekt-Zeichen ihr Stellenwert zuerteilt wird, zum anderen kann er gleichzeitig als repräsentierte Raum-Stelle und Schauplatz, als Ausgangspunkt der Imagination, als Horizont aller Interpretation gesehen werden. Semiotisch betrachtet, kann potentiell jedes einzelne Bildelement (Objekt, Körper, Figur), das im Bildfeld erscheint, zu einem Repräsentanten von Zeichenrelationen werden,[38] d. h. jeder Gegenstand und Körper kann im Relationsgeflecht des Bild-Feldes mit Zeichenfunktion ausgestattet werden – allerdings bedarf es der besonderen Markierung und der privilegierten Positionierung im Zeichenfeld. Als syntaktisches Feld gliedert sich der Bildraum sprachunabhängig/bildspezifisch nach der ursprünglich am Körper gemachten Erfahrung einer räumlichen Orientierung, und zwar nach Indices wie oben/unten, vorn/hinten, links/rechts, horizontal/vertikal und vor allem zentral/peripher und innen/außen. Bekanntlich erfuhren diese Orientierungsdaten im Laufe der Kulturgeschichte unterschiedliche Übersetzungen: vom Körper in den externen Raum, vom Raum in diverse andere symbolische Zeichensysteme.

Im ikonischen Bild-Zeichen-Feld wird so aufgrund dieses primären Raum-Schemas eine Bühne der Differenzen entworfen, der Achsen und Segmente, der Grenzen und Schwellen, der markierten und nicht markierten Orte und Stellen. Es entsteht jenes offene Netzwerk der Relationen, das prinzipiell unabschließbare Interpretations-Prozesse ermöglicht, indem eine Zeichenrelation in die andere übergeht,[39] nach Peirce jener Prozess einer unabschließbaren Semiose, der das Bild-Zeichen mit seinen Kontexten verknüpft. Soweit ich die Einwände der phänomenologischen Bildtheorie verstehe, wird gerade an diesem Moment einer »unabschließbaren Semiose« kritisiert, dass der semiotische Ansatz die Singularitäten, mit denen die Bilder verknüpft sind ... mit der Substitution eines Zeichenbegriffs zu früh überspringe.[40] Das könnte heißen, dass die Semiose viel zu schnell aus dem Bild herausführt und dem Betrachter keine Zeit lässt, sich auf das Ereignis des Zeigens einzustellen.

Zunächst wird man dem entgegenhalten können, dass auch der deiktische Akt des Zeigens sich im Bild nicht anders ereignen kann, als in Vermittlung durch eine zeichenhafte ›Geste‹ deiktischer Markierung oder Hervorhebung. Zum anderen wird gerade die Annahme eines bildspezifischen und bildimmanenten Netzwerkes der Relationen den sog. Singularitäten des Bildes gerecht: Die relationale Sinn-Bildung erfolgt gerade nicht, indem man das Bild »zu schnell mit dem Text liest« und zu früh durchs Bild hindurch auf etwas zuvor Gesagtes hindurchblickt.[41] In der Tat wäre eine derartige Lesart des Bildes reduktiv in der einseitigen Übersetzung ikonischer Zeichen in verbale Zeichen – in der verfehlten Annahme, man könne das Bild als simultane Gestalt nach dem Muster eines sequentiellen Textes lesen. Das räumlich-netzhafte Relationsgeflecht des Bildes legt eine ganzheitliche, simultan-eidetische Form der Betrachtung und des Sinn-Entwurfs nahe, die sich gerade von der rein diskursiv-linearen Verarbeitung im Rahmen von Sprach- und Text-Codes unterscheidet. Ein einseitig sprach-systematischer Zeichenbegriff taugt also von vornherein nicht zu einer Übertragung auf Zeichenverhältnisse im Bild. Der Vorwurf einer dem Primat der Sprache unterworfenen Semiotik geht – was den Peirce'schen Zeichenbegriff betrifft – ins Leere.

Übertragbar scheint allein der von der Literatursemiotik diskutierte Begriff der Konnotation zu sein.[42] Für einen literarischen Sprachtext sprengt die Konnotation im Zeichenverweis auf Bedeutungseinheiten im gesamten soziokulturellen Kontext, im symbolischen Universum überhaupt, die Grenzen des immanenten Text-Raums. Abweichend von sprachlich vorherrschenden denotativ-linearen Sinnbildungsverfahren stellt die Konnotation eine gestalthaft-synthetisch-eidetische Alternative dar: Die Konnotation öffnet einen simultanen Raum des Verweisens auf Bedeutungsfelder, die im Medium der Sprache nicht aktualisiert werden können. Zum Prinzip des konnotativen Verfahrens gehört es somit nicht nur, zur Ausgangsbedeutung zweite, dritte und alle weiteren Bedeutungen in einen umfassenden Sinnbildungsprozess einzubeziehen, sondern immer auch die Ausdrucksgrenzen eines jeweiligen Mediums im Verweis auf das jeweils ›andere‹, ausgeschlossene Medium zu überschreiten.

Kultursemiotisch betrachtet, ist das Bild das konnotative Medium par excellence, der ideale semiotische Ort des konnotativen Verweisens, der konnotativen Öffnung eines weiten Bezugs-Horizonts, schließlich der konnotativen Restitution sinnlich-kognitiver »Ganzheit«. Die Peirce'schen Begriffe v. a. der prinzipiellen Relationalität als fundierendes Prinzip aller Sinnbildung über Zeichen – und der »unabschließbaren Semiose« im Übergang von einer Zeichen-Relation in die andere – eröffnen allein schon genügend Bezüge zum literatursemiotischen Begriff der Konnotation. Schließlich setzen sowohl der konnotative Vorgang als auch der Prozess der unabschließbaren Semiose die konstitutive Leistung des Bewusstseins von Zeichenbenutzern voraus; in den Imaginationen von Erinnerung, Wahrnehmung und Vorstellung vollziehen sich Entwurf und Rezeption des Bild-Zeichens.

V.

Fahrlässig ist es, angesichts der Unterschiedlichkeit von Bildsorten, -typen und -klassen von dem Bild an sich zu sprechen – wie es in bestimmten bildwissenschaftlichen Abhandlungen üblich ist. Schon wenn man Kultbild, Kunstbild und Profanbild unterscheidet, muss auffallen, in welch verschiedenen Interpretationshorizonten der Bildbetrachter hier im Rahmen verschiedener Repräsentationsformen »etwas als etwas« wahrnimmt. Mit dem Erscheinen des technischen Bildes – zunächst der statischen Fotografie – wechselt gegenüber dem traditionellen Tafelbild Ausdrucksform und Ausdruckssubstanz, die Materialität des Zeichen-Repräsentanten und damit der Objektbezug des Zeichens. Als Index stellt das fotografische Bild-Zeichen einen unmittelbaren Bezug her zu einem ganz bestimmten Ort im Raum, zu einer ganz bestimmten Zeitstelle im Zeitfluss. Im raumzeitlichen Bild-Schema ist diese ›reale‹ Orts- und Zeitstelle als vergangen präsent. Auch im traditionell (nicht-technischen) Bild kann z.B. heilsgeschichtlich eine bestimmte Orts- und Zeitstelle eines bestimmten Heilsgeschehens ›mythisch‹ präsent sein, nicht jedoch indexikalisch. Das profane Foto-Bild bezeichnet eine reale Orts- und Zeitstelle eines privaten oder kollektiven Profangeschehens indexikalisch als Spur des ›Realen‹.

Vergleichbar bleibt für das Bild-Zeichen generell der Entwurf eines raumzeitlichen Schemas: eines Schauplatzes, einer Bühne, auf der Körper, Figuren und Objekte signifikant platziert werden. Im technischen Bild aber erscheint der Raum und Ort von vornherein von der Zeit wie aufgesogen. Der im fotografischen Bild indexikalisch entworfene Schauplatz ist von vornherein die Bühne, auf der die Inszenierung der verlorenen Zeit, des verschwundenen Ortes stattfindet und kraft der Erinnerung vergegenwärtigt wird. Mit dem Aufkommen des technisch-bewegten Bildes ereignet sich noch einmal ein revolutionär zu nennender Umbruch in Bezug auf alle Elemente des bildlichen Zeichens, in Bezug auf alle Faktoren der medialen Übersetzung, Kommunikation und Distribution, der Speicherung und Archivierung. Mit dieser technischen Revolutionierung der Ausdrucksmittel des ikonischen Zeichens nach Substanz und Form sind notwendig Veränderungen aufseiten von Inhaltssubstanz und Inhaltsform verbunden. Die fundamentale Raum-Zeit-Relation des Bild-Zeichens erfährt eine folgenreiche Verschiebung. Die nicht-semiotischen Bildwissenschaften wollen in technischen Umbrüchen weder die medien- und zeichengeschichtliche Zäsur, noch den Wandel der Raum-Zeit-Relation im neuen technischen Bild zur Kenntnis nehmen.

Wenn das traditionelle, nicht-technische, perspektivische Bild »Zeit« verräumlicht, ist für das technische Bild – vom unbewegten zum bewegten Bild – in Umkehrung ein Prozess fortschreitender Verzeitlichung des Raums zu beobachten. Die fotografisch repräsentierte Ortsstelle im Raum indiziert von vornherein eine Zeitstelle im Zeitfluss;

den Sequenzen des bewegten filmischen Bildes ist der Zeitfluss immanent; der repräsentierte Bild-Raum begünstigt Raum-Charaktere der Schwelle, der Passage und der Grenze und wird zum Schauplatz von Bewegungen, die zwischen ›innen‹ und ›außen‹, Zentrum und Peripherie, ›diesseits‹ und ›jenseits‹ verlaufen. Externe Bilder sind generalisierend als erinnerungsnahe, wahrnehmungsnahe und vorstellungsnahe Zeichen zu verstehen. Jedes Bild trägt die ursprüngliche Signatur einer Erinnerung an etwas Verlorenes, Vergangenes, Vergehendes, etwas Abwesendes. Verstehen wir die externen Bilder als Transkriptionen der als Bilder-Ströme bewusst werdenden Akte des Erinnerns, Wahrnehmens und Vorstellens, lässt sich erkennen, wie intim die äußeren Bilder auch verknüpft sein müssen mit Formen der Zeit- und Raum-Imagination unseres Bewusstseins. Diese Intimität und Nähe ist es im Übrigen auch, die die Gegner der Semiotik dazu verleiten, von dem Bild als einem Phänomen zu sprechen, das einer Vermittlung durch Zeichen nicht bedarf.

Erinnerung, Wahrnehmung und Vorstellung entwerfen sowohl für den inneren Bilderstrom als auch für die externalisierte Bilder-Welt der Zeichen die Syntax einer Raum-Zeit, in der wir ein Geschehen als ›vergangen‹, als ›gegenwärtig‹ oder als ›zukünftig‹ imaginieren. Die erinnerungs-, wahrnehmungs- und vorstellungsnahen Zeichen noch der technischen Bilder der Fotografie und des Films stiften diese Bezüge zur imaginären Raumzeit unseres Bewusstseins. Die jüngsten algorithmischen Rechenbilder allerdings haben sich von diesen Bezügen gänzlich gelöst und emanzipieren sich prinzipiell von dem begrenzten menschlichen Vermögen, sich zu erinnern, sich etwas vorzustellen oder etwas wahrzunehmen. Digitale Bilder entwerfen sich in abstrakten Daten-Räumen und Daten-Zeiten – jenseits des Analogen.

---

1 Jean Piaget, Bärbel Inhelder: *Die Psychologie des Kindes*. Olten/Freiburg [3]1976, S. 61.

2 Ebd., S. 77.

3 Ebd., S. 62.

4 Hartmut Winkler: *Docuverse. Zur Medientheorie der Computer*. München 1997, S. 53.

5 Ernst Cassirer: *Philosophie der symbolischen Formen*. 1. Teil: *Die Sprache*. Darmstadt [10]1994, S. 22.

6 Ernst Cassirer: *Philosophie der symbolischen Formen*. 2. Teil: *Das mythische Denken*. Darmstadt [9]1994, S. 51.

7 Cassirer, Die Sprache (wie Anm. 5), S. 18.

8 Gerhard Roth: »Wahrnehmung: Abbildung oder Konstruktion« In: R. Schnell (Hg.): *Wahrnehmung – Kognition – Ästhetik*. Bielefeld 2005, S. 29.

9 Ebd.

10 Cassirer, Das mythische Denken (wie Anm. 6), S. 51.

11 Ebd., S. 31.

12 Ebd., S. 284.

13 Ebd., S. 301.

14 Ebd., S. 311.

15 Ebd., S. 307.

16 Hans Belting: *Bild und Kult. Eine Geschichte des Bildes vor dem Zeitalter der Kunst*. München 1991.
17 Cassirer, Das mythische Denken (wie Anm. 6), S. 311.
18 Walter Benjamin: *Das Kunstwerk im Zeitalter seiner technischen Reproduzierbarkeit*. Frankfurt/M. 1976.
19 Cassirer, Die Sprache (wie Anm. 5), S. 51.
20 Ebd.
21 Roth 2005 (wie Anm. 8), S. 30.
22 Gottfried Boehm: *Wie Bilder Sinn erzeugen. Die Macht des Zeigens*. Berlin 2007; Lambert Wiesing: »Das Bild aus phänomenologischer Sicht« In: Klaus Sachs-Hombach (Hg.): *Wege zur Bildwissenschaft*. Köln 2004, S. 152–169.
23 Hans Belting: *Bild-Anthropologie*. München 2001, S. 13.
24 Ebd., S. 14.
25 Boehm 2007 (wie Anm. 22), S. 32; Belting 2001 (wie Anm. 23), S.13.
26 Gerhard Roth: *Das Gehirn und seine Wirklichkeit. Kognitive Neurobiologie und ihre philosophischen Konsequenzen*. Frankfurt/M. 1997, S. 214.
27 Klaus Sachs-Hombach: »Begriff und Funktion bildhafter Darstellungen« In: *Bild – Medien – Wissen. Visuelle Kompetenz im Medienzeitalter*. Hg. von H. D. Huber, B. Lockemann, M. Scheibel. München 2002, S. 18 ff.
28 Belting 2001 (wie Anm. 23), S. 12–14, 20, 22–29.
29 Boehm 2007 (wie Anm. 22), S. 34–53.
30 Belting 2001 (wie Anm. 23), S.13.
31 Ebd., S. 14.
32 Wilhelm Köller: »Der Peircesche Denkansatz als Grundlage für die Literatursemiotik« In: *Literatursemiotik I. Methoden – Analysen – Tendenzen*. Hg. von A. Eschbach, W. Rader. Tübingen 1980, S. 41.
33 Köller 1980 (wie Anm. 32), S. 45.
34 Boehm 2007 (wie Anm. 22), S. 38, 28, 68.
35 Boehm, Gottfried: »Das Paradigma »Bild«. Die Tragweite der ikonischen Episteme« In: *Bilderfragen. Die Bildwissenschaft im Aufbruch*. Hg. von Hans Belting. München 2007, S. 79.
36 Vgl. Köller 1980 (wie Anm. 32), S. 41.
37 Ebd., S. 41.
38 Ebd., S. 42.
39 Ebd., S. 46.
40 Gottfried Boehm: »Das Bild in der Kunstwissenschaft« In: Sachs-Hombach 2004 (wie Anm. 22), S. 18.
41 Ebd., S. 14.
42 Kaspar H. Spinner: »Die Aporien des Konnotationsbegriffs in der Literatursemiotik« In: Eschbach, Rader 1980 (wie Anm. 32), S. 65–84; Karlheinz Stierle: »Versuch zur Semiotik der Konnotation« In: Ders.: *Text als Handlung*. München 1975, S. 131–151.

Gerald Schröder

Der *Schmerzraum* von Joseph Beuys. Zur räumlichen Dimension großer Gefühle

Angefangen mit den so genannten »Plastischen Bildern« der 1950er Jahre über die raumbezogenen Aktionen der 1960er Jahre bis hin zu den Installationen der 1970er Jahre hat Joseph Beuys ein Raumkonzept entwickelt, das existentielle menschliche Erfahrungen wie Trauma und Schmerz ästhetisch vermittelt reflektiert. In gewisser Weise nutzt Beuys den Bereich des Ästhetischen, um traumatisch schmerzhafte Räume zu inszenieren, die darüber hinaus – so zumindest der programmatische Anspruch – auch eine therapeutische Wirkung entfalten sollen. Wie dieses Raumkonzept mit seiner zunächst paradox erscheinenden funktionellen Bestimmung als Diagnose und Therapie genauer zu verstehen ist, soll am Beispiel der Installation *Hinter dem Knochen wird gezählt – Schmerzraum* (1983) untersucht werden.[1] Dabei erweist sich der *Schmerzraum* von Joseph Beuys schließlich als extrem verschachtelt und es gilt somit zu klären, wie atmosphärischer, imaginativer und imaginärer Raum zusammenhängen und in welcher Beziehung sie zum Gedächtnisraum individueller und kollektiver Erinnerung sowie zum aktuellen politischen Raum des Kalten Kriegs stehen.

Von Dezember 1983 bis Februar 1984 präsentierte Joseph Beuys in der Zweigstelle der Düsseldorfer Galerie Konrad Fischer seine Installation *Schmerzraum* (Abb. 1, 2) in den Maßen 5,45 x 7,35 x 2,95 m.[2] Dem Titel stellte er die geheimnisvollen Worte »hinter dem Knochen wird gezählt« voran.[3] Nicht weniger irritierend ist zunächst die Datierung dieser künstlerischen Arbeit, die den weiten Zeitraum von 1941 bis 1983 umfasst. Die Zweigstelle der Galerie befand sich in der Mutter-Ey-Str. 5 und somit direkt hinter der Kunsthalle, wo zeitgleich die große Retrospektive zur Skulptur Picassos gezeigt wurde. Nach Aussagen des Galeristen war die Picasso-Ausstellung auch Anlass gewesen, Beuys um eine parallel stattfindende Ausstellung zu bitten.[4]

Beuys scheint seine Installation weniger als Hommage an den großen französischen Künstler verstanden zu haben, sondern vielmehr als Herausforderung zum künstlerischen Wettstreit. Zwar knüpft er implizit an das politische Engagement Picassos an, doch unterscheidet sich seine Installation gerade durch ihre mediale Qualität vom traditionellen Skulpturbegriff Picassos, der trotz seiner großen Experimentierfreude gerade auf dem Gebiet der Materialcollage doch einer objekthaften Auffassung von Skulptur verhaftet blieb.[5] Demgegenüber schuf Beuys ein Kunstwerk, dem der Betrachter nicht mehr in Distanz gegenübertreten und das er nicht mehr umschreiten kann. In den Schmerzraum muss man hineingehen. Er umgibt einen von allen Seiten und provoziert dadurch eine andere Rezeptionsweise.[6]

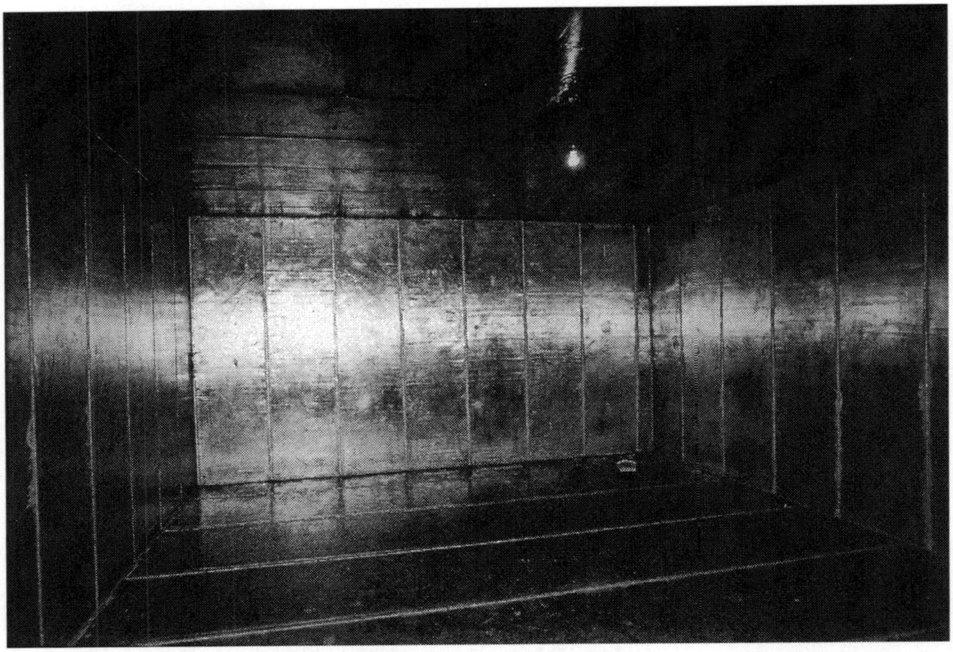

Abb. 1: Joseph Beuys, Hinter dem Knochen wird gezählt – Schmerzraum, 1941–1983, Fundación »la Caixa« Barcelona, © VG Bild-Kunst, Bonn

Was sah nun der kunstinteressierte Betrachter, wenn er durch die Glastüre in den Galerieraum schaute oder diesen gar betrat? Zunächst einmal recht wenig. Denn der Raum ist fast leer und auch ziemlich dunkel. Die gewohnten weißen Wände des Ausstellungsraums zuzüglich Boden und Decke sind komplett mit Bleibahnen verkleidet, wobei der Künstler auf ein handelsübliches Baumaterial zurückgegriffen hat, das normalerweise zur Isolation von Dächern eingesetzt wird. Diese Bleibahnen sind auf ein skelettartiges Stahlgerüst aufgeklebt, das vor die eigentlichen Wände gesetzt worden ist, für den Betrachter allerdings unsichtbar bleibt. An den Kanten sind die einzelnen Bahnen zusammengelötet, so dass sichtbare Nähte entstehen, die den Raum im parataktischen Rhythmus gliedern und mit Richtungsvektoren versehen. So wird durch die Ausrichtung der Nähte die Vertikalität der Wände unterstrichen und die quer zum eintretenden Betrachter angebrachten Bodenplatten scheinen ihm noch weitere Schwellen in den Weg zu legen. Gerade die Leere des Raumes lässt die wenigen Gegenstände besonders hervortreten. Da fällt wohl zunächst das Telefon in der hinteren rechten Ecke auf, das als einziges Element auf die ursprüngliche Funktion des Galerieraums hinweist und von Beuys nicht entfernt worden ist. Von der Decke hängt eine nackte Glühbirne mit geringer Wattzahl, die neben dem durch die Türe fallenden Tageslicht die einzige Lichtquelle im Raum ist. Vielleicht erst auf den letzten Blick fallen die beiden in etwa kopfgroßen Silberreife auf, die Beuys direkt neben der Glühbirne unter der Decke angebracht hat, so dass sie das Licht reflektieren können. Dabei sind die Reife leicht einander zugeneigt und so befestigt, dass sie unter der Decke zu schweben scheinen.

Beuys gestaltete den Raum so, dass er eine bestimmte Atmosphäre entfaltet, die den Betrachter von allen Seiten umgibt und leiblich spürbar wird, indem über die Körper-

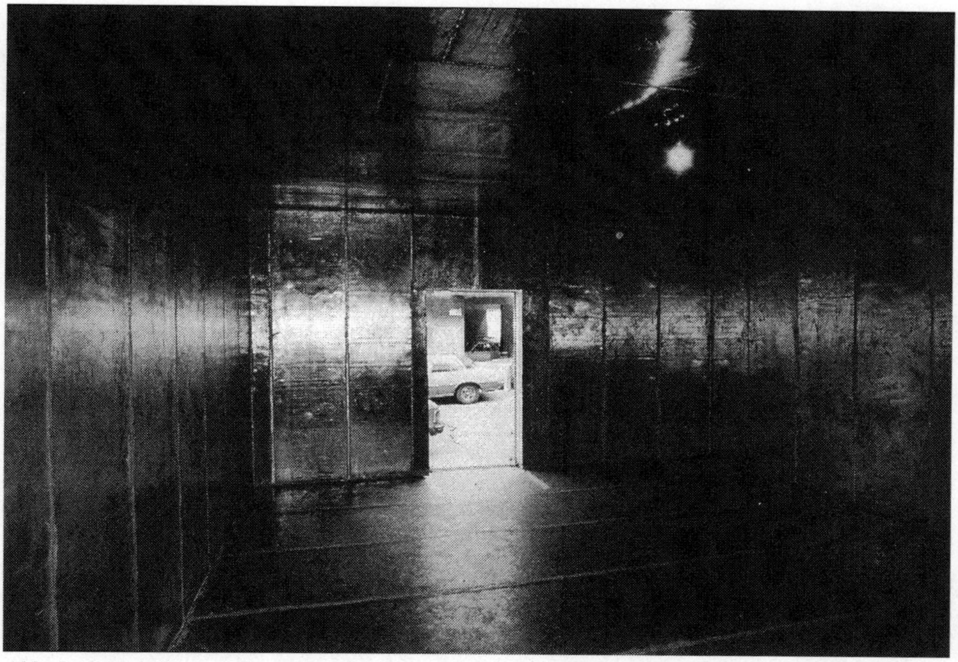

Abb. 2: Joseph Beuys, Hinter dem Knochen wird gezählt – Schmerzraum, 1941–1983, Fundación »la Caixa« Barcelona, © VG Bild-Kunst, Bonn

empfindung bestimmte Emotionen freigesetzt werden, die wiederum die Atmosphäre charakterisieren. Denn, wie Gernot Böhme zu Recht betont hat, verdanken sich Atmosphären gerade dem Zusammenspiel von objektiven Phänomenen und subjektiver Empfindung:

> »Die Atmosphären sind so konzipiert weder als etwas Objektives, nämlich Eigenschaften, die die Dinge haben, und doch sind sie etwas Dinghaftes, zum Ding Gehöriges, insofern nämlich die Dinge durch ihre Eigenschaften – als Ekstasen gedacht – die Sphären ihrer Anwesenheit artikulieren. Noch sind die Atmosphären etwas Subjektives, etwa Bestimmungen eines Seelenzustandes. Und doch sind sie subjekthaft, gehören zu Subjekten, insofern sie in leiblicher Anwesenheit durch Menschen gespürt werden und dieses Spüren zugleich ein leibliches Sich-Befinden der Subjekte im Raum ist.«[7]

Was zeichnet nun die besondere Atmosphäre des *Schmerzraumes* aus und durch welche ästhetischen Qualitäten kommt sie zustande? Indem Beuys den Raum fast leer zeigt und vor allem seine Begrenzungen markiert, macht er ihn als begrenzten Innenraum erfahrbar. Dabei handelt es sich aber beileibe nicht um ein behagliches Interieur. Denn es fehlen die Artefakte, die einen Raum bewohnbar machen. Und der Raum ist gerade groß genug, dass seine Leere spürbar wird. Auch die wenigen Dinge wie Telefon und Lampe, die hier wie Reste einer Einrichtung erscheinen, unterstreichen den Charakter eines ausgeräumten Raumes, der dem Rezipienten ein Gefühl von Verlorenheit und Haltlosigkeit vermitteln mag. Hingegen ist der Raum gerade so klein, dass sich der Besucher auch beengt und eingeschlossen fühlen kann, zumal die Grenzen durch das Blei noch besonders verstärkt werden. Dabei handelt es sich um ein Material, dessen

Schwere sprichwörtlich ist und vor allem durch seine Anbringung an der Decke als lastend und bedrückend empfunden werden muss. Gegenüber dem gewohnten Putz oder gar den Tapeten eines Wohnraums wirken die Bleibahnen hart und kalt. Dies wird verstärkt durch weitere Eigenschaften des Bleis. So trägt seine Funktion als Isoliermaterial dazu bei, ein Gefühl des Eingesperrtseins und der Einsamkeit hervorzurufen, wobei hier auch der akustische Sinn angesprochen wird: Der *Schmerzraum* ist somit auch ein Ort der Stille. Die Isolation wird durch das Material selbst noch einmal buchstäblich reflektiert, wenn das Blei mit der Zeit oxidiert, seinen anfänglichen Glanz verliert, matt und stumpf wird und sich dadurch gleichsam gegenüber dem Umraum abschließt. Auch die graue Farbe des Materials, die – verstärkt durch das dämmrige Licht – eher als Farblosigkeit erscheint, trägt stark zur Tristesse der Atmosphäre bei. Diese muss schließlich regelrecht vergiftet erscheinen, wenn der Besucher sein Alltagswissen um die Schädlichkeit des Schwermetalls in seine Betrachtung mit einfließen lässt.

Die Atmosphäre des Raumes ist also stark durch negative Prädikate bestimmt und kann vielleicht am ehesten als schwermütig, melancholisch, aber darüber hinaus auch als bedrückend, beängstigend und bedrohlich zusammenfassend charakterisiert werden. Daran ändert auch die potentielle Schutzfunktion des Raumes nichts, die der unwirtlichen Atmosphäre des Inneren noch die Bedrohung von außen hinzufügt. Mit Blick auf den Titel der Installation stellt sich die Frage, ob die emotionale Qualität der Atmosphäre auch etwas mit dem Gefühl von Schmerz zu tun hat. Dabei scheint es doch zunächst offensichtlich, dass dem Besucher in diesem Raum kein physischer Schmerz zugefügt wird. Gleichwohl kann der Raum aber eine emotionale Anmutung der räumlichen Dimension des Schmerzes liefern, auf die vor allem Elain Scarry in ihrer kulturanthropologischen Studie *Der Körper im Schmerz. Die Chiffren der Verletzlichkeit und die Erfindung der Kultur* (1985) hingewiesen hat.[8] Denn Scarry beschreibt den physischen Schmerz im Unterschied zur expansiven schöpferischen Tätigkeit des Menschen als räumliche Kontraktion. Im Schmerz werde die Welt um uns herum zum Verschwinden gebracht: »Intensiver Schmerz tilgt die Welt aus.«[9] Indem die Sprache zerstört und die Wahrnehmung zerrüttet wird, verliert der Schmerz empfindende Mensch seinen Bezug zum Umraum, zur Außenwelt. Einsam, von der Welt und den Mitmenschen isoliert, wird er ganz auf seinen eigenen Leib zurückgeworfen, der im eigentlichen Sinne als »Schmerzraum« zu begreifen wäre.[10] Insofern mag der Schmerz zwar zunächst auch den leiblichen Innenraum des Körpers erschließen und in seiner Intensität ein Gefühl körperlicher Präsenz hervorrufen. Doch schließlich macht die negative, kontrahierende Kraft des Schmerzes auch vor diesem leiblichen Innenraum keinen Halt, so dass Scarry den Schmerz zu Recht als »Nachahmung des Todes« und nicht etwa als Intensivierung des Lebens beschreibt.[11] Die hier skizzierte räumliche Struktur des Schmerzes zeigt sich für Scarry exemplarisch in der Folterkammer, weil hier die wohnliche Welt menschlicher Artefakte bereits im Vorhinein vernichtet und in ihr Gegenteil verkehrt worden sei:

> »Der Raum und seine Ausstattung werden zu einer Waffe, die das Opfer mit Vernichtung bedroht und den Kontext der Zivilisation auslöscht; es gibt keine Wand, kein Fenster, keine Tür, keine Badewanne, keinen Kühlschrank, keinen Stuhl, kein Bett mehr.«[12]

Scheint der *Schmerzraum* von Joseph Beuys also atmosphärisch etwas von der räumlichen Dimension dieser körperlichen Empfindung zu vermitteln, so gilt Vergleichbares auch für den psychischen Schmerz des Traumas. Denn auch das Trauma besitzt neben seiner eigentümlichen Zeitstruktur eine räumliche Dimension, wie von der Psychoanalyse im Anschluss an Freuds topisches Modell des psychischen Apparats herausgearbeitet worden ist.[13] Wenn das Ich sich durch schockartige Erlebnisse emotional so überwältigt und bedroht fühlt, dass es diese nicht mehr im Bewusstsein integrieren kann, werden diese Erlebnisse nämlich durch bestimmte Verdrängungsmechanismen quasi eingekapselt und isoliert. Ein Containment entsteht, ein traumatischer Raum, der durch Vernichtungsangst und Schmerz gekennzeichnet ist und stets droht, die ihm gesetzten Grenzen wieder zu durchbrechen. Um diese Grenzen aufrechtzuerhalten, bedarf es eines erhöhten affektiven Energieaufwands des Subjekts, der wiederum in der Folge zu bleibenden pathologischen Veränderungen führen kann wie emotionaler Erstarrung, dem Gefühl innerer Leere sowie eingefrorener Zeit.[14]

Wie bereits erwähnt, liefert die Installation von Joseph Beuys nur eine emotionale Anmutung von physischem und traumatischem Schmerz. Dieser ist im *Schmerzraum* von Beuys gleichsam atmosphärisch verdünnt und ästhetisch distanziert erfahrbar. Dies führt dazu, dass die Atmosphäre auch stimulierend auf die Imagination des Betrachters wirken kann, während real erfahrener Schmerz gerade jegliche Produktivität erlahmen lässt. Es überrascht also nicht, wenn schon die zeitgenössische Kunstkritik die Atmosphäre des Raumes als Assoziationspotential aufgegriffen und den *Schmerzraum* mit unterschiedlichen konkreten Räumen verglichen hat, die sein negatives Potential gleichsam auf den Begriff bringen.[15] So wurden der Gefängnisraum und speziell die berüchtigten Bleikammern des Dogenpalastes in Venedig aufgerufen. Auch das Mausoleum als Ort des Todes und damit der Negation menschlichen Lebens schlechthin. Und schließlich der Bunker als Schutzraum im Krieg und hier speziell der Strahlenschutzbunker, der im Hinblick auf die atomare Bedrohung einen aktuellen Zeitbezug aufwies. Denn Anfang der 1980er Jahre spitzte sich die politische Lage im Kontext des Kalten Krieges zwischen den beiden politischen Machtblöcken bekanntlich noch einmal zu.[16] Den Ausgangspunkt bildeten dabei die neuen atomaren Mittelstreckenraketen SS-20, welche die Sowjetunion Mitte der 1970er Jahre auf Westeuropa ausgerichtet hatte. Als Reaktion darauf setzte sich die Bundesregierung unter Helmut Schmidt für ein neues strategisches Gleichgewicht in Europa ein, was 1979 zum NATO-Doppelbeschluss führte. Dieser setzte der Sowjetunion ein Ultimatum und drohte beim Scheitern der Abrüstungsverhandlungen mit der Stationierung US-amerikanischer Pershing II-Raketen auf dem Territorium der Bundesrepublik. Die festgefahrene und bedrohliche politische Situation führte zu gesellschaftlichen Protesten, die vor allem von der Friedensbewegung getragen wurden und ihren Ausdruck in den großen Demonstrationen in Bonn fanden, an denen auch Beuys als engagierter Bürger und Künstler teilgenommen hat. Auch im Oktober 1983 fand dort eine große Friedensdemonstration statt. Kurz darauf installierte Beuys seinen *Schmerzraum* in Düsseldorf, also genau zu dem Zeitpunkt, als das politisch gesetzte Ultimatum Ende des Jahres auslief. Insofern kann der *Schmerzraum* durchaus als künstlerische Stellungnahme zur aktuellen gesellschaftspolitischen Situation verstanden werden. In ihm ist die gesellschaftlich latent spürbare Atmosphäre der Angst und Bedrohung sowie Erstarrung und Ausweglosigkeit gleichsam ästhetisch verdichtet und damit manifest geworden.

Durch die Datierung der Arbeit von 1941 bis 1983 wird dem *Schmerzraum* ein Zeitraum zugeordnet, der die aktuelle gesellschaftspolitische Situation mit der Geschichte verbindet und dadurch das Assoziationspotential des Raumes noch einmal erweitert. Insofern entfaltet die Installation auch einen Raum der Erinnerung, der individuelles und kollektives Gedächtnis miteinander verschränkt. Im kollektiven Gedächtnis steht das Jahr 1941 vor allem für den Angriff des Deutschen Reiches auf die Sowjetunion und für den Ausbau von Auschwitz zum Vernichtungslager. Durch die mögliche Assoziation dieser beiden historischen Ereignisse wird der Bezug zur aktuellen Situation des Kalten Krieges mit einer historischen Tiefenperspektive versehen. Die militärische Konfrontation von Ost und West kann somit als Analogon oder gar als Resultat der Ereignisse im 2. Weltkrieg verstanden werden und der drohende Schrecken einer atomaren Vernichtung erscheint vor der Folie von Auschwitz, das seit den 1960er Jahren als Synonym für den Holocaust verwendet und bis zum Historikerstreit Mitte der 1980er Jahre immer wieder als Vergleich für den Vietnamkrieg oder eben einen möglichen Atomkrieg herangezogen wurde.[17] So können in der spezifischen Atmosphäre des *Schmerzraums* auch Erinnerungen an konkrete Räume nationalsozialistischer Gräueltaten wach werden wie die Folterkammer oder die Gaskammer.[18] Damit spielt der Bleiraum von Beuys auch auf die »bleierne Zeit« an, eine Metapher Hölderlins, die in den 1970er Jahren zunächst in Italien für die eigene Zeit des inneren Kriegszustands zwischen linksextremen Terroristen und faschistisch beeinflussten Sicherheitskräften angewandt wurde und durch den gleichnamigen und preisgekrönten Film von Margarete von Trotta (1981) auch in der Bundesrepublik neue Aktualität gewann. Nicht nur aufgrund der zeitlichen Nähe und der ästhetischen Qualität des Films, der in Grautönen gezeichnet fast ganz auf bunte Farben verzichtet, bietet sich ein Vergleich mit Beuys an. Denn in Anlehnung an die Biografie von Gudrun Ensslin macht der Film durch das Verfahren der Rückblende deutlich, wie stark Kriegserlebnisse sowie die zunächst verdrängte nationalsozialistische Vergangenheit und ihre spätere Aufarbeitung die Geschichte der Bundesrepublik und speziell das Verhalten der so genannten »68er-Generation« beeinflusst haben. Den Rückblenden im Film entsprechen die imaginativ aufgerufenen Bilder im *Schmerzraum*, denen in diesem Kontext auch Erinnerungen an das Scheitern des deutschen Linksterrorismus und die mit ihm verbundenen Debatten über Recht und Unrecht verschärfter Isolationshaft eingeschrieben sind. Vor allem dieser Aspekt wurde auch ausführlich im Film thematisiert.

Im individuellen Gedächtnis von Joseph Beuys steht das Datum 1941 für den Beginn seiner Rolle als Soldat. So notiert er ganz lakonisch in der ersten von ihm publizierten biografischen Notiz, die er anlässlich seiner Ausstellung im Städtischen Museum Haus Koekoek in Kleve 1961 veröffentlichte: »Soldat 1941, Beginn der Stukazeit 1941 (Hier ist der allgemeine Ausdruck Sturzkampfflieger angebracht, da ich alle Sparten der Waffengattung durchgemacht habe; Funker ist falsch).«[19] In seinen biografischen Angaben spielt die potentielle oder gar faktische Täterschaft allerdings keine Rolle. Stattdessen hebt er bekanntlich eher seinen mit physischem Schmerz verbundenen Opferstatus hervor, wenn er immer wieder seinen Flugzeugabsturz über der Krim erwähnt, der in der Tat historisch verbürgt ist, auch wenn ihn wohl keine Tataren in Filz wickelten und mit Fett einrieben, um ihm das Leben zu retten.[20] Gleichwohl macht diese als Damaskuserlebnis gestaltete Künstlerlegende deutlich, dass der Entschluss, Künstler zu werden, durchaus in die Kriegsjahre fiel oder doch zumindest in dieser Zeit bekräftigt wurde und Beuys bald nach Ende des Krieges das Studium an der staatlichen Kunstakademie in Düsseldorf 1947 aufnahm. Selbstaussagen bestätigen retrospektiv diesen Zusammenhang: »Eigentlich ist dieser Schock nach Ende des Krieges mein Urerlebnis, mein Grunderlebnis, was dazu geführt hat, dass ich überhaupt begonnen habe, mich mit Kunst auseinanderzusetzen, also mich im Sinne eines radikalen Neubeginns wieder zu orientieren.«[21]

Der Schock auf die Erlebnisse im 2. Weltkrieg führte bei Beuys zu einer traumatischen Reaktion in den Jahren 1956 und 1957, die er nicht nur als depressive Erschöpfung und künstlerische Krise, sondern regelrecht als existentielle Bedrohung erlebte. Doch ähnlich wie der physische Schmerz im Krieg wurde auch das Durchleben des traumatischen Schmerzes von Beuys letztlich als positiv und produktiv für seine weitere künstlerische Entwicklung verbucht. Schließlich wurde er bald darauf 1961 als Professor für Bildhauerei an die Kunstakademie Düsseldorf berufen und hatte noch im selben Jahr als Vierzigjähriger seine erste Ausstellung. In diesem Sinne äußert er sich im historischen Rückblick auf die Erlebnisse Ende der 1950er Jahre:

> »[Bei dieser Krise] wirkten zweifellos Kriegsereignisse nach, aber auch aktuelle, denn im Grunde musste etwas absterben. Ich glaube, diese Phase war für mich eine der wesentlichsten insofern, als ich mich auch konstitutionell völlig umorganisiert habe; ich hatte zu lange einen Körper mit mir herumgeschleppt. Der Initialvorgang war ein allgemeiner Erschöpfungszustand, der sich allerdings schnell in einen regelrechten Erneuerungsvorgang umkehrte. Die Dinge in mir mussten sich völlig umsetzen, es musste bis in die Physis hinein eine Umwandlung stattfinden. Krankheiten sind fast immer auch geistige Krisen im Leben, wo alte Erfahrungen und Denkvorgänge abgestoßen beziehungsweise zu durchaus positiven Veränderungen umgeschmolzen werden.«[22]

Künstlerischer Ausdruck dieser traumatischen Reaktion ist die *Gummierte Kiste* (1957) (Abb. 3) in den Maßen 43 x 77 x 91 cm. Dabei handelt es sich um eine schlichte Holzkiste, die mit einer schwarzen Mischung aus Teer und Gummi von allen Seiten bestrichen ist. In Form, Farbe und Materialeigenschaft erinnert der viel später entstandene *Schmerzraum* an dieses frühe Objekt. Ihre besondere Bedeutung erlangt die Kiste im Kontext biografischer Erinnerungen, die davon berichten, wie Beuys sich während seiner depressiven Krise tagelang in der völlig verdunkelten Wohnung eines Freundes eingeschlossen hatte, bis er dort völlig verwahrlost, schon mit Wasser in den Beinen aufgefunden wurde. Dabei äußerte er den Wunsch, sich selbst aufzulösen. Als unmittelbare Reaktion darauf ließ er sich die Holzkiste anfertigen und überzog sie mit dem isolierenden Material:

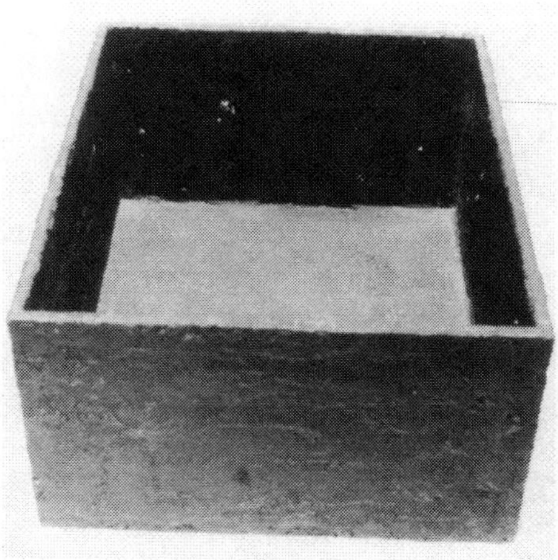

Abb. 3: Joseph Beuys, Gummierte Kiste, 1957, Hessisches Landesmuseum Darmstadt, © VG Bild-Kunst, Bonn

> »Die Kiste sei ein schwarzer, leerer, isolierter Raum, in dem Untersuchungen stattfinden und neue Erfahrungen gemacht werden könnten. Er habe den Zwang gespürt,

> sich in diese Kiste zu setzen, nicht mehr dazusein, einfach mit dem Leben aufzuhören.«[23]

An dieser Kiste scheint Beuys sein therapeutisches Kunstverständnis entwickelt zu haben. Er schuf sich eine sargähnliche Gummizelle, die als Ausdruck des empfundenen Schmerzes, seiner psychischen Bedrohung und sogar Todesnähe zugleich eine erste Distanzierung davon ermöglichte. Einer selbsttherapeutischen Versuchsanordnung vergleichbar, verdrängte Beuys aber nicht seinen Schmerz, sondern wollte ganz buchstäblich in ihn hineingehen und sich in die Kiste setzen. Kunst fungierte bei diesem Experiment gleichsam als Mittel der Distanzierung oder Depotenzierung des Schmerzes. Andererseits schien eine erste Konfrontation mit dem traumatischen Schrecken auch nur in dieser abgeschwächten Weise möglich. Der Bedrohung psychischer Integrität, die als Angst vor körperlicher Selbstauflösung erlebt wurde, wirkte die Kiste auch durch ihre stabilisierenden Wände entgegen. Die hier am eigenen Leib erfahrene therapeutische Wirkung bestimmter Artefakte erhob Beuys später zum programmatischen Anspruch seiner Kunst überhaupt.[24] Dabei griff er aber gerade nicht auf ein psychoanalytisches Vokabular zurück, sondern sprach von Homöopathie und später auch Schamanismus, um die Heilkraft seiner Kunst zu unterstreichen. Denn das Prinzip der Homöopathie – »similia similibus curantur« – findet sich in gewisser Weise auch im magischen Heilritual des Schamanen wieder, wenn dieser sich durch Masken den dämonischen Kräften einerseits mimetisch angleicht und andererseits durch die Theatralik der Maskerade und die Wiederholung des Schreckens in abgeschwächter Form gerade heilsame Distanz zur mythischen Angst schafft.[25] Die Figur des Schamanen bot sich Beuys darüber hinaus auch deshalb an, weil seine besondere Heilkraft – einem Initiationserlebnis vergleichbar – aus der persönlichen Erfahrung von physischem Schmerz und psychischer Instabilität hervorgegangen sei.[26] In diesem Sinne verstand sich Beuys als Künstler der Avantgarde, der unmittelbar auf das Leben einwirken wollte und unterschied sich mit seinem therapeutischen Anspruch wiederum von anderen Strömungen der Neoavantgarde, wie beispielsweise der Fluxusbewegung, in deren Kontext er seine eigentümliche Materialsprache und sein spezifisches aktionistisches Vokabular aber zunächst entwickelt hat. Schmerz und Leid sind in der Biografie von Beuys also nicht nur negativ besetzt, sondern werden wie bei einer Initiation als Katalysatoren persönlicher Entwicklung und vor allem künstlerischer Produktivität aufgefasst.

Im biografischen Kontext fällt auf, wie eng das persönlich erlebte Trauma mit dem gesellschaftlichen Trauma des Holocaust verbunden war. Denn genau in die Zeit seiner traumatischen Krise fiel die erste künstlerische Auseinandersetzung mit Auschwitz: Beuys nahm 1958 am Wettbewerb für ein Mahnmal des ehemaligen Konzentrationslagers teil (Abb. 4). Auch in den 1960er Jahren beschäftigte er sich explizit mit diesem Thema. Die Vitrinen *KZ=Essen 1* und *KZ=Essen 2* (1963) legen ebenso davon Zeugnis ab wie vor allem die Vitrine *Auschwitz-Demonstration* (1956-1964), die Beuys für seine Ausstellung *Sammlung 1968 Karl Ströher* eingerichtet hat.[27]

Mit dem Datum 1941 und dem damit eröffneten biografischen Zeitraum wird implizit deutlich gemacht, dass der *Schmerzraum* auch das eigentümliche Körpergefühl von Joseph Beuys reflektiert, das vielleicht erstmals mit der *Gummierten Kiste* künstlerischen Ausdruck gewonnen hat. Schließlich sprach Beuys in dem bereits erwähnten Zitat zur psychischen Krise von 1957 selbst davon, wie er diese als Transformation

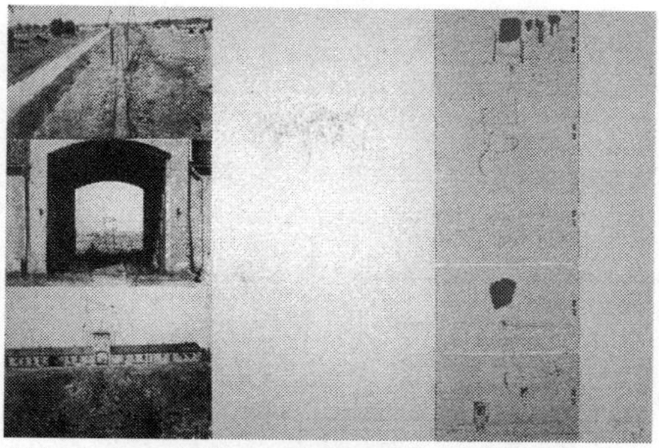

Abb. 4: Joseph Beuys, Entwürfe für Mahnmal Auschwitz, 1957, Stiftung Museum Schloss Moyland – Sammlung van der Grinten, © VG Bild-Kunst, Bonn

seines gesamten Körpers erlebt hat. Die angedeutete körperliche Veränderung könnte grob vereinfacht als Verwandlung eines soldatischen Körperpanzers in eine empfindsame Künstlerhaut beschrieben werden. Paradigmatisch für das Verständnis des soldatischen Körperpanzers ist der Essay von Ernst Jünger *Über den Schmerz* (1934).[28] Darin führt Jünger aus, wie der männliche Körper durch Schmerzerfahrung abgehärtet werden solle. Die Stählung des Körpers sei das Ziel einer kriegerisch-heroischen Disziplin, die mit der Entwicklung eines kälteren Bewusstseins einhergehe. Was hier von Jünger als neuer Menschentypus gefeiert wurde, erkannte Adorno rückblickend zu Recht als zentrale Voraussetzung für die Gräueltaten der Nationalsozialisten:

> »Das gepriesene Hart-Sein, zu dem da erzogen werden soll, bedeutet Gleichgültigkeit gegen den Schmerz schlechthin. Dabei wird zwischen dem eigenen und dem anderer gar nicht einmal so sehr fest unterschieden.«[29]

Adorno machte das von Jünger ausdrücklich gewünschte kältere Bewusstsein als autoritären Charakter kenntlich und erhoffte sich von einer sanfteren Erziehung zusammen mit der Ausbildung eines neuen Körpergefühls auch die Entwicklung »wärmerer« sozialer Fähigkeiten wie Einfühlungsvermögen, Mitgefühl und Liebesfähigkeit.[30] Anknüpfend an Adorno und Wilhelm Reich hat Klaus Theweleit den hier skizzierten Zusammenhang von Soldatenkörper und Faschismus durch sein Buch *Männerphantasien* (1978) populär gemacht.[31] In diesem Kontext verweisen die Bleibahnen des *Schmerzraums* metaphorisch auf die Haut des Künstlers, deren einstmals stählerne Härte durch das Metall noch einmal aufgerufen, aber zugleich durch das weiche Blei transformiert erscheint. Die gelöteten Fugen werden in diesem Bild zu Narben, die auf das Schmerzgedächtnis des Künstlers aufmerksam machen. Dabei wird eine anthropomorphe Lesart des Raumes durch seine Konstruktionsweise unterstützt. Denn – wie bereits erwähnt – überziehen die Bleibahnen das darunter angebrachte Stahlskelett wie eine Haut. Auch die im Anschluss an den *Schmerzraum* aus den übrig gebliebenen Bleibahnen entstandenen *Möbiuswerfer* (Abb. 5) lassen sich wie ein Kommentar auf die hier erfolgte Inversion von innen und außen verstehen. Wie beim Möbiusband, das sich so in den Raum krümmt, dass dieselbe Fläche einmal als Innen- und dann wieder als Außenseite erscheint, können die Bleibahnen im *Schmerzraum* einmal als Begrenzung des Innenraums und metaphorisch als Außenhaut aufgefasst werden. Durch das besonders weiche Metall, das ganz buchstäblich für Eindrücke offen ist, verlieh Beuys dem hautähnlichen Überzug der Wände eine weibliche Qualität, die für die Sensibilität des männlichen Künstlers bürgen soll.[32]

Zusammenfassend kann festgehalten werden, dass sich im *Schmerzraum* von Joseph Beuys ganz unterschiedliche Räume verschachteln. Zunächst ist es der Leibraum des

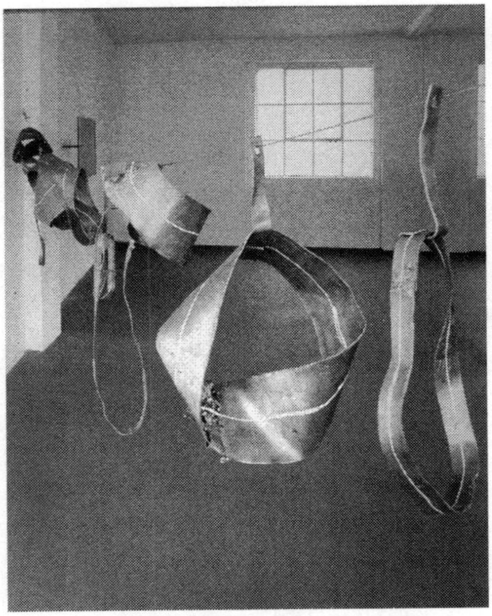

Abb. 5: Joseph Beuys, Möbiuswerfer, 1984, © VG Bild-Kunst, Bonn

Künstlers, der hier eingegangen ist und ästhetisch reflektiert wird. Doch anders als bei der *Gummierten Kiste* beobachtet, zielt die Installation stärker auf den Leib und die Innenwelt des Rezipienten. Die schmerzempfindliche Haut des Künstlers erscheint metaphorisch gewendet und umschließt nun einen Innenraum, in dem der Besucher bestimmte ästhetische Erfahrungen machen kann. Diese Erfahrungen sind zunächst bestimmt durch die dominierende Atmosphäre des Raumes, die vom Rezipienten intuitiv, d. h. unmittelbar leiblich empfunden wird. Neben dem optischen ist dabei auch der akustische Sinn, das Körpergefühl und damit auch stark die Haut des Besuchers angesprochen. So können in diesem atmosphärischen Raum auch synästhetische Effekte entstehen, wie z. B. das Gefühl von Kälte, obwohl der Galerieraum de facto eine Fußbodenheizung besaß und normal temperiert war.

Die Unmittelbarkeit körperlichen und emotionalen Empfindens unterstreicht den aktuellen Zeit- und Raumbezug der Installation. Denn schließlich nimmt der *Schmerzraum* Bezug auf den realen geopolitischen Raum der militärischen Konfrontation westlicher und östlicher Staaten im Kalten Krieg. Doch entscheidend ist, dass dieser Bezug nicht direkt erfolgt, sondern vermittelt über die Atmosphäre, an der sich die Imagination des Betrachters entzünden kann. Der atmosphärische Raum geht also über in einen Imaginationsraum, der als Gedächtnisraum den aktuellen Zeitbezug mit der Historie verknüpft. Streng genommen sind dabei sogar zwei unterschiedliche Imaginationsräume miteinander verschachtelt: Zum einen werden nämlich bestimmte innere Bilder hervorgerufen, die sich zu losen Assoziationsketten verbinden können. Dieser produktive Imaginationsraum ist aber zugleich ein imaginärer Raum, der Realität distanziert oder sogar nichtet.[33] So werden zwar innere Bilder assoziativ beim Betrachter hervorgerufen wie die Gefängniszelle, das Mausoleum, der Bunker, die Folter- oder Gaskammer. Doch gerade dadurch werden die realen Räume auch ästhetisch distanziert. Kurz gesagt, der *Schmerzraum* von Joseph Beuys ist weder ein Gefängnis, noch ein Mausoleum oder ein Bunker, auch keine Folter- oder Gaskammer. Stattdessen ist die Installation ein konkreter ästhetischer Raum, dessen spezifische Atmosphäre einen imaginären Raum hervorruft, der es erlaubt, gesellschaftspolitische Realität in der ästhetischen Distanzierung neu zu reflektieren. Dabei können atmosphärischer und imaginärer Raum durchaus in ein Spiel wechselseitiger Einwirkung treten, insofern die besondere Atmosphäre nicht nur bestimmte imaginative Bilder hervorruft, sondern diese auch wieder auf die atmosphärische Stimmung zurückwirken. In dieser spielerischen Bewegung wird die Semantik des Raumes offen gehalten ohne dabei beliebig zu werden.[34]

Die hier angedeutete doppelte Funktion der Imagination, nämlich einerseits als produktives Vermögen der assoziativen Verbindung innerer Bilder und andererseits als Realität distanzierendes oder gar nichtendes Imaginäres, wird in der Installation selbst noch einmal reflektiert. Zumindest könnte man auf einer strukturellen Metaebene einerseits die Leere des Raumes auch als Reflexion der Welt nichtenden Funktion des Imaginären verstehen. Und andererseits die beiden Silberringe an der Decke als Reflexion des dialektischen Umschlags von einer bedrückenden Atmosphäre in produktive Imaginationstätigkeit. Die Silberringe versinnbildlichen in dieser Hinsicht einen Hoffnungsschimmer im Dunkel des Raumes, sie sind buchstäblich Elemente der Reflexion. Sie versinnbildlichen den Funken, an dem sich die Fantasie des Betrachters entzünden und Assoziationsketten bilden kann. Auch dies geschieht hier buchstäblich: Denn das Silber zeichnet sich gerade im Unterschied zum Blei dadurch aus, dass es Wärme aufnimmt und Energie leitet. Nicht von ungefähr sind die Ringe fast schwebend leicht an der Decke angebracht, so dass der Besucher den Blick heben muss und damit auch körperlich eine erste Bewegung aus der niederdrückenden Atmosphäre heraus vollzieht. Auch sind es zwei Reife, die zudem noch einander zugeneigt sind, so dass auch hierdurch ein Überwinden der atmosphärisch empfundenen Einsamkeit angedeutet wird. Schließlich verweist auch das Telefon ganz offensichtlich auf die Möglichkeit von Kommunikation. Beuys musste hier die Auflage des Galeristen berücksichtigen, der den Raum durch das Telefon funktionstüchtig belassen wollte.[35] Auch wenn das Telefon in der später nach Barcelona verkauften Version nicht mehr vorhanden ist, charakterisiert es doch maßgeblich die Atmosphäre der Düsseldorfer Fassung. Zugleich nutzte Beuys die Vorgabe, um – wie bereits in früheren Arbeiten geschehen – eine kritische Revision von Duchamps Konzept des »ready-made« und seiner spezifischen Rezeption seit den 1960er Jahren zu formulieren.[36] Denn das Telefon ist bei Beuys weder eine anti-künstlerische noch eine institutionskritische Geste, die den Galerieraum als Ort ökonomischen Denkens und Handelns kenntlich machen würde. Dem *Erdtelefon* (1968) vergleichbar, ist der technische Apparat auch hier Stimulans assoziativer Imaginationstätigkeit. Nicht von ungefähr verweist der optisch wahrgenommene Apparat auf das lediglich akustisch vollzogene Telefongespräch, das den Gesprächspartner bildhaft nur in der Imagination erscheinen lässt.

Im künstlerischen Selbstverständnis von Beuys ist der *Schmerzraum* damit auch ein Ort der Transformation und Heilung. Er konfrontiert den Betrachter mit physischem Schmerz und psychischem Trauma, die aber in der ästhetischen Distanzierung quasi homöopathisch verdünnt wie eine Medizin verabreicht werden. In dieser Dosierung kann eine Begegnung mit verdrängten traumatischen Inhalten zugelassen werden und ein erster Schritt zur Integration des Abgespaltenen erfolgen. Auch kann die ästhetische Atmosphäre von Dunkelheit, Härte und Kälte das Bewusstsein für diese Atmosphäre in der Realität schärfen. Doch zielt Beuys mit der Bewusstmachung auch direkt auf eine Veränderung der Realität, die aber weniger bei den gesellschaftlichen Verhältnissen, sondern eher am Individuum ansetzt. In diesem Sinne provoziert der *Schmerzraum* auch einen »Gegenraum«, von dem Joseph Beuys öfter gesprochen hat.[37] Dem physiologisch bedingten Kontrastbild auf der Netzhaut vergleichbar, müsste die Installation demgemäß gerade einen hellen, farbigen und warmen Raum hervorrufen. Im Sinne von Beuys wird nicht nur das Bedürfnis nach diesem Gegenraum wachgerufen, sondern auch die erste Voraussetzung dafür geschaffen. Denn der *Schmerzraum* setzt ganz konkrete

Heilungsprozesse in Gang, indem beim einzelnen Rezipienten die Vermögen intuitiven Empfindens und imaginativer Assoziation aktiviert werden. Beide verstand Beuys nämlich als Remedium gegen identifizierendes Denken und instrumentelle Vernunft, die seiner Meinung nach in unserer Kultur vorherrschen und auch – ganz im Sinne einer Dialektik der Aufklärung – für die gegenwärtige prekäre gesellschaftspolitische Situation mit verantwortlich seien.[38] Intuition und Imagination sollen hingegen dazu beitragen, strategisches Kalkül im Denken und Handeln aufzubrechen und in der Folge eine bessere Welt zu schaffen. Darin liegt das utopische Potential des *Schmerzraums* und der Kunst von Joseph Beuys überhaupt.

Mit seinen Anspielungen auf die nationalsozialistische Vergangenheit sowie die gegenwärtige politische Situation der Bundesrepublik steht der *Schmerzraum* von Joseph Beuys freilich nicht isoliert. Spezifisch ist in diesem Kontext jedoch das gewählte Medium. Denn im Unterschied zu Georg Baselitz und Gerhard Richter sowie Jörg Immendorff, Markus Lüpertz und Anselm Kiefer, deren figurative Tafelbilder gerade zu Beginn der 1980er Jahre als spezifisch westdeutscher Beitrag zur Entwicklung der Kunst auch international gewürdigt wurden, schuf Beuys mit dem *Schmerzraum* eine Installation, die seine raumbezogenen Arbeiten der 1960er und 1970er Jahre konsequent fortsetzt.[39] Grundlegend war dabei für ihn zunächst die dadaistische und surrealistische Materialästhetik, die er – typisch für die westdeutsche Kunst der späten 1950er Jahre – vermittelt durch die Collagen und Assemblagen Robert Rauschenbergs sowie des Nouveau Réalisme rezipierte und für seine so genannten »Plastischen Bilder« nutzte. Im Kontext der Fluxus-Bewegung übertrug Beuys die im kleinen Format der »Plastischen Bilder« erprobte Zusammenstellung heterogener und oft obsoleter, beschädigter Dinge, die den Betrachter aufgrund ihrer Ekel erregenden Materialität eher abzustoßen als anzuziehen scheinen, auf den Galerieraum, der nun aber als Aktionsraum genutzt wurde. Durch die psychophysische Dimension der verwendeten Materialien einerseits und durch die formale Gestaltung des Raumes andererseits, der performativ und kompositorisch erschlossen wurde, unterscheiden sich Beuys' Aktionen von denjenigen anderer Vertreter der Fluxus-Bewegung, die sich entweder – wie Wolf Vostell – am Happening von Allan Kaprow orientierten und somit eine direkte Partizipation des Publikums anstrebten oder – wie dies von George Maciunas gefordert wurde – die eher kurze und konzentrierte Aktionsform des Events von George Brecht zum Vorbild nahmen. Bereits bei seinen Aktionen verlieh Beuys dem Galerieraum durch schwarzen Anstrich eine unheimliche und triste Atmosphäre oder suchte solche Räume auf, die – wie Keller oder Bunker – von vornherein über eine entsprechende Atmosphäre verfügten.[40] Richtungsweisend für die Installationen der 1970er Jahre waren neben den Aktionen auch die Ausstellungen der 1960er Jahre, bei denen Beuys seine Objekte als räumliche Ensembles arrangierte. Dabei orientierte er sich auch an den raumbezogenen Arbeiten von Robert Morris und setzte sich zugleich wieder davon ab, indem er die programmatisch geforderte Buchstäblichkeit der Minimal Art durch eine semantische Konnotation der verwendeten Materialien konterkarierte und damit auch die phänomenologisch begründete, bloß leiblich fundierte Wahrnehmung zugunsten einer imaginativen Wahrnehmungsweise erweiterte. Auch wenn Beuys den weißen Galerie- und Museumsraum zunehmend in Frage stellte oder sogar ganz verließ, unterscheidet er sich doch von institutionskritisch perspektivierten Installationen, die in den 1970er Jahren den »white cube« des Galerie- und Museumsraums explizit zum Thema machten.[41] Dabei ging es

Künstlern wie Daniel Buren, Marcel Broodthaers und Hans Haacke um eine kritische Hinterfragung der Autonomie moderner Kunst, indem sie den Galerie- und Museumsraum als konstitutiven Ort ihrer Genese freilegten und damit zugleich die verborgenen Machtstrukturen des »white cube« auf der formalästhetischen, epistemologischen sowie ökonomischen und gesellschaftspolitischen Ebene deutlich machten. Beuys hingegen stellt mit der Installation des *Schmerzraums* die Galerie als Ort des Warenverkehrs unter dem Deckmantel künstlerischer Autonomie nicht in Frage, sondern nutzt die vermeintliche gesellschaftliche Ausgrenzung des Kunstraums, um diesen als Raum einer psychischen Abspaltung, eines traumatischen Containments, zu inszenieren und dabei zugleich zum Ort einer besonderen ästhetischen Erfahrung zu machen, die sich durch ein komplexes Wechselspiel von sinnlich-leiblicher Empfindung sowie Imagination und Reflexion auszeichnet und von Beuys aufgrund ihrer distanzierenden und integrierenden Kraft als Therapeutikum verstanden wird.

---

1 Zu dieser Arbeit siehe v. a. Armin Zweite: »Die plastische Theorie von Joseph Beuys und das Reservoir seiner Themen« In: Ausst.-Kat. *Joseph Beuys. Natur, Materie, Form.* Düsseldorf (Kunstsammlung Nordrhein-Westfalen 30. Nov. 1991 – 9. Feb. 1992). Hg. v. Armin Zweite. München 1991, S. 13–29. – Barbara Strieder: »›Zeige deine Wunde‹ – Joseph Beuys und der Schmerz« In: *Schmerz-Symposium.* 26. Juli 1998, Parkhotel Schweizerhaus, Kleve. Hg. v. Prof. Dr. med. Heribert J. Hinckers. Kleve 1998, S. 67–89. – *Fundación »la Caixa«.* Catálogo de la Colecciòn de Arte Contemporáneo. Barcelona 2000, Bd. 1, S. 106–112. – Gene Ray: »Joseph Beuys and the After-Auschwitz Sublime« In: *Joseph Beuys. Mapping the Legacy.* New York 2001, S. 55–74.

2 Die Installation wurde 1985 von der Sparkassenstiftung in Barcelona erworben. Siehe Fundación »la Caixa« 2000 (wie Anm. 1).

3 Der Titel geht auf ein Ölbild von 1961 zurück, das in der Ausstellung im Haus Koekkoek (1961) zu sehen war. Vgl. Ausst.-Kat. *Joseph Beuys. Zeichnungen, Aquarelle, Oelbilder, Plastische Bilder aus der Sammlung van der Grinten.* Kleve (Städtisches Museum Haus Koekkoek, 8. Okt. – 5. Nov. 1961). Kleve 1961, Nr. 226.

4 Vgl. Zweite 1991 (wie Anm. 1), S. 47.

5 Vgl. v. a. Werner Spies: *Picassos Skulpturen.* Ostfildern-Ruit 2000.

6 Zur Rezeption der raumbezogenen Arbeiten von Joseph Beuys allgemein siehe v. a. Melitta Kliege: *Funktionen des Betrachters. Modelle der Partizipation bei Joseph Beuys und Antoni Tàpies.* München 1999 (= Diss. Univ. Berlin 1996), S. 97–184.

7 Gernot Böhme: *Atmosphäre.* Frankfurt/M. 1995, S. 33/34.

8 Elaine Scarry: *Der Körper im Schmerz. Die Chiffren der Verletzlichkeit und die Erfindung der Kultur* (1985). Frankfurt/M. 1992. Zur kritischen Revision der Thesen Scarrys siehe auch Patrick McGee: »Theory in Pain« In: *Genre*, 20/1987, S. 67–84. Und: Aleida Assmann: »Die Häuslichkeit der Welt. Zu Elaine Scarrys *The Body in Pain*« In: Delfin, 6/1988/89, S. 37–46. Sowie: Jakob Tanner: »Körpererfahrung, Schmerz und die Konstruktion des Kulturellen« In: *Historische Anthropologie*, 2/1994, S. 489–502.

9 Scarry 1992 (wie Anm. 8), S. 47.

10 In diesem Sinne verwendet Merleau-Ponty diesen Begriff: »Vielmehr will ich sagen, dass der Schmerz selbst seinen Ort anzeigt, also einen ›Schmerzraum‹ konstituierend.« Siehe Maurice Merleau-Ponty: *Phänomenologie der Wahrnehmung* (1945). Berlin 1966, S. 119.

11 Scarry 1992 (wie Anm. 8), S. 49.

12 Ebd., S. 63.

13 Zusammenfassend siehe v. a. Werner Bohleber: »Die Entwicklung der Traumatheorie in der Psychoanalyse« In: *Psyche. Zeitschrift für Psychoanalyse und ihre Anwendungen*, 54/2000, Heft 9/10, S. 797–839.

14 Ebd., S. 831.

15 Vgl. Heiner Stachelhaus »Der ganze Schmerz der Zeit« In: *Neue Ruhr-Zeitung*, 31. Dez. 1983, wieder abgedruckt in: Ders.: *Joseph Beuys*. München 1988, S. 199/200; und in Götz Adriani, Winfried Konnertz und Karin Thomas: *Joseph Beuys*. Köln 1994, S. 192. Vgl. auch die kurze Rezension in der *Süddeutschen Zeitung* vom 19. Jan. 1984.

16 Vgl. Bernd Stöver: *Der Kalte Krieg*. München 2003, S. 98–100.

17 Hans Magnus Enzensberger sprach 1964 vom »Prinzip Auschwitz«, stellte eine Beziehung zum drohenden Atomkrieg her und rückte Auschwitz damit in eine generalisierende Perspektive. Bereits damals wurde an diesem Umgang mit der deutschen Geschichte Kritik geübt, so von Hannah Arendt und Jürgen Habermas. Siehe Habbo Knoch: *Die Tat als Bild. Fotografien des Holocaust in der deutschen Erinnerungskultur*. Hamburg 2001, S. 906/907.

18 Zu diesem Bezug siehe Ray 2001 (wie Anm. 1). Die Lesart von Ray ist allerdings zu ikonographisch und eindimensional. Sie berücksichtigt nicht das breitere Assoziationspotential der Installation, das eine semantische Festlegung gerade verhindert.

19 Joseph Beuys: »Notizzettel Josef [sic!] Beuys« In: Ausst.-Kat. Kleve 1961 (wie Anm. 3), o.S. Überraschenderweise verschwindet dieses Datum im nachfolgenden *Lebenslauf – Werklauf* von 1964 und in den späteren Ergänzungen.

20 Zur Kritik an dieser Künstlerlegende siehe v. a. Benjamin Buchloh: »The Twilight of the Idol« In: *Artforum*, 18/1980, Heft 5, S. 35–43. Sowie die sehr polemisch formulierte Biografie von Frank Gieseke und Albert Markert, Flieger: *Filz und Vaterland. Eine erweiterte Beuys-Biografie*. Berlin 1996.

21 Joseph Beuys, in: *Penthouse*, 106/1980, Heft 98, zit. nach Mario Kramer: »Joseph Beuys: „Auschwitz Demonstration" 1956–1964« In: Ausst.-Kat. *deutschlandbilder: Kunst aus einem geteilten Land*. Berlin (Martin-Gropius-Bau 1997/1998). Hg. von Eckhart Gillen. Frankfurt/M. 1997, S. 293.

22 Joseph Beuys in: Götz Adriani, Winfried Konnertz und Karin Thomas: *Joseph Beuys. Leben und Werk*. Köln 1981, S. 66/67. Neu abgedruckt in Adriani u. a. 1994 (wie Anm. 15), S. 40.

23 Heiner Stachelhaus: *Joseph Beuys*. Düsseldorf 1988, S. 64.

24 Zum medizinischen Aspekt im Werk von Beuys siehe v. a. Axel Hinrich Murken: *Joseph Beuys und die Medizin*. Münster 1979.

25 Vgl. Max Horkheimer und Theodor W. Adorno: »Der Schamane bannt das Gefährliche durch dessen Bild. Gleichheit ist sein Mittel.« (*Dialektik der Aufklärung*, 1947) In: Max Horkheimer: *Gesammelte Schriften*. Hg. von Gunzelin Schmid Noerr. Bd. 5. Frankfurt/M. 1987, S. 39.

26 Vgl. v. a. Mircia Eliade: *Schamanismus und archaische Ekstasetechnik* (1957). Frankfurt/M. 1975, S. 43–76.

27 Siehe dazu v. a. Kramer 1997 (wie Anm. 21), S. 293–303.

28 Ernst Jünger: »Über den Schmerz« (1934) In: Ders.: *Werke*. Bd. 5. Stuttgart 1960, S. 151–198. Zur Auseinandersetzung von Beuys mit den Schriften Jüngers siehe Hans van der Grinten: »Beuys und Jünger« In: *Joseph Beuys-Tagung*. Basel 1.–4. Mai 1991. Hg. von Volker Harlan, Dieter Koepplin u. a. Basel 1991, S. 7–12.

29 Theodor W. Adorno: »Erziehung nach Auschwitz« (1967) In: Ders.: *Gesammelte Schriften*. Hg. von Rolf Tiedemann. Bd. 10/2. Frankfurt/M. 1977, S. 682.

30 Vgl. Margarete und Alexander Mitscherlich: *Die Unfähigkeit zu trauern. Grundlagen kollektiven Verhaltens* (1967). München 1982, S. 77–83.

31 Klaus Theweleit: *Männerphantasien*. Bd. 1 u. 2. Frankfurt/M. 1978.

32 Zu diesem Aspekt allgemein vgl. Gabriele Winter: »Elemente des Weiblichen im Werk von Joseph Beuys« In: *Vorträge zum Werk von Joseph Beuys*. Hg. v. Arbeitskreis Block Beuys Darmstadt im Verein der Freunde und Förderer des Hessischen Landesmuseums in Darmstadt e.V. Göttingen 1995, S. 35–44.

33 Vgl. Jean-Paul Sartre: *Phänomenologische Psychologie der Einbildungskraft* (1940). Hamburg 1971, S. 279–292.

34 Iser beschreibt das Zusammenspiel zwischen Fiktivem und Imaginärem mit Blick auf die Literatur. Vgl. Wolfgang Iser: *Das Fiktive und das Imaginäre. Perspektiven literarischer Anthropologie*. Frankfurt/M. 1981, S. 377–411.

35 Gespräch mit Frau Fischer im Dezember 2004.

36 Zur Rezeption des »ready-made« von Marcel Duchamp siehe v. a. William A. Camfield: *Marcel Duchamp. Fountain*. Houston, Texas 1989. Und Dieter Daniels: *Duchamp und die anderen. Der Modellfall einer künstlerischen Wirkungsgeschichte in der Moderne*. Köln 1992, S. 166–232.

37 Zum Begriff des Gegenraums mit Blick auf die Partiturzeichnung zur Aktion *Infiltration-Homogen für Konzertflügel, Der größte Komponist der Gegenwart ist das Contergankind, Division of the Cross* (1966) siehe v. a. Mario Kramer: *Klang & Skulptur. Der musikalische Aspekt im Werk von Joseph Beuys*. Darmstadt 1995 (= Diss. Univ. Hamburg 1993), S. 81/82.

38 Beispielhaft für die vielen Äußerungen von Beuys, die in diese Richtung gehen, sind folgende Sätze von 1970: »Ein Bild kann nicht sprechen. Ein Bild muß sich ganz anders mitteilen. Es müssen Kräfte davon ausgehen, die ganz andere Informationen davon abgeben können als zum Beispiel erklärende Sprache. Es ist wirklich Imagination im Spiel, und Imagination verstehe ich nicht als etwas Unklares, sondern als ein Mittel, etwas Komplexeres auszusagen als einen Gedanken, der mehr oder weniger logisch aufgebaut sein muß. Ich komme also insofern immer ein Stück über mein Denken hinaus.« Zit. nach Uwe Schneede: *Joseph Beuys. Die Aktionen*. Ostfildern-Ruit 1994, S. 234.

39 Zur sogenannten »Nazismusdebatte« in der westdeutschen Kunst um 1970 siehe Cornelia Gockel: *Zeige deine Wunde. Faschismusrezeption in der deutschen Gegenwartskunst*. München 1998. – Stefan Germer: »Die Wiederkehr des Verdrängten. Zum Umgang mit deutscher Geschichte bei Georg Baselitz, Anselm Kiefer, Jörg Immendorff und Gerhard Richter« (1994) In: *Germeriana. Unveröffentlichte oder übersetzte Schriften von Stefan Germer zur zeitgenössischen und modernen Kunst*. Hg. v. Julia Bernard, Jahresring 46, Köln 1999, S. 39–55.

40 Für seine Aktion *Manresa* (1966) ließ Beuys den Raum der Galerie Schmela in Düsseldorf schwarz streichen. *Action the dead mouse* (1971) fand im Keller der Düsseldorfer Kunstakademie statt und für die Aktion *Celtic* (1971) wählte Beuys die Zivilschutzräume in Basel als Aufführungsort.

41 Zur künstlerischen Reaktion auf den weißen Museumsraum siehe Brian O'Doherty: *In der weißen Zelle*. Hg. von Wolfgang Kemp. Berlin 1996. – Benjamin Buchloh: »Von der Ästhetik der Verwaltung zur institutionellen Kritik. Einige Aspekte der Konzeptkunst von 1962–1969« In: Ausst.-Kat. *um 1968. konkrete utopien in kunst und gesellschaft*. Düsseldorf (Städtische Kunsthalle, 27. Mai – 8. Juli 1990). Hg. von Marie Luise Syring. Köln 1990, S. 86–99.

Anna Greve

Ein Schwarzer als Repräsentant der *weißen* Stadt Dresden?*

Dresden ist in den letzten Jahren zu einer Stadt der kulturellen Superlative geworden. Im Jahr 2004 wurde das nach dem neusten Stand der Museumstechnik eingerichtete Neue Grüne Gewölbe im ersten Obergeschoss des Dresdner Residenzschlosses – dessen Gesamtsanierung bis 2013 abgeschlossen sein soll – eröffnet. Im Jahr 2005 katapultierte die Wiederweihe der Frauenkirche die Stadt in das internationale Bewusstsein. Zeitgleich öffnete die Kunsthalle im Lipsiusbau erstmals seit 1945 wieder ihre Türen. Ebenso wie mit der im gleichen Jahr erfolgten Gründung des Gerhard Richter Archivs sollte damit neben dem Image als Barockstadt dasjenige eines Zentrums der Gegenwartskunst etabliert werden. Nicht zuletzt die viele Monate im Voraus zu buchenden Karten machen den Besuch des 2006 eröffneten Historischen Grünen Gewölbe zu einem exklusiven Erlebnis. Es ist an seinem Ursprungsort im Erdgeschoss des Residenzschlosses zu finden, weitestgehend an dem Zustand von 1733 orientiert. Auch die Präsentationen in Kupferstich-Kabinett und Porzellansammlung wurden in dieser Zeit grundlegend überarbeitet, derzeit werden der Mathematisch-Physikalische Salon im Zwinger sowie Skulpturensammlung und Galerie Neue Meister im Albertinum generalüberholt. Neben diesen Ereignissen vor Ort stellten sich die Staatlichen Kunstsammlungen Dresden mit Großausstellungen im Ausland vor: *The Glory of Baroque Dresden* (Jackson 2004), *Dresden. Spiegel der Welt* (Toyko und Kobe 2005), *Pincely Splendor. The Dresden Court 1580-1620* (Rom 2005, Versaille 2006), *From Caspar David Friedrich to Gerhard Richter. German Paintings from Dresden at The J. Paul Getty Museum* (Los Angeles 2006). Die gemeinsam mit den Staatlichen Museen zu Berlin – Preußischer Kulturbesitz und der Bayerischen Staatsgemäldesammlung in München ausgerichtete Ausstellung *Blicke auf Europa. Europa und die deutsche Malerei des 19. Jahrhunderts* in Brüssel anlässlich der deutschen EU-Ratspräsidentschaft führte endgültig eine kulturpolitische Gleichrangigkeit Dresdens mit den führenden deutschen Kunstzentren Berlin und München vor. Die anhaltenden Debatten um die Waldschlösschen Brücke, deren Realisierung den Verlust des UNESCO-Weltkulterbetitels bedeuten würde, scheinen dem keinen grundlegenden Schaden zuzufügen.

Ohne Frage sind dies nicht zuletzt Verdienste des Generaldirektors Martin Roth, der sich und seine Institution durch beharrliche Öffentlichkeitsarbeit und unermüdliche Verhandlungen innerhalb lokaler, bundesweiter und internationaler politischer Strukturen profiliert. Dieser Erfolgsgeschichte soll ein anderer Aspekt an die Seite gestellt werden: die Subordination der kunsthistorischen Interpretation unter die Marketingstrategie. Demonstriert werden soll dies im Folgenden anhand der gegenwärtigen Rezeption eines Werkes aus dem Grünen Gewölbe.

I.

Die aus Birnbaumholz geschnitzte und mit Edelsteinen besetzte Skulptur *Mohr mit Smaragdstufe*[1] (um 1724) von Balthasar Permoser und Johann Melchior Dinglinger war zentrales Werbemotiv bei den oben genannten Ereignissen. Ihre Genese kann an dieser Stelle nur zusammengefasst werden: Im Auftrag von August dem Starken und anlässlich der Neuaufstellung des Grünen Gewölbes im Jahre 1733 entstand sie als Trägerfigur für eine aus den Anfängen der Dresdner Kunstkammer stammende Smaragdstufe, die Kaiser Rudolf II. im Jahr 1581 dem sächsischen Kurfürsten August geschenkt hatte. Bis auf einen Lendenschurz und den Schmuck ist die Figur nackt. Da die Stufe aus den Minen bei Muzo (im heutigen Kolumbien) stammte, lag eine Gestaltung der Trägerfigur in Anlehnung an eine Amerika-Darstellung nahe und so lassen sich die Tätowierungen auch auf Kupferstiche des 2. Teils der *India Occidentalis* (1591) aus der Werkstatt von Theodor de Bry über die indigenen Völker Floridas zurückführen. Die Physiognomie der Skulptur weicht deutlich von den Kupferstichvorlagen ab, denn dort weisen die Dargestellten trotz feinster technischer Ausführung weder Hautfarben noch einer geografischen Herkunft zugeschriebene spezifische Gesichtszüge auf. Der »Mohr« ist somit die europäische Konstruktion eines Afroamerikaners. Es ist zu vermuten, dass die Anwesenheit von Savase Oke Charnige und Tusské Stannagée in Dresden zwischen 1722 und 1725, zweier »amerikanischer königlicher Printzen«, wie es im *Sächsischen Kern-Chronicon* von Johann Christian Crell heißt,[2] zu der Idee für das Werk und sein Pendant *Mohr mit Landsteinstufe*[3] führte. Durch diese zweite Figur mit verschiedenfarbigen, vorwiegend sächsischen Steinen sollte dem sagenhaften Reichtum der außereuropäischen Welt ein würdiges Gegenüber geschaffen werden, das die Konkurrenzfähigkeit des einheimischen Bergbaus bewies, wie ich an anderer Stelle gezeigt habe.[4] In den beiden Figuren manifestiert sich ebenso wie in anderen Darstellungen von Schwarzen im Bestand des Grünen Gewölbes das Verlangen der *weißen* Europäer nach Exotik.[5] Nicht reale – ins höfische Leben integrierte – Schwarze standen Pate,[6] sondern die aus älteren Bildtraditionen und illustrierter Reiseliteratur gespeisten Vorstellungen und Konstruktionen außereuropäischer Menschen, wie es sich beispielsweise auch in Bezug auf Kokosnusspokale und Faltgloben nachweisen lässt.[7] Es zeigt sich sowohl ein Gefühl der Bedrohung und Inferiorität der *weißen* Europäer als auch ihre symbolische Aneignung der außereuropäischen Welt. Entscheidend ist dabei, dass die Darstellung eines Königs verwendet wurde, dessen dunkle Hautfarbe für sein außereuropäisches Herrschaftsgebiet steht.

II.

Die Faszination für die ästhetische Kraft des Werkes *Mohr mit Smaragdstufe* aus *weißer* Perspektive hat sich bis heute gehalten. So erschien die Figur zwischen 1998 und 2004 alljährlich auf dem Werbeplakat für das Dresdner Stadtfest, jeweils mit etwas unterschiedlichen Hintergründen (Abb. 1).[8] Hat sich die Wahrnehmung der über 280 Jahre alten Skulptur angesichts anhaltender Debatten über Globalisierung und Migration verändert? Auf dem Plakat sind vor der grau abgesetzten Altstadtsilhouette Dres-

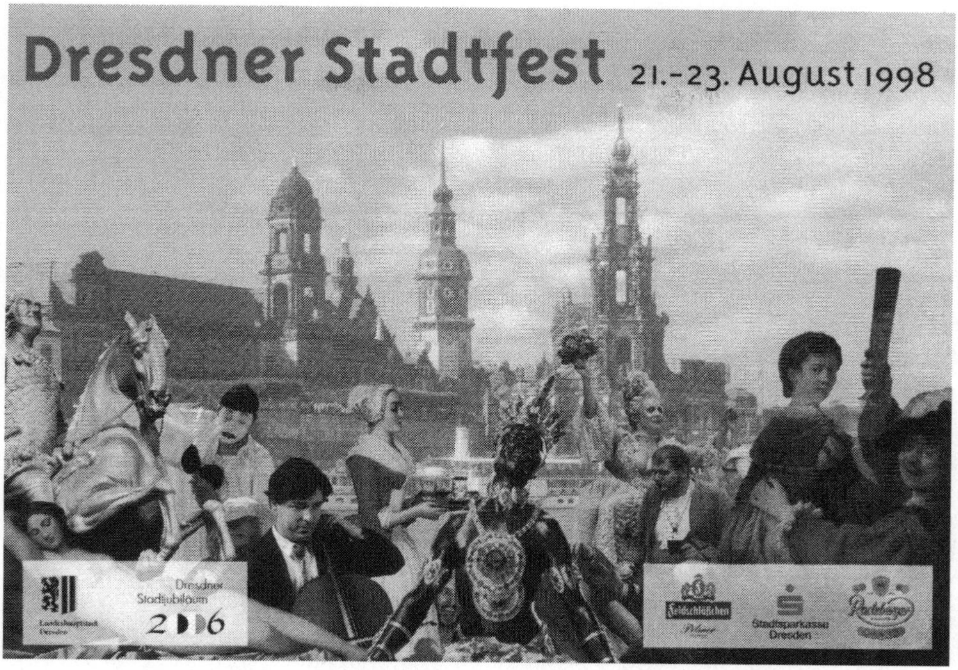

Abb. 1: Postkarte Dresdner Stadtfest 1998

dens, unter blassblauem Himmel, in der unteren Bildhälfte – von links nach rechts – elf Figuren zu sehen: Das vergoldete Reiterstandbild von August dem Starken (1736), das sich auf der Neustädter Seite Dresdens befindet, die hellhäutige »schlummernde Venus« aus dem Gemälde von Giorgione (um 1508/10) in der Gemäldegalerie Alte Meister, ein Pantomime-Schauspieler mit weißer Maske, ein hellhäutiges kleines Mädchen, ein hellhäutiger Cellist, das blasse »Schokoladenmädchen« aus dem Bild von Jean-Etienne Liotard (um 1744/45) aus der Gemäldegalerie Alte Meister, der dunkelhäutige »Mohr«, eine mit Rouge geschminkte hellhäutige Schauspielerin, davor ebenfalls im historischen Kostüm eine hellhäutige männliche Person und das Doppelporträt von Rembrandt mit seiner Frau Saskia (um 1635) aus der Gemäldegalerie Alte Meister. Es handelt sich also um Vertreter der Dresdner Kunst- und Kulturszene aus den Staatlichen Kunstsammlungen, dem Schauspielhaus und der Semperoper. Sieht man von dem goldenen August, der nackten hellen Venus und der dunkelhäutigen Gestalt mit ihrer spärlichen Bekleidung ab, ist nicht sofort erkennbar, ob es sich um reale, verkleidete Personen oder Figuren aus berühmten Gemälden der Kunstgeschichte handelt. In ihrer Zusammenstellung repräsentieren sie die europäische *weiße* Kultur. Wieso wird die Darstellung eines Schwarzen als geeignetes Aushängeschild für die Stadt Dresden mit einer mehrheitlich *weißen* Bevölkerung ins Zentrum gerückt, flankiert von zwei aus Mann und Frau bestehenden Gruppen? Am linken Bildrand blickt Kurfürst August voller Tatendrang mit erhobenem Haupt gen Himmel. Die schlummernde Venus liegt hingegen völlig passiv und wehrlos zu seinen Füßen, während die Hufe des Pferdes über ihrem verletzlichen Körper schweben und drohen ihre Schamgegend brutal zu treffen. Durch die teilweise Bedeckung von Venus und Pferdehufen mit dem Logo der

Stadt wird dieses Moment etwas zurückgenommen. Die Nacktheit der Venus entspricht dem Typus des Idealschönen der Hochrenaissance und unterscheidet sich damit deutlich von der stereotypen wilden Nacktheit des Schwarzen, der wiederum gar nicht verletzlich wirkt. Der polarisierten Geschlechterkonstellation am linken Bildrand ist ein ganz anderes Geschlechterverhältnis am rechten Bildrand gegenüber gestellt: Rembrandt, mit seiner Frau Saskia auf dem Schoss, erhebt fröhlich sein Glas. Auch hier dominiert der Mann, die Frau strahlt jedoch ein eigenes Selbstbewusstsein aus. Die Begegnung zwischen Mann und Frau, als unvereinbare andersartige Wesen, in allen ihren Nuancen scheint ein unabdingbarer Aspekt des Feierns zu sein, was das zentrale Thema des Plakates ist. In der zentralen Figur des Plakates, die sich zwischen diesen Gruppen befindet, kristallisiert sich eine weitere Fassette von Andersartigkeit. Sie sticht durch ihre dunkle Hautfarbe, den besonderen Körperschmuck und die Nicht-Bekleidung, die Freiräume links und rechts von ihr und ihre Haltung hervor. Letztere suggeriert, sie würde inmitten dieser fröhlichen Gesellschaft Bildbetrachtern und Bildbetrachterinnen ein Tablett hinhalten. Von der Smaragdstufe die sie in dem realen Kunstwerk hält ist auf dem Plakat kaum etwas erkennbar. So erfüllt diese Figur wie das Mädchen mit dem exotischen Getränk Schokolade links dahinter eine dienende Funktion, sie nimmt nicht als Gast an der Festgesellschaft teil. Ihr Körper ist Träger kostbarer Edelsteine, die einen besonderen finanziellen, künstlerischen und exotischen Reichtum Dresdens suggerieren. Durch den Kontext der anderen Figuren ist dieser Reichtum nun sächsisch und nicht mehr außereuropäisch, wie im Falle des realen Kunstwerkes, wie oben dargelegt wurde. Potenziert wird dieses Moment durch die Tatsache, dass nicht der heimischere *Mohr mit Landsteinstufe*, sondern der explizit außereuropäische Afroamerikaner in Gestalt des *Mohren mit Smaragdstufe* gewählt wurde. Der Prozess der Aneignung des Fremden zur eigenen Identitätskonstruktion hat sich im 21. Jahrhundert somit gegenüber dem 18. Jahrhundert zugespitzt.

Sieben Jahre lang hatten die Dresdner jeden Sommer dieses Plakat vor Augen. Wie im 18. Jahrhundert, als das Werk *Mohr mit Smaragdstufe* entstand, macht der Schwarze die Figurenansammlung bunter und erfüllt eine Rolle als Diener und Exot, der die *weißen* Betrachterinnen und Betrachter belustigt. Entsprechend hatte der Ausländerrat Dresden zur Entstehungszeit des Plakates Einspruch dagegen erhoben, der aber von Seiten der Plakatproduzenten mit dem Hinweis, es würde sich bei der Skulptur um die Darstellung eines amerikanischen Prinzen handeln, als mangelnde Souveränität im Umgang mit Kunstwerken abgewiesen wurde.[9] Nach Auskunft der Hersteller sei eine Auswahl aus den prominentesten Dresdner Werken getroffen worden. Diese Figur hätte sich ästhetisch am besten in den Bildaufbau fügen lassen. Dadurch, dass alle übrigen Personen eine sehr helle Hautfarbe haben, wirkt die Figur im Zentrum nicht dazugehörig und findet keine aktuelle Anbindung, wie im Fall der anderen Figuren aus Gemälden, die weitestgehend als kulturelle Vorfahren und Dresdner Persönlichkeiten behandelt werden. Diese Figur gehört einer vergangen Zeit an, die Gesellschaftsposition des Schwarzen hat sich im heutigen Kontext noch verschlechtert, da er seinen einstigen Königsstatus gänzlich verloren hat. Die Figur soll nur ästhetischen und kulinarischen Genuss versprechen. Der Körper wird als Träger dieser Botschaft benutzt, eine individuelle Persönlichkeit – wie dem Herrscher August dem Starken am linken oder dem Maler Rembrandt am rechten Bildrand – wird ihr abgesprochen, obwohl das Werk wie oben dargelegt durchaus mit den konkreten Biografien von Savase Oke Charnige und

Tusské Stannagée in Zusammenhang gebracht werden kann. Das Plakat wurde nicht bewusst mit dieser Intention gestaltet. Die Einzelmotive wurden aber ausgewählt und nach einem ästhetischen Empfinden arrangiert, das eine strukturelle *weiße* Privilegierung und Dominanz reproduziert und nicht in Frage stellt. Die Tatsache, dass das Plakat über einen so langen Zeitraum immer wieder verwendet wurde, spricht nicht nur für ökonomisches Marketing sondern auch für die allgemeine Akzeptanz der Darstellung. Der bis heute anhaltende Reproduktionsprozess der bekanntesten Dresdner Repräsentation eines Schwarzen unterstreicht paradoxerweise das Weißsein der Stadt Dresden.[10]

III.

Auf dem Werbeplakat für die Ausstellung *The Glory of Baroque Dresden* im Jahr 2004 in Jackson/Mississippi ist die Figur *Mohr mit Smaragdstufe* alleine zu sehen. Diese von den Staatlichen Kunstsammlungen ausgerichtete Ausstellung sollte die Kunst Dresdens und damit auch Dresden als attraktive Tourismusstadt darstellen. Warum wurde dafür ausgerechnet die Darstellung eines Schwarzen verwendet? Laut der Dresdner Projektmanagerin entschied der Direktor der Mississippi Commission for International Cultural Exchange, Jack Kyle, dass aufgrund eines Bevölkerungsanteils von 70% Schwarzen in Mississippi keine Kunstwerke mit Darstellungen von Schwarzen gezeigt werden sollten, da diese darauf zumeist eine dienende Funktion erfüllten.[11] Die Furcht vor negativen Schlagzeilen und der allgemein geringe Wissensstand über europäische Kunst seien der Grund gewesen, die Thematik in Ausstellung und Katalog zu umgehen. Der Kunsthistoriker Wolfgang Kemp kommentiert in seiner Rezension der Ausstellung ironisch: »Beim Gala-Empfang aus Anlass der Eröffnung und des Besuchs von Kanzler Schröder war die mehrheitlich schwarze Bevölkerung des Bundesstaates durchaus vertreten; hinter den Schanktischen und als Wachpersonal.«[12]

Angesichts der Tatsache, dass im Vorfeld der Ausstellung vereinbart wurde keine Werke mit der Darstellung von Schwarzen zu zeigen, erstaunt die Wahl des Werkes *Mohr mit Smaragdstufe*. Dass der Dargestellte gar kein Schwarzer sei wurde im Kontext der Ausstellung mit derartiger Vehemenz betont, dass der – in Anlehnung an Kupferstiche über die indigenen Völker Nordamerikas – Gestaltete in den pädagogischen Begleitpublikationen zur Ausstellung zum Südamerikaner wurde.[13] Die Wahl dieses Werkes als Aushängeschild für die Ausstellung lässt sich somit durch den Reiz der Ambivalenz erklären: es ist eines der Hauptwerke des Grünen Gewöbes das auf den ersten Blick durch seine dunkle Hautfarbe die Aufmerksamkeit für die Ausstellung in Jackson in besonderem Maße erregte, jegliche Empfindlichkeit bezüglich der Darstellung eines Schwarzen jedoch schnell durch den Entstehungskontext des Werkes abgewehrt werden konnte, da es sich ja »eigentlich« um einen *weißen*, königlichen Amerikaner handeln würde. In Dresden wurde hingegen explizit mit den kolonialistischen Assoziationen zum Begriff »Mohr« für das Ausstellungsprojekt geworben.[14] Ähnlich wie im Fall des Plakates für das Dresdner Stadtfest, wurde im Fall der Ausstellung in Jackson offensichtlich die doppelte Fremdheit von außereuropäischem Anderen und geschlechtlichem Anderen als besonders werbewirksam empfunden, denn das zweite, wesentlich umstrittenere Plakat zeigte einen Ausschnitt aus dem Gemälde *Bei der Kupplerin* von Jan Vermeer van Delft (1656).[15]

Nicht nur als beliebtes Plakatmotiv in Mitarbeiterinnenbüros und als Buchcover, etwa des Sammlungsführers des Grünen Gewölbes oder des Gesamtverzeichnisses 2006/2007 des Deutschen Kunstverlags, sondern auch als zehn Meter großes Transparent an der gerade geschlossenen Ostfassade des Residenzschlosses und in eben dieser Größe in vierfacher Ausführung an den Fahnenstangen links und rechts der Augustusbrücke vor dem Georgentor, dem einstigen Stadtzugang, war das Werk *Mohr mit Smaragdstufe* im Jahr 2006 anlässlich der Eröffnung des Historischen Grünen Gewölbes in Dresden massiv präsent. Hätte es angesichts von über 4000 Objekten nicht auch eine andere Figur sein können? Heute stehen sich die Figuren *Mohr mit Smaragdstufe* und *Mohr mit Landsteinstufe* wie 1733 im Pretiosensaal des Historischen Grünen Gewölbes gegenüber und weder Beschriftung noch Audioguide-Text verraten etwas über die hier dargelegte Problematik. In dem darauf folgenden und den Rundgang durch das Historische Grüne Gewölbe abschließenden Bronze-Raum begegnen wir der »so genannten Negervenus«, wie auf dem Beschriftungsschild einer weiblichen Figur zu lesen ist und die in dem ursprünglichen Inventarbuch als *Mohrin mit Spiegel* bezeichnet wird. Auch über sie und ihre Rezeption ließe sich eine Geschichte erzählen, die das Weißsein der Künstler, der Ausstellungsmacher und der intendierten Bildbetrachter sichtbar machen würde.

IV.

Eine Nachlässigkeit sowohl im Umgang mit der eigenen *weißen* Perspektive als auch mit der Darstellung von »Fremden« zeigt sich in Dresden allerdings nicht nur im Bereich der bildenden Kunst. So fanden die Dresdner Musikfestspiele im Jahr 2005 unter dem Motto »Lust am Fremden« statt. Zur Begründung dieser Themenwahl hieß es in dem Programmheft: »Die Anregung zu diesem Thema kam aus der Kultur, der Tradition und der Geschichte Dresdens, die sich fremden Einflüssen mit Aufgeschlossenheit und Neugierde stellt. Denken Sie nur an das Meißner Porzellan, das Japanische Palais, Schloss Pillnitz und die Einflüsse, welche die Dresdner Musikgeschichte aus anderen Ländern und Kulturen bezogen hat.« Wie im Fall der aufgezählten historischen Objekte, bot das Musikprogramm den lustvollen Konsum fremder Kunstfertigkeit ohne die Reflektion der eigenen Auseinandersetzung mit den Fremden, die vor Ort leben. Angesichts des triumphalen Einzuges der Rechtsextremen NPD in den sächsischen Landtag, den 9,2 % der Wähler im Jahr 2004 ermöglichten, erstaunt es, dass die Dresdner Kulturszene nicht die Chance ergriff, um anlässlich des Stadtfestes, der Ausstellung in Jackson, der Musikfestspiele oder der Eröffnung des Historischen Grünen Gewölbes eine aktuelle Positionierung des eigenen Deutsch- und Weißseins innerhalb der globalen multikulturellen Gesellschaft vorzunehmen. Nicht einmal anlässlich der Ausstellung *Deutschland und Äthiopien. Sehnsucht nach der Ferne* der Staatlichen Kunstsammlungen Dresden im GRASSI Museum für Völkerkunde zu Leipzig im Jahr 2006, die aller zaghafter kritischer Äußerungen enthoben 2007 im Goethe-Institut Gebrekristos Desta Center in Addis Ababa zu sehen war, erfolgte dies. Die politische Empfindlichkeit der äthiopischen Partner und die Autonomie der Kunstwerke gegenüber der Politik hätten dies verboten.[16]

In mehrfacher Hinsicht ist das Werk *Mohr mit Smaragdstufe* tatsächlich repräsentativ für die *weiße* Stadt Dresden: Die Smaragdstufe verweist auf die Anfänge der Kunstkammer und die politische Bedeutung des Kurfürstentums Sachen im Heiligen Römischen Reich Deutscher Nation im 16. Jahrhundert, die im 18. Jahrhundert angefertigte Trägerfigur ist ebenso in Zusammenhang mit der Konzeption des Grünen Gewölbes unter August dem Starken wie mit seinen Ambitionen in Übersee verknüpft. Die *weiße* Bevölkerung Dresdens kann sich heute mit dieser glanzvollen Vergangenheit gut identifizieren und besteht auf der Unsichtbarkeit der eigenen Farbe als System der Privilegierung und Dominanz. Einmal mehr dient ein entpersonalisiertes und seines Kontextes beraubtes Fremdes als Folie für die eigene Identitätskonstruktion.

---

* Dieser Beitrag wäre undenkbar ohne die Diskussionen mit Peggy Piesche über die Genese des Bandes *Mythen, Masken und Subjekt. Kritische Weißseinsforschung in Deutschland*, hrsg. von Maureen Maisha Eggers, Grada Kilomba, Peggy Piesche und Susan Arndt, Münster 2005. Für kritische Anmerkungen danke ich außerdem Dr. Peter Plaßmeyer, Direktor des Mathematisch-Physikalischen Salons, Staatliche Kunstsammlungen Dresden. Verfasst habe ich diesen Text aus meiner eigenen *weißen* Perspektive, die ich erst beginne zu reflektieren. Ich folge dem oben genannten Band in der Großschreibung von Schwarz als Eigenbezeichnung, der ein Widerstandspotenzial innewohnt, und *weiß* als andersartiger sozialer Konstruktion aus der hegemonialen Position heraus.

1 Balthasar Permoser/Johann Melchior Dinglinger: *Mohr mit Smaragdstufe*, um 1724. H. 63,8 cm. Staatliche Kunstsammlungen Dresden, Historisches Grünes Gewölbe, Inv.-Nr. VIII 303.

2 Vgl. Johann Christian Crell: *Kurtzgefaßtes Sächsisches Kern-Chronicon*. 3. Paquet, 28. Couvert, Leipzig 1722, S. 35–37; 5. Paquet, 62. Couvert, Leipzig 1725, S. 559–562.

3 Balthasar Permoser/Johann Melchior Dinglinger: *Mohr mit Landsteinstufe*, um 1724. H. 67 cm. Staatliche Kunstsammlungen Dresden, Historisches Grünes Gewölbe, Inv.-Nr. V 156.

4 Siehe ausführlicher zur Geschichte dieser Skulptur: Anna Greve: »Das Grüne Gewölbe in Amerika – Amerika im Grünen Gewölbe?« In: *Dresdener Kunstblätter*, 1, 2005, S. 39–47.

5 Vgl. Anna Greve: »Das europäische Verlangen nach Exotik: Die afrikanischen Krieger im Grünen Gewölbe« In: *Dresdener Kunstblätter*, 2, 2006, S. 81–86.

6 Vgl. Ingeborg Kittel: »Mohren als Hofbedienstete und Soldaten im Herzogtum Braunschweig-Wolfenbüttel« In: *Braunschweigisches Jahrbuch*, 46, 1965, S. 78–103. – Wolfram Schäfer: »Von ›Kammermohren‹, ›Mohren‹-Tambouren und ›Ost-Indianern‹. Anmerkungen zu Existenzbedingungen und Lebensformen einer Minderheit im 18. Jahrhundert unter besonderer Berücksichtigung der Residenzstadt Kassel« In: *Hessische Blätter für Volks- und Kulturforschung*, 23, 1988, S. 35–79. – Peter Martin: *Schwarze Teufel, edle Mohren*, Hamburg 1993. – Josef Kandert: »Africa and African People in Rudolfine thought« In: Ausst. Kat. *Rudolf II. Prague and the World*, Prag 1998, S. 166–168. – Ausst. Kat. *Exotisch – höfisch – bürgerlich. Afrikaner in Württemberg vom 15. bis 19. Jahrhundert*, hrsg. von Monika Firla, Stuttgart 2001. Für den sächsischen Hof liegt bisher keine detaillierte Studie vor.

7 Vgl. Anna Greve: »Die Welt aus der Tasche gezogen. Ein neu erworbener Faltglobus im Mathematisch-Physikalischen Salon« In: *Dresdener Kunstblätter*, 5, 2005, S. 298–306. – Anna Greve: »Die Kolonisation Brasiliens auf einer Nuss« In: *Dresdener Kunstblätter*, 4, 2006, S. 205–210.

8 Ich danke Frau Christine Rothenberg, Förderverein Dresdner Stadtjubiläum 2006, die mir das Plakatmotiv zur Verfügung stellte.

9 Ich danke Herrn Stellmacher, Michel Sandsteinverlag Dresden, für das Gespräch am 11. April 2005.

10 Wie Homi K. Bhabha überzeugend darlegte, zeichnen sich die kolonialen Stereotypen eben nicht durch gleich bleibende Klischees aus. Die ihnen innewohnenden Macht der Ambiva-

lenz sichert ihnen ihre Wiederholbarkeit in sich wandelnden historischen und diskursiven Zusammenhängen. Homi K. Bhabha: *The location of culture*, London 1994.

11 Ich danke Frau Dr. Sabine Siebel, Ausstellungssekretärin der Staatlichen Kunstsammlungen Dresden, für das Gespräch am 12. Februar 2005.

12 Vgl. Wolfgang Kemp: »Jetzt sind wir König« In: *Die Zeit*, 4. März 2004.

13 Vgl. Mississippi Commission of International Cultural Exchance (Hg.): *The Glory of Baroque. Student Guide*, Jackson 2003, S. 11. – Mississippi Commission of International Cultural Exchance (Hg.): *The Glory of Baroque. Theacher's Guide*, Jackson 2003, S. 48. – Mississippi Commission of International Cultural Exchance (Hg.): *The Glory of Baroque.* Exhibition Catalogue, Jackson 2004, S. 177.

14 Vgl. »Ein Mohr geht auf Reisen. Dresdner Kunstschätze in den USA« In: *Dresdner Morgenpost*, 28. Januar 2004.

15 Wolfgang Kemp kommentiert den symbolischen Gehalt dieses Gemäldes als Aushängeschild für die Ausstellung: »Schade nur, dass Schröder und Bush nicht, wie ursprünglich geplant, die Ausstellung gemeinsam eröffnet haben und unter dem Bild [einer Bordellszene, A.G.], im Zeichen der Kunst, wieder zusammengekommen sind [nach den Differenzen bezüglich des Irak-Krieges, A.G.]«. Kemp 2004 (wie Anm. 12).

16 Ich danke Frau Dr. Kerstin Volker-Saad, Projektleiterin der Ausstellung, für das Gespräch am 7. Januar 2005.

Matthew Beaumont, Andrew Hemingway, Esther Leslie, John Roberts (Hg.): As Radical als Reality Itself. Essays on Marxism and Art for the 21st Century. Oxford et. al.: Peter Lang 2007

Als vor einigen Jahren der Chefvolkswirt der Deutschen Bank, Norbert Walter, in einem Interview zum Thema »Forschungslenkung über Drittmittelförderung« gefragt wurde, ob die Deutsche Bank Einfluss auf die Forschung nehme, räumte er freimütig ein, dass »gewisse Schwerpunktsetzungen« vorgenommen würden, um deutlich zu machen, »was sie [die Bank] für wichtig hält« (*Forschung & Lehre*, 2002, H. 1, S. 6–7). Rechtfertigend schob er nach: »Der fatale Einfluß des Kommunismus auf die Geistes- und Sozialwissenschaft ist in allzu frischer Erinnerung.« Darüber hinaus müsse es »im Eigeninteresse von Forschung liegen, jene Hygienevorstellungen zu entwickeln, die zur Sicherung von Qualität und Regulation unabdingbar sind«. Kapitalismuskritik war offenbar mit den ›Hygienevorstellungen‹ der Deutschen Bank nicht vereinbar und mithin ein Ausschlusskriterium für eine Forschungsförderung durch die Wirtschaft, so das Signal, das Walter, auch in seiner Funktion als Leiter von Deutsche Bank Research, nach eigener Aussage einem »der weltweit bedeutenden Think Tanks für Trends in Wirtschaft, Gesellschaft und Finanzmärkten«, in diesem Interview aussendete.

Während in Deutschland – durch die rotgrüne Regierung eher befördert als bedauert – Politik, Wissenschaft und Kultur zunehmend in den Klammergriff der Wirtschaft geraten waren und es dieses Signals kaum bedurft hätte, konnte man in den angelsächsischen Ländern, in denen der globale Kapitalismus mit seinen sozialen und kriegspolitischen ›Nebenwirkungen‹ zu dieser Zeit weiter fortgeschritten war, Ansätze einer Neuformierung der früheren ›Neuen Linken‹ bzw. ihrer Nachfolgegeneration beobachten. Auf dem Feld der Kunstgeschichte setzte der Radical Art Caucus auf der Jahrestagung der College Art Association im Februar 2000 in New York mit einer Session über »Marxism and Art History Today« ein erstes Zeichen (vgl. *Kunst und Politik*, 3/2001, S. 139–144). Es folgte im April 2002 die von der British Academy und dem Lipman-Miliband Trust geförderte internationale Konferenz »Marxism and the Visual Arts Now« am University College in London, aus der der vorliegende Band *As Radical as Reality Itself* (2007) hervorgegangen ist. Inhaltlich knüpft dieses Buch an den von Andrew Hemingway herausgegebenen Sammelband *Marxism and the History of Art* an, der 2006 in London erschienen ist.

Marxism and the History of Art war, in der Perspektive eines »Projekts marxistische Kunstwissenschaft«, der Versuch, sich der theoretischen und historischen Grundlagen einer marxistischen Kunstwissenschaft zu vergewissern. Anders als es der Titel des Bandes vermuten ließ, ging es dabei weniger um die Rekonstruktion einer marxistischen Tradition in der Kunstwissenschaft, sondern eher um eine kritische Revision der von der »Neuen Linken« in den 70er Jahren rezipierten (neo)marxistischen Texte zur Ästhetik, Kunst- und Kulturtheorie aus der Mitte des letzten Jahrhunderts. Ein Beitrag über William Morris, der den Auftakt bildete, fiel konzeptionell und zeitlich aus dem Rahmen, deutete aber die Absicht des Herausgebers an, den Schwerpunkt auf eine (weitgehend) unabhängige, tendenziell dissidente Tradition innerhalb der marxistischen

Ästhetik zu setzen. Untersucht wurden die ästhetischen Konzeptionen und methodischen Ansätze von Michail Lifschitz, von Mitgliedern des früheren Budapester Sonntagskreises (Frederick Antal, Arnold Hauser, Georg Lukács), von Vertretern der Frankfurter Schule (Walter Benjamin, Theodor W. Adorno), von marxistischen Kunsthistorikern und Kunstkritikern wie Francis Klingender, Max Raphael und Meyer Schapiro sowie Intellektuellen wie Henri Lefebvre, der seine kulturtheoretischen Ideen in direktem Kontakt mit der künstlerischen Avantgarde entwickelte. Die letzten drei Beiträge des Bandes widmeten sich der jüngeren Geschichte der marxistischen Kunstwissenschaft. Andrew Hemingway skizzierte die ›New Left Art History‹ in Westdeutschland, Großbritannien und den USA, Jutta Held fokussierte die Auseinandersetzung der kritischen Kunstgeschichte mit dem Faschismus und Otto Karl Werckmeister beschrieb unter dem Titel »The Turn from Marx to Warburg in West German Art History« die Entpolitisierung von Teilen der der ›Neuen Linken‹ in Westdeutschland nach der konservativen Wende in den 80er Jahren und der deutschen Vereinigung von 1990.

Nach der theoretischen und historischen Revision in *Marxism and the History of Art* unternimmt der Band *As Radical as Reality Itself*, den die Herausgeber dem Andenken an Jutta Held gewidmet haben, nun den nächsten Schritt auf dem Weg zum angestrebten Projekt einer marxistischen Kunstwissenschaft und Kunstkritik. Die Aktualität marxistischer Kultur- und Gesellschaftstheorien steht für die Herausgeber angesichts der Krise des Kapitalismus außer Frage. Auf dem Feld der Theorie wollen sie einen Gegenakzent zur Dominanz postmoderner Konzepte setzen (Matthew Beaumont). Marxistische Theorien sollen neu erarbeitet (»reworked«) und im Theorienspektrum neu positioniert (»repositioned«) werden, so der Anspruch. Die Diskussionskultur soll neu belebt und um kritische Elemente erweitert werden, Argumentation und Konfrontation die postmoderne Suche nach dem allgemeinen Konsens ablösen (John Roberts). Dem Vorwurf, ›theoretisch unterentwickelt‹ zu sein, begegnen die Herausgeber mit dem Gegenhinweis, dass der Marxismus in der gegenwärtigen Diskussion allenfalls als stalinistische Karikatur existiert und eine intellektuelle Auseinandersetzung nicht stattfindet. Ihrerseits versuchen sie, die Position einer marxistischen Kunstgeschichte in Abgrenzung zu verwandten kulturtheoretischen und kulturgeschichtlichen Ansätzen zu entwickeln (Andrew Hemingway). Aus britischer Perspektive sind es vor allem die in ihrer antimarxistischen Diktion als widersprüchlich erachteten Cultural Studies bzw. die neueren Visual Culture Studies, zu denen die Grenze gezogen wird (Esther Leslie).

Angesichts der Position des Marxismus in den hegemonial geführten politischen und intellektuellen Debatten der 80er und 90er Jahre wundert es nicht, dass die Herausgeber noch teilweise aus der Defensive argumentieren. Andererseits markieren sie offensiv die Felder, für die sie eine Kernkompetenz marxistischer Kunst- und Gesellschaftstheorie in Anspruch nehmen. Dazu gehören (neben der eigenen Theoriegeschichte) das Verhältnis von Kunst und Staat, die Praxis künstlerischer Repräsentation im öffentlichen Raum, die Ästhetik der sozialistischen und postsozialistischen Staaten, die symbolische Repräsentation der Arbeit (bzw. der Nicht-Arbeit) in der Kunst und nicht zuletzt die Praxis einer künstlerischen Gesellschaftskritik. Diese Themen werden exemplarisch von Autorinnen und Autoren aus den Bereichen der Kunst, der Kunstgeschichte, der Literaturwissenschaft, der Philosophie, der Mediengeschichte und der Kommunikationswissenschaft behandelt. In Orientierung an der Kritischen Theorie werden die Erkenntnisse vor allem in der Auseinandersetzung mit den künstlerischen Avantgarden gewonnen. Darüber hinaus wird ein besonderer Akzent auf die Fokussierung subkultureller und subversiver Praktiken innerhalb der visuellen Kultur der Gegenwart gesetzt, insbesondere von den jüngeren Autorinnen und Autoren, der dem ›neuen‹ marxistischen Ansatz eine besondere Spezifik, Aktualität und Attraktivität verleiht.

As Radical as Reality Itself ist Ausdruck einer sehr lebendigen, kritisch-marxistischen Diskussion innerhalb der Kunst- und Kulturwissenschaften, die sich von London aus international und transdisziplinär vernetzt und durchaus das Potenzial hat, das Interesse neuer, auch jüngerer Kreise zu gewinnen. Dass Projekte wie dieses nicht in Gefahr stehen, von globalen Konzernen wie der Deutschen Bank gefördert zu werden, versteht sich von selbst. Die Beteiligten wird es in ihrer Arbeit bestätigen und bestärken.

Martin Papenbrock

»Jud Süß« – Propagandafilm im NS-Staat. Ausstellung im Haus der Geschichte Baden-Württemberg, Stuttgart, 14. Dezember 2007 bis 3. August 2008. Katalog hg. von Ernst Seidl, Stuttgart 2007, 152 S., zahlreiche, durchgehend farbige Abb., ISBN 978-3-933726-24-7

Es ist kein einfaches Thema, dem sich die Sonderausstellung im Haus der Geschichte Baden-Württemberg widmete: Wie präsentiert man einen Film aus dem Dritten Reich, der unter Vorbehalt steht und nur mit Kommentar öffentlich gezeigt werden darf? Einen Film, der nicht nur einer der erfolgreichsten Propagandafilme im NS-Reich war, sondern *der* antisemitische Hetzfilm überhaupt? Einen Film, der jedoch kein plumper Propagandafilm war, sondern ein professionell gedrehter Historien-Kostümfilm mit Starbesetzung?

Tatsächlich war Veit Harlans *Jud Süß*, der im Herbst 1940 in die Kinos kam, opulent ausgestattet und fortschrittlich produziert. Er bot den Zuschauern »großes Unterhaltungskino« und vermittelte doch unter dem Deckmantel einer angeblichen historischen Realität schwerste propagandistische Verhetzungen gegen die »jüdische Rasse«. Der Film wurde zwischen 1940 und 1945, während der Zweite Weltkrieg und die Vernichtung der europäischen Juden in vollem Gange waren, von etwa 40 Millionen Menschen in Europa, davon 20 Millionen im »Reich«, also knapp einem Drittel der damaligen Bevölkerung, gesehen. Er wurde gezielt zur antisemitischen Stimmungsmache der NS-Einsatzgruppen eingesetzt. *Jud Süß* ist damit einer der »erfolgreichsten« Filme überhaupt.

Den Ausstellungsmachern ist es gelungen, das heikle Thema so aufzubereiten, dass nicht nur deutlich wird, wie raffiniert die Nationalsozialisten das Medium Film für ihre Propaganda benutzt haben, sondern auch, wie ein historischer Stoff zur Projektionsfläche unterschiedlichster Interpretationen werden konnte. In sieben Abteilungen wird die Fragestellung übersichtlich und mit ausgewählten Exponaten und Filmausschnitten präsentiert. Dabei haben die Kuratoren auch manch überraschendes Dokument entdeckt. Der Katalog zur Ausstellung, auf den sich diese Besprechung konzentriert, erläutert und ergänzt die Ausstellung durch wissenschaftlich fundierte und dabei gut lesbare

Beiträge, welche die Problematik eindringlich vor Augen führen, ohne mit erhobenem Zeigefinger zu dozieren. Es zeichnet die Publikation aus, dass sie das ernste Thema nicht nur gründlich erforscht, sondern es auch versteht, die komplexen und oft kritischen Inhalte so zu präsentieren, dass sie einem großen Publikum über die Grenzen der Wissenschaft hinaus zugänglich werden.

Gegliedert in zwei große Teile, kann die erste Hälfte des Katalogs, die den Aufbau der Ausstellung in sieben Kapiteln widerspiegelt, wie ein Begleiter durch die Schau gelesen werden. Sehr viele der gezeigten Exponate werden näher besprochen. Hervorzuheben ist an dieser Stelle die Qualität der Abbildungen: Unter den präsentierten Objekten sind zahlreiche Schriftquellen, die so gut reproduziert wurden, dass die Schriftstücke auch im Katalog lesbar sind. Weitere Exponate werden in den vier Textbeiträgen im zweiten Katalogteil näher erläutert; diese Essays fassen die wichtigsten Erkenntnisse der Ausstellung zusammen und veranschaulichen sie durch die Verbindung mit konkreten Belegen. Darüber hinaus ist es den Ausstellungsmachern in der Sonderschau gelungen, erstmals insgesamt zweiundzwanzig Minuten des Harlan-Films öffentlich zu zeigen. Im Katalog werden Filmstills relevanter Szenen mit einer kurzen Transkription der entsprechenden Drehbuchszene an den Anfang jedes Kapitels gestellt.

Ausstellung wie Katalog beginnen mit einer Annäherung an die historische Figur des Joseph Süß Oppenheimer, dessen Biografie schon zu Lebzeiten besonders durch sein spektakuläres Ende großes publikatorisches Interesse erregt hat. Als Hoffaktor – dem Volksmund geläufiger als »Hofjude«, der die fürstlichen Finanzgeschäfte führte, ohne Teil der Beamtenschaft zu sein – für den württembergischen Herzog Karl Alexander machte er zwischen 1734 und 1737 eine kurze, aber steile Karriere. Süß Oppenheimer wusste die kostspielige Hofhaltung des Herzogs durch eine geschickte und sicher nicht immer unproblematische Fiskalpolitik zu finanzieren. Nach dem Tod des Herrschers wird »Jud Süß« von den Ständen gefangengesetzt. Obwohl keiner der gegen ihn erhobenen Vorwürfe wie Amtshandel, Bestechlichkeit und sexueller Umgang mit Christinnen nachgewiesen werden konnte, wurde Süß Oppenheimer nach monatelanger Haft in einem Käfig gehängt.

Bereits mit dem Verfahren gegen Süß setzte die publikatorische Aufarbeitung und Verbreitung des Geschehens ein: Zahlreiche Traktate und Flugschriften erschienen, die Geschichte wurde oft reißerisch ausgeschlachtet – ganz nebenbei bietet dieser Teil auch einen Einblick in die mediale Kultur der Frühen Neuzeit. So wurden die eigentlichen Ereignisse schnell überdeckt, »Fakten und Fiktion vermischten sich von Anfang an« (S. 88). Der historische Wahrheitsgehalt ist heute nicht mehr feststellbar. Die Figur Joseph Süß Oppenheimer ist daher nur schwer zu fassen und bietet Interpretationen und Spekulationen großen Raum.

Mit dieser Problematik setzt sich der erste Beitrag von Ernst Seidl auseinander, der einen Überblick über die zahlreichen Publikationen zum Thema im Laufe der Jahrhunderte bis heute gibt und einige exemplarisch bespricht; am bekanntesten wohl die Novelle *Jud Süß* von Wilhelm Hauff, erschienen 1827, sowie Lion Feuchtwangers gleichnamiger Roman aus dem Jahr 1925, die meist verkaufte literarische Bearbeitung der Geschichte. Feuchtwangers Roman war bereits 1934 Grundlage für eine britische Verfilmung durch Lothar Mendes, die sich gegen den erstarkenden Antisemitismus wandte. Es ist bezeichnend, wie unterschiedlich der fiktional aufgeladene Stoff um die historische Figur des »Jud Süß« gedeutet werden kann.

Ende der 1930er Jahre entstand das Drehbuch zum nationalsozialistischen Film, das im Spätherbst 1939 von Veit Harlan zur Vorlage für seine Verfilmung gemacht wurde. Vorgeblich will sich der Film auf die historische Realität stützen. Abgesehen davon, dass sich eine solche unter der Publikationsflut nicht mehr herausschälen lässt, war es dem Filmteam wohl kaum möglich, an einem einzigen Nachmittag – wie Briefe der Terra Filmkunst in der Ausstellung belegen – die mehrere Regalmeter umfassenden Akten zum Fall Josef Süß Oppenheimer im Hauptstaatsarchiv Stuttgart zu sichten. »Das fiktionale Drehbuch wurde unter propagandistischen, rassenpolitischen und vor allem antisemitischen Gesichtspunkten umgeschrieben und umgesetzt« (S. 98): In Harlans Film schleicht sich ein als Höfling getarnter »Jud Süß« (gespielt von Ferdinand Marian) in die christliche Welt, indem er den Herzog (Heinrich George) gezielt in finanzielle Abhängigkeit bringt. Er nimmt unbescholtenen Bürgern ihr Hab und Gut und schottet seinen Fürsten nicht nur durch schmeichlerische Reden von den Untertanen ab, sondern unterstützt auch dessen unmoralischen Lebenswandel. »Jud Süß« ist es auch, der das unschuldige Christenmädchen Dorothea (Kristina Söderbaum) bedrängt und vergewaltigt. Die weiß sich daraufhin in ihrer (Rassen-)Schande nicht mehr zu helfen und geht ins Wasser – die Parallelen zur nationalsozialistischen Ideologie von der »Rassenschande« als schlimmster Bedrohung des »arischen Volkes« sind unübersehbar; fünf Jahre zuvor waren die »Nürnberger Gesetze« erlassen worden. Dorotheas Ehemann und die aufgebrachte Menge fordern nach ihrem Freitod den Kopf des Verantwortlichen. Oppenheimer wird gefangengesetzt, der »Rassenschändung« für schuldig befunden und hingerichtet. Im Anschluss wird ein Judenbann über das Land ausgesprochen – auch hier sind die Analogie zur nationalsozialistischen Propaganda von der »Rassenreinheit« und der damit verbundenen Vertreibung der Juden unübersehbar. Der Höhepunkt des Films liegt in den Ereignissen zwischen »Jud Süß« und Dorothea, der Vergewaltigung, ihrem Selbstmord und der Hinrichtung des Täters.

Fiktive Frauenfiguren haben in allen literarischen Behandlungen des Stoffes eine wichtige Rolle gespielt, wie der Essay von Cornelia Hecht ausführt. Ihr Vergleich von Wilhelm Hauffs Novelle, Feuchtwangers Roman und Harlans Drehbuch und Film macht jedoch deutlich, dass erst und nur in der Verfilmung von 1940 die »Sexualisierung der Figur« (S. 113) Oppenheimers ins Zentrum der Handlung gerückt wurde. »Jud Süß« wurde gezielt negativ und bedrohlich gezeichnet, um die »jüdische Rasse« zu diskreditieren, Ängste zu schüren und Stimmung zu machen. »Der Film arbeitete bewusst mit Figurenkonzeptionen und kulturellen Annahmen der antisemitischen Vorstellungswelt« (S. 111). Dieser »Konstruktion eines Feindbildes« wendet sich das zweite Kapitel der Ausstellung zu. Beleuchtet wird zunächst die pseudowissenschaftlich aufbereitete antisemitische Ideologie der Nazis, etwa in den rassentheoretischen Büchern von Alfred Rosenberg. Auch angebliche physiognomische Unterschiede wurden in der nationalsozialistischen Propaganda verstärkt eingesetzt, wie mehrere Plakate zeigen.

Erwartungsgemäß stark überzeichnet werden die Juden im Harlan-Film dargestellt, wie der zweite Essay von Ernst Seidl ausführt. Neben einem bedrohlich dargestellten »Jud Süß«, der sich so gut anpasst, dass er sich äußerlich nicht von den christlichen Höflingen unterscheidet, im Gefängnis aber seine »Maske« verliert und wieder die befremdlichen jüdischen Züge offenbart, werden stereotype »Ostjuden« mit überzeichneten Zügen wie der gebogenen Nase, abstehenden Ohren, einem verschlagenen Blick unter Hängelidern und einer hängenden Unterlippe gezeigt. Im Harlan-Film werden sechs jüdische Figuren von Werner Krauß, einem der renommiertesten deutschsprachigen Schauspieler des 20. Jahrhunderts, verkörpert, der die stereotypen Klischees »perfektioniert«. Es ist allerdings nicht klar, inwieweit Krauß selbst antisemitisch eingestellt war. Mit Sicherheit hat er jedoch »die Juden nicht sehr geliebt«, wie ein Zitat von Erich Kästner belegt. Nach dem Ende des »Dritten Reiches« wird Krauß im Rahmen der Entnazifizierung mehrfach vor Gericht gestellt, bis er schließlich als »Mitläufer« eingestuft und zu einer Geldstrafe verurteilt wird. Seine Bemühungen um Rehabilitation durch namhafte Entlastungszeugen, in der Ausstellung belegt durch mehrere Briefwechsel – etwa mit George Bernard Shaw –, zeigen exemplarisch, wie leicht vielen der ideologische Umschwung vom Kollaborateur zum Nazi-Gegner nach Kriegsende gefallen ist: Krauß selbst behauptete, die Teilnahme am Film wäre ihm aufgezwungen worden; schon seine »überzeugenden« Darstellungen in der Verfilmung stehen dem jedoch entgegen.

Es ist ebenso interessant wie schockierend zu sehen, mit welch simplen Strategien die nationalsozialistische Propaganda gearbeitet hat, wie Seidls Essay herauszustellen weiß. Dabei war die Verunglimpfung einer ganzen Menschengruppe aufgrund ihrer Religionszugehörigkeit zu einer vermeintlich andersartigen, gefährlichen »Rasse« mit visuellen Mitteln keinesfalls eine Erfindung des Dritten Reichs. Schon die Flugblätter aus dem 18. Jahrhundert, welche die Geschichte von »Jud Süß« verbreiteten, haben mit Typisierungen gearbeitet. Im Nationalsozialismus wurde diese visuelle Propaganda-Strategie zur »Perfektion« gebracht. Ihr Erfolg dürfte im »eindeutigen Primat des Visuellen vor dem Reflexiven der menschlichen Wahrnehmung liegen« (S. 134) – eine Beobachtung, die heute eine umso größere Gültigkeit hat. Durch die Allgegenwart von Werbung, Internet und Fernsehen sind die Menschen mehr denn je der Macht der Bilder ausgesetzt.

Diese theoretischen Beobachtungen werden in Ausstellung wie Katalog durch Ausschnitte und Beschreibungen von Filmszenen und den darin angewandten filmischen Methoden verdeutlicht. Harlan arbeitet verstärkt mit dem Bild-Gegenbild-Verfahren, in dem durch Überblendungen von einem Bild zum nächsten übergeleitet wird – etwa vom »verkleideten« Höfling Oppenheimer zum Gefangenen, der wieder »typisch« jüdische Züge zeigt. Gezielt eingesetzt wird darüber hinaus auch die Filmmusik: Szenen im Judenviertel werden etwa mit bedrohlich-fremd klingenden jiddischen Gesängen hinterlegt. Auf subtile Weise wird dem Betrachter so eine Botschaft untergeschoben, die ihm im aufwändig produzierten Kostümfilm kaum bewusst wird – eine Methode, die für den heutigen Betrachter, der um die historischen Hintergründe wissen und im Umgang mit Bildern geübter sein sollte, eine schon ans Paradoxe grenzende Offensichtlichkeit in den Absichten zeigt, zugleich aber immer noch verblüffend und erschreckend »gelungen« wirkt.

Die nächsten drei Kapitel der Ausstellung sowie der Essay von Immo Wagner-Douglas thematisieren die Entstehungsgeschichte des Films sowie seine Verbreitung und Auswirkungen. Die Nationalsozialisten haben die Möglichkeiten des Mediums Film erkannt und gezielt eingesetzt. Das Kino bot durch die Wochenschau vor Filmbeginn mehr oder weniger die einzige Informationsquelle der Zeit. Mehr als 1,1 Milliarden Menschen gingen 1942 im NS-Reich ins Kino – zum Vergleich: heute sind es in Deutschland nur 140 Millionen. Die Filmwirtschaft wurde unbemerkt von der Öffentlichkeit verstaatlicht und Teil des Propagandaministeriums unter Joseph Goebbels.

Antisemitische Filme wurden als »Volksführungsmittel« (S. 38) in Auftrag gegeben; *Jud Süß* galt als besonderer »Meisterwurf«, für den viele bekannte Schauspieler verpflichtet wurden. Schon vor der deutschen Erstaufführung am 24. September 1940 wurde der Harlan-Film mit größtem Aufwand beworben; der Film wurde synchronisiert und in verbündeten, abhängigen und besetzten Ländern gezeigt. Die Publikumsreaktionen wurden heimlich überwacht; vielfach kam es im direkten Anschluss an den Film erwartungsgemäß zu Ausschreitungen gegen Juden.

Gegen Ende wendet sich die Ausstellung der Zeit nach dem Dritten Reich zu. Was geschah nach Kriegsende mit den Filmleuten? Waren sie sich ihrer Funktion, die ihnen speziell durch die Mitwirkung an einem Film wie *Jud Süß* zukam, bewusst? Hervorzuheben ist hier vor allem der Regisseur Veit Harlan: Wie Krauß bemühte sich auch Harlan schon im Mai 1945 um Entlastungszeugen. Seine Prozesse enden mit Freisprüchen, da angeblich »keine Kausalität zwischen Film und der Ermordung der Juden« (S. 72) festzustellen war – ein Fehlurteil, wie die Ausstellung erhellt. Auch von Seiten der Schauspieler hat keine richtige Auseinandersetzung mit ihrer Rolle bei der Verfilmung stattgefunden.

Ein – noch – recht knappes Kapitel zu »Jud Süß heute« zeigt, dass der historische Stoff um die Figur Josef Süß Oppenheimer nach 1945 völlig vom Harlan-Film verdeckt wird. Erst in den 1970er Jahren setzt wieder eine wissenschaftliche Auseinandersetzung mit dem Thema ein; hinzu kommen in den letzten Jahren verstärkt literarische und dramatische Verarbeitungen.

Im Anhang bietet der Katalog neben einem umfangreichen Literaturverzeichnis auch eine ausführliche Besetzungs- und Mitarbeiterliste des Veit-Harlan-Films *Jud Süß*, einen Überblick über die Erstaufführungen sowie über die beteiligten Personen und eine Filmografie von Harlan.

Es bleibt die Frage, warum ein solches Machwerk wie Veit Harlans *Jud Süß* überhaupt zum Thema einer eigenen Ausstellung gemacht werden sollte. Müsste ein so durch und durch antisemitischer Propagandafilm wie *Jud Süß*, der unter Vorbehalt steht, nicht ein- für allemal unter Verschluss gehalten werden? Nach einem Besuch der Ausstellung und der Lektüre des Katalogs fällt die Antwort eindeutig aus: Nein. Denn die sachliche, wissenschaftliche Auseinandersetzung mit einem derartig heiklen Thema dient dem demokratischen Gemeinwesen sehr viel mehr, als wenn es verschwiegen und mystifiziert wird. Dies gilt auch und gerade für Themen aus dem Dritten Reich. Zwar wird in der öffentlichen Debatte immer wieder Bezug auf Themen der NS-Diktatur genommen, allerdings befassen sich solche Verweise nur selten eingehend mit den komplexen historischen Hintergründen. Dies belegte erst kürzlich die Debatte über die nationalsozialistischen Autobahnen oder die ideologisierte Familienpolitik des Dritten Reiches. Nach wie vor besteht also großer Bedarf an nüchterner und fundierter Aufarbeitung der jüngeren Vergangenheit.

Simone Kraft

Kommentierte Bibliografie »Bildwissenschaften in der Diskussion«

Hans Belting (Hg.): *Bildfragen: die Bildwissenschaften im Aufbruch*, Paderborn 2007. 357 Seiten.

Die Publikation geht auf die Tagung *Bildwissenschaft? Eine Zwischenbilanz* im Jahr 2005 am Internationalen Forschungszentrum für Kulturwissenschaften (IFK) in Wien zurück. Ziel war es, die Wortführer der Debatte um die Bildwissenschaften ins Gespräch miteinander zu bringen und »das Bildermachen als Kulturpraxis zu deuten«, wie es in der Einleitung heißt. Vorwiegend Kunsthistoriker, aber auch Ethnologen, Philosophen und Psychologen befassen sich in den Aufsätzen mit der Bedeutung der Bilderfrage als Thema der Kulturwissenschaft. Dabei werden das Verhältnis von Bild und Sprache, Bilder als Artefakt und Vorstellungen, die Notwendigkeit einer »globalen Kritik der visuellen Kultur« und die Differenzen bzw. Überschneidungen zwischen Kunstgeschichte und Medienwissenschaft diskutiert. Enthalten ist der auf der Tagung vereinbarte Briefwechsel zwischen Gottfried Boehm und William J. Thomas Mitchell über den *iconic* bzw. *pictural turn*. Weitere Autoren: Ilka Brändle, Peter Geimer, Hans Dieter Huber, Klaus Krüger, Christiane Kruse, Thomas Macho, Birgit Mersmann, Reinhart Meyer-Kalkus, Jean-Luc Nancy, Elisabeth von Samsonow, Martin Schulz, Serge Tisseron, Horst Wenzel, Beat Wyss.

Mathias Bruhn (Hg.): *Bilder ohne Betrachter* (= Bildwelten des Wissens. Kunsthistorisches Jahrbuch für Bildkritik; 4,2), Berlin 2006. 120 Seiten.

Angesichts der Tatsache, dass den wenigen Ikonen der Bildkommunikation ein gewaltiger Vorrat ungezeigter Formen gegenüber steht, auf die sie bezogen sind und ohne die sie nicht existieren würden, widmen sich in diesem Band vorwiegend Kunsthistoriker den unterschiedlichen Zuständen in denen diese Formen bestehen können, »die für kurze Zeit oder dauerhaft ohne Betrachter sind und die dennoch als ›Bilder‹ angesprochen werden«. Dabei werden in Vergessenheit geratene Bildprodukte der Massenmedien, durch einen Auswahlprozess verloren gegangene wissenschaftliche Aufzeichnungen ebenso wie nach dem Gebrauch abgestoßene Objekte berücksichtigt. Autoren: Peter Geimer, Vinzenz Hediger, Martina Heßler, Tom Holert, Lothar Ledderose, Kelly Wilder.

Hubert Burda und Christa Maar (Hg.): *Iconic Turn. Die neue Macht der Bilder*, Köln 2004. 452 Seiten.

Die Publikation geht auf die Vorlesungsreihe *Iconic Turn – das neue Bild der Welt* zurück, die von der Burda-Akademie zum Dritten Jahrtausend in Kooperation mit dem Humanwissenschaftlichen Zentrum an der Ludwig-Maximilians-Universität München in den Jahren 2002 und 2003 durchgeführt wurde. Dies war die erste umfassende Zusammenführung spezieller Blickwinkel auf die heutige Allgegenwart von Bildern von Seiten der Ägyptologie, Biologie, Computerwissenschaft, Kunstgeschichte, Mathematik, Medienwissenschaft, Medizin, Philosophie und Physik. Autoren: Jan Assmann, Hans Belting, Gottfried Boehm, Reinhard Brandt, Stephan Brunfels, Horst Bredekamp,

Bazon Brock, Franziska Brons, Norman Foster, Britta Glatzeder, Wolfgang M. Heckl, Stefan Heidenreich, Martin Kemp, Friedrich Kittler, Hans-Otto Peitgen, Rolf Pfeifer, Willibald Sauerländer, Wolf Singer, Peter Sloterdijk, Barbara Maria Stafford, Bill Viola, Peter Weibel, Wim Wenders, Anton Zeilinger, Semir Zeki.

Markus Buschhaus: *Über den Körper im Bilde sein. Eine Medienarchäologie anatomischen Wissens*, Bielefeld 2005. 353 Seiten.

Im Sinne einer Bildwissenschaft, die wissenschaftliche Bilder als integralen Bestandteil mit einschließt, und mit einem erweiterten Kulturbegriff, der auch Praktiken der *hard sciences* – wie die Anatomie – als kulturell bedeutende Phänomene versteht, widmet sich die Dissertation anatomischen Darstellungen mittels Zeichnungen, Fotografien, Röntgenaufnahmen, Computertomographien und Visible Human Projects vom 16. Jahrhundert bis heute. Dabei wird insbesondere nach der Funktion von Bildern für die Produktion und Organisation von Wissen gefragt.

Markus Buschhaus und Inge Hinterwalder (Hg.): *The Picture's Image. Wissenschaftliche Visualisierung als Komposit*, München 2006. 321 Seiten.

Der Band geht zurück auf die gleichnamige Tagung des von Hans Belting gegründeten Graduiertenkollegs *Bild – Körper – Medium. Eine anthropologische Perspektive* im Jahr 2005. Versammelt sind Beiträge aus den Bereichen Kunst- und Medienwissenschaft sowie Anglistik, Biologie, Germanistik, Physik und Soziologie. Zum einen wird nach dem Stellenwert des Bildes innerhalb der verschiedenen Disziplinen gefragt, zum anderen werden die bild- und medientheoretischen Ansätze der letzten Jahre an medizin- und wissenschaftshistorischen Untersuchungsgegenständen bzw. Fragestellungen erprobt. Die Herausgeber heben hervor, dass gerade die Differenzierung zwischen *image* und *picture* es erlaube, »wissenschaftliche Visualisierung als Komposit in den Blick zu nehmen und damit sowohl artefakt- als auch praxisbezogene Ansätze zu berücksichtigen«. Autoren: Harun Badakhshi, Olaf Breidbach, Hans H. Diebner, Stefan Ditzen, Manfred Faßler, Erna Fiorentini, Jochen Henning, Anette Hüsch, Tanja Klemm, Karin Leonhard, Roland Meyer, Barbara Orland, Hans Ulrich Reck, Gunnar Schmidt, Albena Yaneva.

Anne von der Heiden (Hg.): *Per imaginem. Bildlichkeit und Souveränität*, Berlin 2005. 224 Seiten.

Die Publikation geht auf eine Tagung im Rahmen des Kollegs Friedrich Nietzsche der Stiftung Weimarer Klassik im Jahr 2002 zurück. Eine grundsätzliche Parallele von Bildlichkeit zu Souveränität sieht die Herausgeberin darin, dass das Bild für sich in Anspruch nimmt, das Wesen erscheinen zu lassen und damit zugleich von dem Erscheinenden verschieden ist. »Damit vollzieht es eine ähnliche Ausschlussbewegung wie der Souverän, der mit dem Akt der Ausschließung Unterschiedenes durch seine Definition zugleich einschließt und so seine Ordnung durchsetzt.« Der Aspekt des Gewordenen verweise in beiden Fällen auf einen Ursprung und die Entstehung in einem Prozess, der nicht unabhängig zu denken sei. Versammelt sind Beiträge aus den Bereichen Kunstgeschichte, Medienwissenschaft, Medizin, Literaturwissenschaft und Philosophie. Autoren: Claudia Blümle, Beate Fricke, Alexander García Düttmann, Johan F.

Hartle, Hans-Hager Hildebrandt, Ulrike Kadi, Renate Kappes, Barbara Kösters, Rut Blees Luxemburg, Anna Marx, Armin Schäfer, Alenka Zupančič.

Philine Helas, Maren Polte, Claudia Rückert und Bettina Uppenkamp (Hg.): *Bild/Geschichte. Festschrift für Horst Bredekamp*, Berlin 2007. 589 Seiten.

Die Sammlung hauptsächlich kunsthistorischer Beiträge repräsentiert die zentralen Forschungsfelder Bredekamps vom Mittelalter bis zum technischen Bild und seine These, »dass eine kritische Wissenschaft des Bildes notwendig Bildgeschichte ist, deren methodisches Handwerkszeug die Kunstgeschichte bereithält«, wie es die Herausgeberinnen formulieren. Sowohl die Geschichtlichkeit von Bildern als auch ihre Rolle als »Akteure« in der Geschichte sind zentrale Fragestellungen in Bredekamps Arbeiten. Die Möglichkeit eines kritischen Verständnisses von Bildern sieht er an die grundsätzliche Koppelung von Bild und Geschichte gebunden. Die zu seinen Ehren verfassten Aufsätze thematisieren in diesem Sinne Positionierungen der Kunstgeschichte innerhalb der aktuellen Wissenschaftslandschaft, unterschiedliche Medien der Wissenschaften als »Wissensträger«, Rollen von Bildern als Impuls, Medium und Produkt von Denkprozessen, Prozesse der Umformung und Umdeutung, Wechselverhältnisse zwischen künstlerischen, sozialen und politischen Prozessen sowie Selbstbilder von Künstlern und Wissenschaftlern. Autoren: Herbert Beck, Andreas Beyer, Hartmut Böhme, Jochen Brüning, Hubert Burda, Werner Busch, Karl Clausberg, Peter Cornelius Claussen, Michael Diers, Susanne Falkenhausen, Frank Fenrenbach, Monika Flacke, Jörg Friedrich, Thomas W. Gaehtgens, Dieter Grimm, Dorothee Haffner, Wolfram Hogrebe, Berthold Hinz, Stephan von Huene, Elisabeth Kieven, Petra Kipphoff, Friedrich Kittler, Sybille Krämer, Adam Labuda, Irvin Lavin, Marilyn Aronberg Lavin, Thomas Macho, Jürgen Mittelstraß, Herbert Molderings, Jürgen Müller, Ulrich Raulff, Ulrich Reinsisch, Werner Röcke, Charlotte Schoell-Glass, Eva-Maria Schön, Peter Seiler, Barbara Maria Stafford, Ruth Tesmar, Monika Wagner, Ingeborg Walter, Horst Wenzel, Otto Karl Werckmeister, Matthias Winner, Gerhard Wolf, Henning Wrede, Roberto Zapperi, Frank Zöllner.

Torsten Hoffmann und Gabriele Rippl (Hg.): *Bilder. Ein (neues) Leitmedium?*, Göttingen 2006. 232 Seiten.

Der Band geht auf eine im Wintersemester 2005/06 vom Zentrum für komparatistische Studien an der Georg-August-Universität Göttingen gemeinsam mit der Amerikanistik der Universität Bern veranstalte Ringvorlesung zurück. In ihrer Einleitung konstatieren die Herausgeber eine deutliche Diskrepanz zwischen einer wachsenden Bildermacht einerseits und einem Mangel an praktischer und theoretischer Bildkompetenz andererseits. Die versammelten Aufsätze von Historikern, Kunsthistorikern, Literaturwissenschaftlern, Medienwissenschaftlern und Philosophen sollen einen interdisziplinären Überblick zur aktuellen Debatte um die Bildwissenschaft geben. Sie diskutieren die Frage, ob Bilder das (neue) Leitmedium westlicher Kulturen sind, das andere Medien wie die Schrift langsam verdrängt. Autoren: Gilbert Hess, Kai Kirchmann, Habbo Knoch, Sybille Krämer, Christiane Kruse, Walter Leimgruber, Gerald Moers, Klaus Sachs-Hombach, Carsten Peter Warncke.

Hans Dieter Huber: *Bild, Beobachten, Milieu: Entwurf einer allgemeinen Bildwissenschaft*, Ostfildern-Ruit 2004. 223 Seiten.

Huber geht von drei zentralen Bereichen für das Verstehen von Bildern aus: das Bild, der Beobachter und das Milieu. In einem ersten Schritt definiert er Bilder als Systeme und unterschiedet drei Ebenen des Bildes: den physischen Bildträger, die bildliche Darstellung und die Bildreferenz. In einem zweiten Schritt werden Imagination, Projektion, visuelles Unbewusstes und Erfahrung der Betrachter als entscheidend für das Verstehen von Bildern thematisiert. Drittens werden soziale Milieus, Schichten, Lebensstile, strukturelle Koppelungen und operationale Schließungen als »Kontrollfelder« einer Einstellung, Steuerung und Kontrolle der Erfahrung von Bildern analysiert.

Thomas Knieper und Marin G. Müller (Hg.): *War Visions: Bildkommunikation und Krieg*, Köln 2005. 432 Seiten.

Der Band geht auf die gleichnamige Tagung im Hamburger Warburg-Haus zurück. Nach historischen Rückblicken bis ins 16. Jahrhundert wird die Rolle des heutigen Bildjournalismus im Krieg, die Darstellung von Krieg in Comics und Computerspielen sowie die Ikonisierung des Krieges vorwiegend von Kommunikationswissenschaftlern untersucht. Es wird nach dem Kalkül von Terroristen mit den massenmedialen Bildern gefragt, nach der Beweiskraft der Schreckensbilder, nach den ihnen inhärente visuelle Authentizität und nach ihrer Inszenierung. In der Einleitung formulieren die Herausgeber das Ziel der Publikation, »Perspektiven für eine kritische Auseinandersetzung mit den Bildern des Krieges« zu eröffnen. Autoren: Michael Beuthner, Petra Dorsch-Jungsberger, Kathrin Fahlenbrach, Till Fischer, Ursula Frohne, Christoph Klimmt, Ansgar Koch, Sebastian Köhler, Tim Kuhrcke, Stefan Leifert, Peter Ludes, Michaela Maier, Agnes Matthias, Marion G. Müller, Ralf Palandt, Gerhard Paul, Karl Nikolaus Renner, Steffen Sommer, Beate Spindler, Reinhold Viehoff, Stephan Alexander Weichert, Hans-Jürgen Weiss, Elke Anna Werner, Adalbert Wilhelm, Jürgen Wilke.

Birgit Mersmann und Martin Schulz (Hg.): *Kulturen des Bildes*, München 2006. 472 Seiten.

Der Band versammelt Beiträge der Stipendiatinnen und Stipendiaten der ersten Förderungsphase des von Hans Belting gegründeten Graduiertenkollegs *Bild – Körper – Medium. Eine anthropologische Perspektive*. Interdisziplinär werden das Verhältnis von Bild und Sprache, die Frage nach dem Ort der Bilder und diejenige nach der spezifischen Bildlogik in unterschiedlichen Medien, Soziokulturen und Wissenschaftsdiskursen diskutiert. Im Zentrum steht das Interesse an einer spezifischen Kultur der Bilder im Unterschied zu textlichen Medien, wobei die kulturelle Vielfalt der Bilder eine einheitliche Bildtheorie zugleich verbiete, wie die Herausgeber betonen. Der Ansatz sei nicht zu verwechseln mit der »unverbindlichen und undisziplinierten Pluralität«, die zuweilen den angloamerikanischen *visual culture studies* vorgeworfen werde. Das Verbindende Element der Aufsätze sei das dynamische Wechselverhältnis von Bild, Medium und Körper und die Betonung des spezifischen Umfeldes der Bilder, in dem sie ihre Wirkung, Funktion und Bedeutung entfalten. Autoren: Kerstin Adermann, Nicola Behrmann, Ilka Brändle, Markus Buschhaus, Barbara Filser, Elke Gaugele, Julia Glesner, Julia Gelshorn, Martin Gieselmann, Inge Hinterwaldner, Anette Hüsch, Annamira Joachim, Katrin Kärcher, Karin Krauthausen, Karin Leonhard, Katharina Lorenz, Kristin

Marek, Dominic Olariu, Raphaèle Preisinger, Marius Rimmele, Matthias Weiß, Caroline Wesenberg.

Helga Mitterbauer und Ulrich Tragatschnig (Hg.): *Iconic turn? (= Moderne. Kulturwissenschaftliches Jahrbuch*; 2), Innsbruck 2006. 260 Seiten.

Die Herausgeber legen in ihrer Einleitung dar, dass es ihnen mehr als fraglich erscheint, »ob die Kunstwissenschaft den Anspruch einer neuen Leitdisziplin stellen kann.« Angesichts der Tatsache, dass »in der kulturwissenschaftlichen Globalisierungsdebatte das Bild zum definitorischen Kriterium geworden« sei, könne es nicht mehr nur Gegenstand der bildzentrierten Forschungsdisziplinen sein. Germanisten, Historiker, Kunsthistoriker, Philosophen, Politikwissenschaftler und Soziologen zeigen mit ihren Aufsätzen die vielfältigen Möglichkeiten einer breit angelegten und interdisziplinären bildwissenschaftlichen Forschung auf bzw. welche Rolle das Bild als Forschungsobjekt in den diversen Disziplinen inzwischen einnimmt. Autoren: Benjamin Drechsel, Sebastian Grevsmühl, Jürgen Joachimsthaler, Karl R. Kegler, Bernhard Langer, Thomas Lenz, Jasmin Mersmann, Martin Mittelmeier, Mario Pellin, Joachim Penzel, Dominik Schnetzer, Anne Tilkorn, Nicole Zillien.

Ingeborg Reichle, Steffen Siegel und Achim Spelten (Hg.): *Verwandte Bilder: die Fragen der Bildwissenschaft*, Berlin 2007. 328 Seiten.

Die Publikation der interdisziplinären Arbeitsgruppe *Die Welt als Bild* der Berlin-Brandenburgische Akademie der Wissenschaften versammelt Beiträge aus den Bereichen Archäologie, Geschichte, Kommunikationswissenschaft, Kunstgeschichte, Literaturwissenschaft, Medienwissenschaft, Philosophie und Wissenschaftsgeschichte. Davon ausgehend, dass Bildlichkeit von einer Madonnenskulptur bis zu einer Radaraufnahme sehr unterschiedlich ist und es dennoch eine mediale Verwandtschaft gibt, wird ein Netz von Bildverwandtschaften gezeichnet. Die Herausgeber formulieren die These, dass Bilder nicht schon deshalb zu Bildern werden, »weil sie Familienähnlichkeiten mit anderen Bildern haben, sondern weil durch diese Familienähnlichkeiten ein Ganzes geschaffen wird, zu dem das einzelne Bild sich jeweils verhält. Bildlichkeit ist die Eigenschaft, eine Stellung in der Familie der Bilder einzunehmen«. Autoren: Viktor Bedö, Jan Peter Behrendt, Sebastian Bucher, Marcel Finke, Sebastian Gießmann, Sebastian Vincent Grevsmühl, Barbara Kopf, Alexandra Lembert, Roland Meyer, Marius Rimmele, Michael Rottmann, Nina Samuel, Silvia Seja, Achim Spelten.

Klaus Sachs-Hombach (Hg.): *Bild und Medium. Kunstgeschichte und philosophische Grundlagen der interdisziplinären Bildwissenschaft*, Köln 2006. 278 Seiten.

Die Publikation geht zurück auf das Symposium *Kunstgeschichtliche Hermeneutik und bildwissenschaftliche Systematik* in Magdeburg im Jahr 2004. Ziel war es, das Verhältnis von Kunstgeschichte zu anderen an Bildern interessierten Disziplinen in Hinblick auf eine zukünftige allgemeine, interdisziplinär ausgerichtete Bildwissenschaft zu klären. Neben zahlreichen kunsthistorischen Beiträgen finden sich in dem Band solche von Seiten der Germanistik, Informatik, Kommunikationswissenschaft, Medienwissenschaft und Philosophie. Autoren: Horst Bredekamp, Martina Dobbe, Klaus Forster, Gustav Frank, Hans Dieter Huber, Thomas Knieper, Christiane Kruse, Simone

Mahrenholz, Hans Ulrich Reck, Pablo Schneider, Jörg R. J. Schirra, Stephan Schwan, Steffen Siegel, Jörg Trempler, Carmen Zahn.

Martin Schulz: *Ordnungen der Bilder: Eine Einführung in die Bildwissenschaft*, München 2005. 163 Seiten.

Im Zentrum stehen die Theorien und Methoden des ›iconic turn‹, der auf das sprachanalytische Paradigma des ›linguistic turn‹ anspielt und die Aufmerksamkeit auf eine Wende lenkt, die bereits in mehreren Disziplinen stattgefunden hat: die Macht der Bilder wird verstärkt analysiert und der Textaussage gleichwertig anbei gestellt. Schulz diskutiert die Fragen nach und Kontroversen um eine entsprechend neue Bildwissenschaft. In Anlehnung an das von Hans Belting gegründete Graduiertenkolleg spielen dabei die drei historisch variablen und sich wechselseitig bedingenden Parameter »Bild, Körper, Medium« eine entscheidende Rolle. Der Autor kommt zu dem Schluss, dass es eine »Superdisziplin Bildwissenschaft«, die allen angeschlossenen Disziplinen den theoretischen und methodischen Rahmen gibt, nicht geben kann. Stattdessen plädiert er für eine interdisziplinäre und integrative Bildwissenschaft, »für die eine große Fakultät erst noch erfunden werden müsste«.

Beat Wyss: *Vom Bild zum Kunstsystem*, Köln 2006. 2 Bände. 319 und 188 Seiten.

Es handelt sich um einen Abriss der Kunstgeschichte als Bildergeschichte, wobei das Schlagwort der Bildwissenschaft bewusst vermieden wird, da es durch den darin festgeschriebenen Singular die Gefahr laufe, »falsifizierte Einsichten von gestern für nichtig zu erklären«. Aufschlussreicher sei es, »die Wege zwischen entdeckter Wahrheit und der Einsicht seines Irrtums« nachzuzeichnen. Von zentraler Bedeutung der Bildergeschichte hin zum Bild als autonomes Kunstwerk in der Moderne sei demnach die Geschichtlichkeit der Bilder und »deren zeitlich begrenzte Gültigkeit als Medium, Welt glaubhaft zu zeigen.« Wyss knüpft an Hans Beltings anthropologischen Ansatz an und kombiniert ihn mit Charles S. Peirces Semiotik, Sigmund Freuds Psychoanalyse und Niklas Luhmanns Systemtheorie.

Anna Greve

Autorinnen und Autoren

MARKUS BUSCHHAUS, geb. 1973, Studium der Germanistik, Romanistik, Pädagogik und Philosophie in Düsseldorf und Lyon. Ehemaliger Stipendiat des DAAD und der DFG (Doktorand und Postdoktorand am Karlsruher Graduiertenkolleg *Bild-Körper-Medium. Eine anthropologische Perspektive*), 2004 Promotion in Medienwissenschaften. Lehrveranstaltungen an der Heinrich-Heine-Universität Düsseldorf und der HfG Karlsruhe. Mitarbeit an hochschulpolitischen Projekten, Akkreditierungsverfahren und Evaluationen. Forschungsschwerpunkte sind: Bild- und Medientheorien, dabei insbesondere die Funktionshorizonte der Bildwissenschaften in der und für die Wissens- bzw. Wissenschaftsgeschichtsschreibung; medizinische Bildkulturen (Anatomie, Pathologie, klinische Diagnostik); Geschichte wissenschaftlicher Publikationsformen; Projekt zu einer Ikonotopie (Frage nach den Orten der Bilder und den von ihnen begünstigten kulturellen Handlungen). Seit 2006 hauptberuflich im Schuldienst (Gymnasium) tätig.

MAGGIE GRAY is a PhD student in the History of Art department at University College London. Her research focuses on the work of British comics writer Alan Moore from the late seventies to mid-eighties, tracing the trajectory of his career in relation to both the broader historical development of British comics and the political and social context of Thatcherism. Her main concerns are questions about the possibility of cultural resistance and counter-hegemonic intervention through mass culture. Her previous research has addressed US superhero comics and Cold War ideology, and the emergence of the term »graphic novel« in relation to the so-called »adult revolution« of the 1980s and specifically Neil Gaiman's *Sandman.*

GÖTZ GROSSKLAUS, geb. 1933, Studium der Germanistik, Geschichte, Philosophie, Kunstgeschichte (1954–1961) an den Universitäten München, Freiburg und Hamburg. 1961 Staatsexamen an der Universität Hamburg (Deutsch/Geschichte). 1961–1967 berufliche Tätigkeit (Gymnasium, Rundfunk, Verlag). 1966 Promotion (Dr. phil.) an der Universität Freiburg. 1968 Wissenschaftlicher Assistent an der Universität Karlsruhe (TH). 1973 Habilitation an der Universität Karlsruhe (TH). 1974 Professor für Neuere Deutsche Philologie ebd. 1996 Assoziierter Profesor für Mediengeschichte an der Staatlichen Hochschule für Gestaltung Karlsruhe. 1999 Emeritierung.

ANDREW HEMMINGWAY, born 1950 Harrogate, Yorkshire. 1968–71 University of Hull: B.A. Honours, History (upper second class); 1972–74 University of East Anglia: M.A., History of Art; 1977–89 University College London (part-time): Ph.D., History of Art (Thesis title: *Discourses of Art and Social Interests: The Representation of Landscape in Britain, c.1800-1830*). 1974-87 Lecturer/Senior Lecturer in History of Art Ealing College of Higher Education, London; 1987–93 Lecturer in History of Art University College London; 1993–2003 Reader in History of Art University College London; 2003 – to date Professor in History of Art University College London. 1988–97 and 2007 to date Member of the Editorial Group of the *Oxford Art Journal*; 1997–2007 Advisory

Editor, *Oxford Art Journal*; 1998 – to date Member of Editorial Board of *Kunst und Politik. Jahrbuch der Guernica-Gesellschaft.*

ASKO LEHMUSKALLIO studied Cultural Anthropology, Science of Religions and Peace- and Conflict Studies at the Philipps-University Marburg and Photography at the Universidad Complutense de Madrid. He has worked with a 3-year scholarship at the DFG-postgraduate program »Image. Body. Medium. An anthropological perspective« at the New Media School in Karlsruhe, and the year 2005–2006 as Researcher in Residence at the Finnish Museum of Photography. Since 2006 he works as a researcher at the Helsinki Institute for Information Technology. His research focuses on why and how do people picture public urban spaces, including pictures on the Web, and how do new information and communication technologies change the actual possibilities and practices related to picturing one's environment.

STEWART MARTIN is Programme Leader of BA Fine Art and Critical Theory and Lecturer in Modern European Philosophy, Aesthetics and Art Theory at Middlesex University London. He is a member of the editorial collective, and reviews editor, of the journal *Radical Philosophy*. Stewart Martin's principal research interests are in the philosophical critique of capitalist culture; the relation between theories and practices of contemporary art and post-Kantian philosophies of art; Frankfurt School Critical Theory, particularly Adorno. Stewart Martin is currently working on a book entitled *Art of Capital*.

MARIUS RIMMELE, Studium der Kunst- und Medienwissenschaft, Deutschen Literatur und Philosophie an der Universität Konstanz. 2002 Mitarbeiter im SFB »Literatur und Anthropologie« im Teilprojekt »Historische Anthropologie westlicher Bildmedien« an der Universität Konstanz. 2003–2006 Stipendiat am Graduiertenkolleg *Bild – Körper – Medium. Eine anthropologische Perspektive* (Hochschule für Gestaltung Karlsruhe). Promotion 2007 mit einer Arbeit über die Semantisierung von Triptychen und anderen klappbaren Bildträgern. Derzeit wiss. Mitarbeiter (Assistent) in der Kunstwissenschaft an der Universität Konstanz. Forschungsinteressen: Bild und Frömmigkeitspraxis im Mittelalter, auf den Träger des Bildes gerichtete Selbstreflexivität, Formen von Sinnschichtungen und Tropik im Bild, Semantik von Kleidung im Bild.

GERALD SCHÖDER ist seit März 2008 als Akademischer Oberrat am Kunstgeschichtlichen Institut der Ruhr-Universität Bochum beschäftigt. Zuvor war er hier als Wissenschaftlicher Mitarbeiter angestellt. Seine eingereichte Habilitationsschrift trägt den Titel *Schmerzensmänner – Trauma und Therapie und der westdeutschen und österreichischen Kunst der 1960er Jahre*. Die Promotion erfolgte im Jahr 2000 mit einer Arbeit über den Florentiner Gelehrten und Kunstschriftsteller des 16. Jahrhunderts Francesco Bocchi: *Der kluge Blick – Studie zu den kunsttheoretischen Reflexionen Francesco Bocchis*. Publiziert hat Gerald Schröder darüber hinaus zu den Themenfeldern Surrealismus und Minimal Art sowie zur Kunsttheorie und Skulptur des ausgehenden 16. Jahrhunderts.

PETER SMITH, Principal Lecturer in Art History and Cultural Theory, Programme Leader for MA in Photography. Qualifications: MA in Art History, the Courtauld Institute of Art; Architectural Association, Graduate School Diploma; BA Hons in Fine Art, Coventry University.

Abbildungsverzeichnis und -nachweis

Beitrag Peter Smith:

Abbildung 1: Jeff Wall, *The Storyteller,* 1986 (courtesy of the artist)
Abbildung 2: Barbara Kruger, *Untitled (I Shop Therefore I Am)*, 1987 (courtesy of the Mary Boone Gallery New York)
Abbildung 3: Walker Evans, *Let Us Now Praise Famous Men*, 1939
Abbildung 4: Allan Sekula, *Shipwreck and Workers*, Part of *Titanic's Wake*, 1998/2000 (courtesy of Christopher Grimes Gallery Santa Monica, CA)

Beitrag Maggie Gray:

Abbildung 1: Linder, *Untitled*, 1978, Image courtesy of Stuart Shave/Modern Art
Abbildung 2: *Sounds* cover, March 19th 1977
Abbildung 3: Curt Vile (Alan Moore), *Roscoe Moscow, Who Killed Rock 'n' Roll?,* Episode 30 »Washing the Detective!!«, Sounds, 27th October 1979, © Alan Moore
Abbildung 4: Curt Vile (Alan Moore), *Roscoe Moscow, Who Killed Rock 'n' Roll?*, Episode 53 »Working for the Clampdown« Sounds, 10th May 1980, © Alan Moore
Abbildung 5: Curt Vile (Alan Moore), Roscoe Moscow. Who Killed Rock 'n' Roll?, Episode 54 »State of the Nation!« Sounds, 17th May 1980, © Alan Moore

Beitrag Asko Lehmuskallio:

Abbildung 1: Pia Lindman, *New York Times 09/02–09/03*, 2002–2003, video still of re-enacting gestures depicted in newspaper photographs in front of a video camera
Abbildung 2: Pia Lindman, *New York Times 09/02–09/03*, 2002–2003, a pencil drawing on vellum paper made from the video still
Abbildung 3: Chappatte, *Cartoon War*, 2006, www.globecartoon.com, © Chappatte

Beitrag Hille Koskela:

Abbildung 1: Wolfgang Staehle, *Empire 24/7*, 1999, www.medienkunstnetz.de/works/empire24-7/
Abbildung 2: Ken Goldberg, *Demonstrate*, 2004, demonstrate.berkeley.edu/signin.htm
Abbildung 3: Janet Cardiff, *Eyes of Laura*, www.eyesoflaura.org/index3.php
Abbildung 4: Cheryl Sourkes, *Homecammer*, www.cherylsourkes.com/homecammer.htm

Beitrag Markus Buschhaus:

Abbildung 1:	Alessandro Allori, Beinstudie, 1560er Jahre
Abbildung 2:	Bildtafel aus *De humani corporis fabrica* von Andreas Vesalius, 1543
Abbildung 3:	Torsten Seidel, Portrait of this mortal coil #7, 2003
Abbildung 4:	Torsten Seidel, Portrait of this mortal coil, 2003, Installation, Dresden Hellerau
Abbildung 5:	Tafel 75 zu Aby Warburgs Bilderatlas *Mnemosyne*

Beitrag Gerald Schröder:

Abbildung 1:	Joseph Beuys, *Hinter dem Knochen wird gezählt – Schmerzraum*, 1941–1983, Fundación »la Caixa« Barcelona, © VG Bild-Kunst, Bonn 2008
Abbildung 2:	Joseph Beuys, *Hinter dem Knochen wird gezählt – Schmerzraum*, 1941–1983, Fundación »la Caixa« Barcelona, © VG Bild-Kunst, Bonn 2008
Abbildung 3:	Joseph Beuys, *Gummierte Kiste*, 1957, Hessisches Landesmuseum Darmstadt, © VG Bild-Kunst, Bonn 2008
Abbildung 4:	Joseph Beuys, *Entwürfe für Mahnmal Auschwitz*, 1957, Stiftung Museum Schloss Moyland – Sammlung van der Grinten, © VG Bild-Kunst, Bonn 2008
Abbildung 5:	Joseph Beuys, *Möbiuswerfer*, 1984, © VG Bild-Kunst, Bonn 2008

Beitrag Anna Greve:

Abbildung 1:	Postkarte *Dresdner Stadtfest 1998*

Themenschwerpunkt des nächsten Bandes:
Politische Raumtypen